SPA STYLE

ASIA-PACIFIC

THERAPIES • CUISINES • SPAS

SPA STYLE

ASIA-PACIFIC

Thames & Hudson

First published in the United Kingdom in 2006 by
Thames & Hudson Ltd, 181A High Holborn, London WC1V 7QX

www.thamesandhudson.com

British Library Cataloguing-in-Publication Data
A catalogue record for this book is available from the British Library

ISBN-13:   978-0-500-28620-3
ISBN-10:   0-500-28620-5
Printed and bound in Singapore

Before following any advice or practice contained in this book,
it is recommended that you consult your doctor. The publisher
cannot accept responsibility for any injuries or damage incurred
as a result of following any of the suggestions, preparations or
procedures described in this book, or by using any of the
therapeutic methods that are mentioned.

Every effort has been made to ensure the accuracy of the information
in this book at the time of going to press. Some details are liable
to change and the publisher recommends calling ahead to verify
information with the respective properties.

*The authors would like to thank the following for their help and
contribution: Greg Payne; Gayle Heron and Angela Tabart at
Li'Tya; Dr Jaime Galvez Z. Tan; Cathy Brilliantes-Palma and Paulo
Sambile at Nurture Spa; Jennifer J. Sanvictores at The Farm;
Terry and Cathy Maloney, Kelda Maloney and Richard
Schoonraad at Daintree Eco Lodge and Spa.*

Contents

Introduction

With probably the richest spa culture in the world, it comes as no surprise that Asian spas continue to dominate global spa awards and there's every reason why. Asia is more than a destination; it's a cradle of some of the world's oldest civilizations, home to the globe's largest population and collection of cultures so rich, deep and varied. Teeming with life, it is the most vibrant corner of the planet.

What is natural and instinctive in Asia others spend millions trying to copy. The past decade alone has seen spas from New York to London and Paris decked out with Buddha statues, incense and bamboo in an effort to bring as much Asian spirituality as possible to the spa experience. But Asian spas recognize the importance of local grooming and tradition and base their physically and spiritually healing therapies around indigenous ingredients and age-old cures.

The following pages offer an insight into these ancient healing practices, from India and China to Indonesia, Thailand, Philippines and Japan, therapies that form the basis of treatments offered in the majority of spas throughout the region. Indigenous Aboriginal therapies are included too as Aboriginal tribal Elders are finally starting to share their time-honoured healing secrets with the world. While many of the more modern therapies appearing in spa menus worldwide have their roots firmly grounded in traditional Eastern medicine, they also avail of the more Western scientifically-based tools to enhance the overall experience. Not surprising then is the emergence of a new style of therapy, the contemporary cosmopolitan—or a fusion of East and West—which features treatments that are firmly grounded in the ancient principles of balance and harmony yet with an extra dimension. While *Spa Style Asia-Pacific* primarily focuses on the spa traditions of the region, it adds this new cosmopolitan dimension to widen readers' perspectives and offer a more complete overview of the numerous therapies on offer.

To enhance the wellness experience at home, Spa Cuisine presents healthy recipes from established spas across the region. To plan your very own spa journey, Spa Digest provides essential information on the region's top spas. Spa Speak explains frequently used spa, treatment and fitness terms and the comprehensive Spa Directory is a handy guide with full contact details of spas around the region.

Spa Style Asia-Pacific will deepen your appreciation of today's spa treatments, allowing you to learn about their roots in traditional healing systems and actually try the experience at home. The exotic blend of ancient time-honoured and truly unmatched natural therapies will soothe and enrich body, mind and spirit.

Spa Therapies

Asia-Pacific's healing traditions adopt a holistic approach of treating the body, mind and spirit as one, tackling the root cause of the problem and viewing the body as capable of healing itself. These time-honoured traditions are based on the fundamental principle of a 'life-force' which flows through the body, an imbalance of which is believed to be the cause of illness; and a balance the cause of health and well-being.

The following pages give a background to the ancient healing practices of the Asia-Pacific region. Spanning east from India and China to Japan and heading south towards Thailand, Indonesia, the Philippines and Australia, the philosophies form the basis of treatments and therapies offered by many spas in the region. The Cosmopolitan section draws from spa traditions that are found all over the world.

Each section includes some simple recipes enabling a spa experience at home.

Ayurveda

INDIA'S KEYS TO HEALTH AND REJUVENATION

India's cultural and historical legacy is second to none. The traditions of this vast subcontinent predate that of the Ancient Egyptians and its architectural heritage is almost impossible to match with its beautiful and inspiring palaces, unique authenticity and minimalist modernity.

Translated from the ancient Indian language of Sanskrit, ayurveda is the 'science of life' (ayur meaning life, veda meaning knowledge) and is regarded by scholars as the oldest healing system in the world. It remains the prime healing tradition adopted by the people of India, Sri Lanka and Nepal and over the years, thanks to the teachings of holistic lifestyle guru Deepak Chopra and the adoption of an ayurvedic lifestyle by a clutch of celebrities, the secrets of this ancient discipline (especially regarding rejuvenation and longevity) have found their way into spas worldwide.

Those who practice this self-healing philosophy understand it to be a long-term lifestyle choice, with the full benefits reaped only if its principles are followed in every single respect.

| The resplendent Taj Mahal in Agra, a masterpiece of Mughal architecture, conjures a sense of serenity and peace. || Incense and spice at an Indian spa.

A Cultural Perspective

Legend has it that some three millennia ago, 52 rishis (wise old sages and religious leaders of ancient India) left their villages and gathered high in the Himalayas to seek enlightenment. Troubled by the problems of their people and widespread illness, they sought to learn from Brahma, the creator god, how to eradicate illness in the world. They were touched by divine inspiration while meditating and gathered their thoughts into a series of Vedic texts—ancient Sanskrit books that are today revered as the original Hindu tomes of knowledge. These volumes reveal a healing system steeped in Hindu philosophy on which the basic paradigm and practice of ayurveda is based.

According to ayurvedic belief, everything was 'one' in the beginning when the first sound, om, was heard. Its vibrations resulted in the creation of the five elements—air, ether (or space), fire, heat and water—from which everything in the universe is made.

At the heart of ayurvedic philosophy is the concept that our bodies are a microcosm of the universe with three universal governing forces at work: vata (air), pitta (fire) and kapha (earth). These forces are called doshas and, just as each of us has an individual face or thumbprint, we also have a unique pattern of energy that corresponds with these doshas, a combination of physical, mental and emotional characteristics that is our inherent constitution. Achieving balance and harmony between the doshas is the aim of therapy and the foundations of health and well-being in ayurvedic medicine (see box). However, diagnosing a dosha is not as simple as it may

| The luxuries of space and peacefulness abound in the Himalayan mountains. || Cymbals are used to note the end of a treatment or meditation session. ||| The sacred lotus, a common image at the spa and India's national flower.

Be the change you want to see.

Mahatma Gandhi

seem as, although a particular one may be dominant in the body, ayurveda believes that all individuals possess all three (vata, pitta and kapha) to certain degrees.

We are said to be in good health when all three doshas are properly balanced. The proper amount of vata promotes creativity and flexibility, pitta generates understanding and analytical ability, and kapha engenders stability, affection and generosity. Imbalances in the doshas are thought to disrupt the flow of prana, the 'life force' that enters the body through food and breath, and impede agni, the fire that provides energy for digestion, metabolic processes, the immune system, and the processes of thought and feeling. The key to ayurveda is treating the body, mind and spirit as a unified entity to maintain health, balance and harmony.

An ayurvedic consultation begins the minute you walk through the door, with the practitioner observing gait and general appearance. Questioning and palpation enables the practitioner to determine

dosha type and the nature of the client's problem. Unlike Western diagnoses that attempt to identify illness through common symptoms, the ayurvedic system is highly individualized and holistic in approach. An examination of the pulse, eyes, tongue and overall physical appearance is incomplete without a thorough assessment of the client's emotional and spiritual well-being. The ayurvedic practitioner's task is to re-balance body, mind and spirit according to each person's unique 'pattern', so they can resume harmony once again with the universe. Therapies are generally divided into curative or preventive, all following the essential self-healing philosophy and self-care techniques that are a fundamental part of ayurveda. A typical regime could include a series of luxurious massages, oil therapy, vegetarian diet, consumption of healthy herbal tonics and a daily routine of yoga and meditation. For those who are in good health, preventive measures that revitalize and protect the body may be prescribed.

	Vata	Pitta	Kapha
Physical Make-up	small boned and light	medium bone structure	strong boned and prone to weight gain
Disposition	friendly, sociable, fast learner, artistic fast eater, prone to constipation	ambitious, passionate, hot tempered, intelligent, exudes wisdom, generally eats sensibly with a tendency to diarrhoea	earth mothers, loving, truthful, resourceful, nurtures and provides, enjoys food and eating
Skin Type	tendency towards dry skin and fine lines	normal/combination skin, tendency towards oiliness	skin can be oily

Treatments & Therapies

Abhyanga

This traditional synchronized ayurvedic massage is performed by two therapists using rhythmic strokes and a dosha-specific essential oil blend. It helps to cleanse the body while also improving circulation and inducing a real feeling of peace and calm. To uphold ayurvedic tradition, it is recommended that same gender therapists are used for the massage.

Ayurvedic Massage

Traditional ayurvedic massage uses medicated herbal oils specifically selected based on the body's dosha. The massage is done directly on the skin, and is aimed at loosening the excess doshas and directing them towards the organs of elimination. It also promotes circulation, increases flexibility and relieves pain and stiffness. Massage can be performed by one or more therapists in tandem (abhyanga) and techniques range from kneading to rubbing and squeezing with the hands. The feet are sometimes used in chavutti pizhichil, a specialized technique where the therapist suspends himself by a rope from the ceiling to apply extra pressure with his feet to undo stubborn aches.

Champissage

Champissage (Indian head massage) has been used in India for centuries to banish headaches, muscle tension, eye strain and stiff neck. It remains as popular as ever today, especially amongst Indian women who believe that a regular head massage, along with natural vegetable oils, keeps their hair healthy, shiny and really strong.

Traditional Indian head massage combines physical massage with the more subtle form of chakra or 'energy centre' balancing. With its firm yet gentle rhythm, the massage helps unknot blockages, relieve tension and rebalance the body's energy with powerful effects. Advocates swear that just 30 minutes a week makes life brighter and better. But the real beauty of the technique rests in its simplicity—it can be done anywhere as long as there is a comfortable chair and a willing pair of healing hands.

The Five Phases of Detoxification:

Nasya (nasal scenting): A few drops of medicated oil are applied to the nose, after which the mucous membrane, neck and shoulders is gently massaged. Nasya helps clear the nasal passages and alleviate kapha-oriented imbalances such as headaches, allergies, sinusitis and nasal congestion.

Raktamokshana (blood-letting): Raktamokshana uses surgical instruments or leeches to drain the body of impure blood. It is used for pitta conditions such as skin problems, boils and abscesses.

Vamana (emetic vomiting): The ancient rishis believed it was beneficial to the body to induce vomiting through consumption of special potions. Vamana does just this and clears excess kapha in the body. It is recommended for treating bronchitis and for throat, chest and heart problems.

Vasti (enema): Vasti is recommended for treating disorders arising from vata imbalance. Anuvasana

vasti (oily enemas) are used to treat skin dryness and digestive imbalances, while asthapana vasti (decoction enemas) are used to treat nervous problems and fatigue.

Virechana (gentle purging): A herbal tea, which acts as a safe and mild laxative, flushes the digestive tract completely. Virechana cleanses the pitta, and helps treat conditions such as skin diseases, fevers, intestinal worms and irritable bowel syndrome.

Marma Point Massage

Marma means secret, hidden and vital, and marma points are essentially vital energy points in the body where prana gathers, much like the acupoints of traditional Chinese medicine. Ayurveda's ancient treatises state that the human body contains 107 marma points, which, when struck or massaged, can either injure or heal. For example, the lohit, a marma point on the leg, may be massaged to treat paralysis. Conversely, if the same point is struck, it may induce severe damage even paralysis. Today marma point massage is most frequently practised in South India and is believed to work best for vata types as it heals and increases flexibility.

The massage is performed with the thumb or index finger. Beginning with small clockwise circles, the therapist will gradually increase both the motion and pressure that are applied. A marma point that is either blocked or out of balance will cause some discomfort when massaged. Traditionally, ayurvedic medicated herbal oils were used in the massage although essential oils such as lavender, eucalyptus or peppermint are also beneficial.

Mukh Lepa

Used for centuries as a beauty ritual for women, this traditional facial treatment uses specific massage techniques and herbal ingredients to cleanse, tone, nourish and hydrate the face. A dosha-specific herbal lepa (or plaster) is applied to the face to completely cleanse and renew the skin from within.

| A marma point massage works to unblock or rebalance the energy points that are situated all over the body. || An ayurvedic neem wood treatment table. ||| The pleasures of a warm climate allowing you to shower in the great outdoors. |||| Mukh lepa is a traditional facial treatment customized for specific doshas.

Samana (Herbal Medicine)

Samana or herbal medicine is prescribed individually to correct imbalances in the doshas. It is taken as a liquid or as dried herbs, powders or in tablet form. Some of the more commonly used herbs include:

Aloe Vera: Aloe is called kumari (the maiden) in ayurveda, which suggests its beneficial effects for women. It is excellent for regulating the female monthly cycle as well as easing menstrual-related

| Traditional Indian style with a contemporary twist. || Aloe vera's multitude of uses makes this plant a vital ingredient whether it's a liquid, gel or lotion. ||| All-natural ingredients of the Samana (herbal medicine).

Panchakarma

One of ayurveda's most effective regimes is panchakarma or full detoxification therapy. Comprising several steps, panchakarma involves the complete removal of toxins at the deepest internal levels with the aim of rebalancing the body's inherent equilibrium and doshas. It can be prescribed as a series of individual treatments or as a combination with another therapy depending on individual doshas and needs. Therapy normally takes a minimum of two weeks and is not advised for those suffering from anaemia or weakness, for pregnant women, or the very young and very old.

Purvakarma

This pre-operative phase of panchakarma comprises oil and sweat therapy to soften and cleanse the skin in preparation for detoxification.

Snehana (oil therapy): A mixture of herbs, oils and natural ingredients is carefully blended based on the client's dosha and gently massaged over the body, face and neck to stimulate or soothe, depending on individual requirements. The oils may also be taken orally or introduced as enemas.

Svedana (sweat therapy): A cross between a steam bath and sauna, svedana is a method of body purification that deeply cleanses and relaxes. After massage, the client steps into a giant steam box. Through perspiration, the body clears the toxins that have been brought to the upper layers of the skin during massage. Apart from the elimination of wastes, svedana also warms the muscles, relieves bloating and improves the radiance and condition of the skin.

pain. Aloe soothes and heals the body and, applied as fresh aloe gel on the skin, it is great for healing burns, rashes, skin inflammation, insect bites and other painful conditions while acting as a nourishing moisturizer on the face. It is also effective for relieving 'acid' stomach, gastritis and for cooling pitta in the liver, blood, eyes and digestion.

Brahmi: Known as gotu kola in the West, brahmi (centella asiatica) balances the doshas and stimulates the circulation, especially the blood vessels of the skin and mucous membranes. It rejuvenates and revitalizes, strengthens memory and intelligence, improves concentration, physical strength, digestive power and the complexion. It is most often taken as tea or medicated ghee.

Musta: Known as nutgrass or knotgrass in the United States, where it is a rampant weed, musta (cyperus rotundus) reduces pitta and kapha and regulates the menses. As a weak decoction in water it is used for treating fevers, diarrhoea, dysentery, indigestion and haemorrhoids.

Shatavari: The root of shatavari (asparagus racemosus) is a member of the asparagus family and excellent for controlling the doshas (especially vata and pitta). It is usually taken as a powder, medicated

ghee or simmered in milk and is an excellent female blood rejuvenator while also helping to strengthen the immune system, urinary tract and the body as a whole.

Triphala (three fruits): A multi-purpose herbal remedy, triphala can be eaten or used as a shampoo, body wash or douche, a laxative or emetic, as eye drops, a gargle or snuff for the nose. It helps calm inflammation, scrapes excess fat from the body, rebalances the doshas and maintain a youthful countenance. It is an ingredient common to a number of medicines and its three constituents (amalaki, haritaki and bibhitaki) can be made into a number of rejuvenating preparations.

Jeti Neti

Jeti neti, or yoga's nasal douche, is a nasal cleansing therapy that douches the nasal passages with a saline solution. By dislodging mucus it is excellent for clearing blocked sinuses while also clearing the eye passages and airways and improving circulation. A jeti neti vessel is shaped like a small teapot with an extra-long spout.

Shirodhara

Shirodhara, sometimes referred to as the 'massage of the third eye', is a powerful and uniquely ayurvedic therapy designed to relieve mental tensions and provide a calm state of mind. A steady stream of warmed medicated oil is slowly poured over the third eye on the forehead. Shirodhara can be performed at the end of panchakarma or as a healing therapy on its own to rebalance the mind and revitalize the senses.

Takradhara

Similar to Shirodhara, this calming therapy uses medicated buttermilk, which is poured on the third eye to bring relief to those suffering from insomnia, depression and other stress related problems.

Yoga and Meditation

In Indian philosophy, therapies that pamper the mind and spirit are of equal importance as physical treatments. Yoga, the Hindu method of body-mind integration, was originally practiced by ancient Hindu sages to help achieve enlightenment. These days, it

Basil Leaf Tea
Helps ease coughs and sore throats

7 g (¼ oz) basil leaves
2 cloves
1½ tsp ginger juice

Steep ingredients in hot water for one minute. Drink while hot.

is no longer guru-oriented or religion-based and with the help of its celebrity endorsement, yoga has become a mainstay of many seeking a more centred lifestyle. With advocates such as Madonna and Christy Turlington, former catwalk queen and now one of the most recognized faces of yoga East and West, proving that regular practice makes for a strong, supple and healthy body.

Much of what is known of yoga today is derived from the *Yoga Sutra*, yoga's classical and seminal text, written in the third century BC by Yogi Patanjali. Focusing primarily on matters of the spirit, the science of yoga consists of eight 'limbs': yama (laws of life), niyama (rules for living), asana (the physical postures), pranayama (breath control), pratyahara (the drawing of one's attention to silence), dharana (concentration), dhyana (meditation) and samadhi (spiritual union). Reaching the bliss and peace of samadhi is the ultimate goal.

While all yoga styles seek to balance body, mind and spirit they go about it in various ways. They may differ in how the asanas are carried out and where attention is focused (on mastering the holding of the posture or on breathing or alignment). Some use props while others crank up the temperature and go for the sweat. No particular style is the best. It's

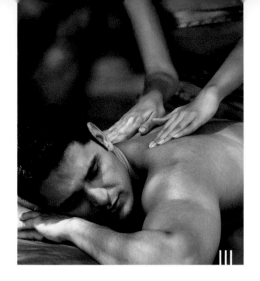

As long as there is breath in the body, there is life. When breath departs, so too does life. Therefore, regulate the breath.

The Hatha Yoga Pradipika

down to personal preference. The following is a guide to the more common styles of yoga that are now practised all around the world.

Ashtanga: This physically demanding yoga was developed by K. Pattabhi Jois to build strength, flexibility, and stamina. Not for the weak, ashtanga yoga offers a fast-paced series of sequential poses beginning with sun salutations. Students move from one posture to another in a continual flow and movements are very much linked to correct breathing. Power yoga is based on ashtanga.

Bikram: Bikram Choudhury, guru to the stars, developed this hot yoga practice where the room temperature remains between 29°C and 38°C (85°F and 100°F). In this hot and steamy environment, students vigorously perform (always in the same order) 26 poses designed to cleanse the body from the inside out.

Jeti Neti

2 tsp salt
4 glasses of warm water

Fill jeti neti pot with 2 glasses of water and 1 tsp salt. Tilt head to the left and place the spout in the right nostril. The water should flow through the right nostril and out the left. Breathe through the mouth to prevent the discomfort of water in the nasal passages. Refill the pot and repeat on the other side.

To clear any residual water from the nostrils a technique called Bellows Breath or Bhastrika is used. While standing, put your hands on your hips. Bend forward until the torso is parallel to the floor bending the knees slightly. Keep the eyes open and mouth closed. Breathe deeply through the nostrils relaxing the stomach. Breathe out with force, pulling in the diaphragm. Do this continuously and quickly 25 times, turning the head right, left, up and down for one breath in each direction.

| Shirodhara, the most recognizable of the ayurvedic therapies. Warm oil flows steadily onto the third eye to relieve mental tension. || Pranayama, meaning breath control, constitutes one of the eight limbs of yoga. ||| A massage is administered with medicated herbal oil that is specifically selected for the body's dosha.

Hatha: Nearly all yoga styles are rooted in hatha—yoga's physical discipline that focuses on developing control of the body through a series of asanas and pranayama or breathing techniques. In Sanskrit ha represents the sun and tha, the moon. Much like the yin and yang of TCM, hatha represents the duality of life and it leads the way to balancing these opposing forces in the body and in life.

Iyengar: B.K.S. Iyengar developed this style of yoga which stresses a deeper understanding of how the body works. Students focus on symmetry and alignment, using props such as straps, blankets, wooden blocks, and chairs to achieve postures with each pose being held for a longer amount of time than in most other styles of yoga.

Kundalini: Once a guarded secret in India, kundalini yoga arrived in the West in 1969, when Sikh Yogi Bhajan began to teach it publicly. This practice is designed to awaken kundalini energy, which is stored at the base of the spine and often depicted as a coiled snake. Kundalini mixes chanting and breathing practice with yoga asanas.

Sivananda: Founded by Swami Vishnu-devananda, sivananda's gentle approach takes students through the twelve sun salutation postures and incorporates chanting, meditation and deep relaxation. Students are encouraged to embrace a healthy lifestyle and vegetarian diet with positive thinking and meditation.

Tantra: Routinely misunderstood, tantra is less about sexual indulgence and more about discovering and stimulating sensual spirituality. It works with the highly charged kundalini energy and teaches practitioners how to use this energy not only for sexual pleasure, but also for bringing joy and wholeness to everyday life, and for aiding spiritual evolution. Tantra yoga includes visualization, chanting, asana, and strong breathing practices.

Meditation

Considered by many as the highest form of yoga, meditation calms and stills the mind like no other known practice. During meditation, the pulse slows, blood pressure drops and the brain relaxes, eliminating stress and providing a sense of peace and tranquillity.

The best way to learn to meditate is by joining a class. Wear loose clothing during a session, which should take place in a warm and quiet atmosphere. Do not force meditation longer than is comfortable and do not attempt to meditate after eating or when tired. In the rare instance that disturbing memories surface, stop immediately.

Breath Awareness Meditation:

- Find a quiet place where you are unlikely to be interrupted
- Sit in a cross-legged or lotus position on the floor or alternatively on a chair with both feet on the ground. Make sure you are comfortable.
- Observe the flow of breath without trying to change it.
- If the mind wanders gently bring it back to the breath.
- Do this for about 20 minutes, but never to the point where it is forced.

Breath can also be focused by:
- Concentrating on the sound of the breath
- Counting each breath as it is inhaled and exhaled. Count from one to 10 focusing on the breath and the numbers.
- Focus on the sensation of the breath flowing in and out of the nostrils.

| The tree pose. This asana will strengthen the body and improve your sense of balance. To deepen, try it with your eyes closed and learn to balance without any reference to the outer environment. || Just 20 minutes of meditation every day will change your life with a highly relaxed and calm mind and body.

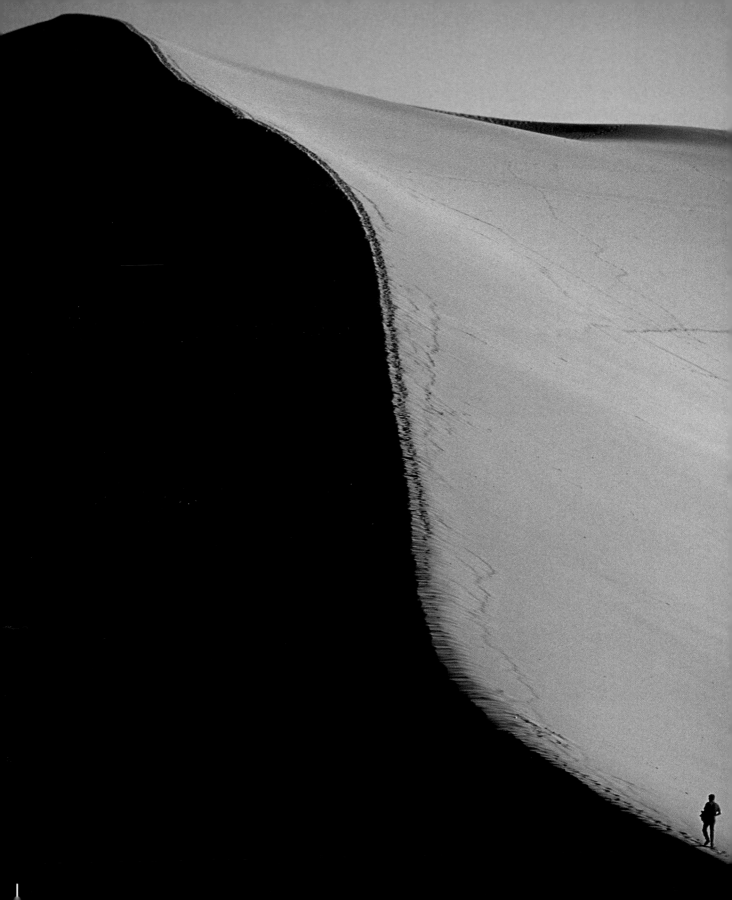

Traditional Chinese Medicine

BALANCING THE LIFE FORCE WITHIN

"In the universe and in life, great achievements may easily be accomplished by starting with small actions." Lao Tzu, Tao Te Ching (c.1066-770)

With the present shift from Western thinking to a more integrative mind and body approach of the East, Taoism, the fundamental philosophy of the world's oldest civilization is as relevant today as it was in classical China.

When the World Health Organization (WHO) first began endorsing traditional healing systems, traditional Chinese medicine, or TCM, was top of their list. Hardly surprising, as its influence has spread further and wider than any other complementary therapy. Many spa treatments enjoyed in Asia and indeed globally, have roots in ancient Chinese healing philosophies and, while the practices may vary slightly due to the availability of ingredients and therapists, the fundamental conceptual paradigms adopted are very much the same. Chinese medicine embraces the Taoist holistic and preventive approach to health by focusing on diet, movement, and spiritual and emotional well-being. It treats the body as a whole and aims to prevent illness by maintaining overall health and balance.

| The shady yin and the sunny yang of the vast and impressive sand dunes in China | | The five elements of earth, fire, metal, water and wood that, according to traditional Chinese medicine (TCM), keep the body in balance.

Whoever wishes to investigate medicine should proceed thus: In the first place consider the seasons of the year and what effect each of them produces.

Hippocrates (c.500BC)

A Cultural Perspective

Chinese legend attributes the foundations of early medicine to the classics of two emperors—Red Emperor Shen Nong's script *Shen Nong Ben Cao Jing* (*Classic of Herbal Medicine*) and Yellow Emperor Huang Di's *Huang Di Nei Jing* (*The Yellow Emperor's Canon of Internal Medicine*). Although archaeological evidence suggests that the roots of Chinese medicine date back almost 5,000 years, the most significant periods in medical history are the Shang (1766-1100BC) and early Zhou (1027-221BC) dynasties, which saw the development of pre-scientific supernatural medicine, and the late Zhou and early Qin (221-207 BC) dynasties during which the foundations of TCM were established.

Then, medicine was based on ancestral worship, shamanism and magic. The living would consult their ancestors whose displeasure at certain events resulted in illness. Prayer and ritual sacrifice were the cures. This early period also witnessed the beginnings of various philosophical traditions which sought rational and scientific explanations based on empirical observations of nature. These theories, brought together by Confucian theory, laid the foundation for scientific-based medicine.

In Taoist belief, the universe exists as a unified whole, comprising two opposing yet complementary forces known as yin and yang. The interplay between these forces governs qi, the energy that powers the universe and suffuses every living cell. The philosophy of yin and yang is further refined into the theory of the five elements of earth (tu), fire (huo), metal (jin), water (shui) and wood (mu), with each nurturing, supporting, and—where appropriate—controlling one another to keep the body in balance, health and harmony. Everything in the universe corresponds with one of the five elements which helps to explain the effect of sounds, smells, food, the planets, seasons and emotions on the body.

From acupuncture to qi gong, the cultivation of these ancient practices is encouraged not only as therapy, but as an essential component of daily living to preserve vitality, longevity and good health.

Qi

The concept of qi, the 'vital energy' or 'life force' that sustains life is fundamental to the understanding of Chinese healing. The ancients believed that getting vital air or qi to the tissues and cells through a continuously circulating blood supply was the basic physiological function of the body. Together with jing (essence) and shen (mind or spirit), they comprise the 'three treasures' with qi being the organizing principle; jing the governor of vitality and longevity; and shen responsible for consciousness and mental ability.

When a person is in good health the movement of qi and blood through the body is harmonious. However, if qi or blood is blocked or slowed, the organs, tissues and cells will be deprived of the power needed to function at their best. Traditional therapies such as acupuncture, moxibustion, acupressure, reflexology and tui na, or exercise routines such as qi gong and tai chi, work towards removing blockages and encouraging a smoother flow of qi.

Yin and Yang

In ancient Taoist belief, the universe exists as a unified whole, comprising two opposing yet complementary forces called yin and yang. Originally

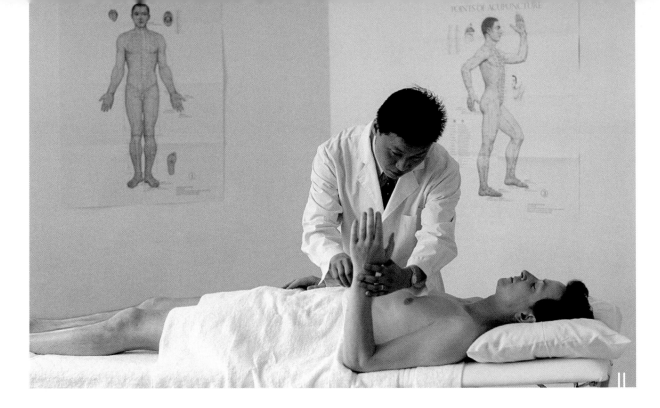

depicted as the shady (yin) and sunny (yang) sides of the mountain, together they represent poles of the same basic energy, much like the positive and negative poles of an electric current. As with everything in the natural world, both men and women each contain aspects of yin and yang. Yin is feminine, with cold, dark, quiet, static and wet properties, while yang is masculine, with warm, bright, dynamic and dry properties. When yin and yang forces are in balance, there is health and harmony. However, this dynamic equilibrium is easily disrupted by forces from within (such as grief, joy, shock, anger) and external environmental factors (such as cold, heat, dampness and dryness) that can leave the body susceptible to illness and disease.

Meridians

Qi flows along a network of channels or meridians to empower each and every organ in the body. The meridian network, much like a cobweb of crawling capillaries, comprises a system of 12 main channels (six yin and six yang channels) and eight 'extraordinary channels' that are spread throughout the body with each channel corresponding to an organ whose name it carries. Situated along the meridians are vital points called acupoints. It is at these strategic locations that qi can be stimulated through the traditional techniques of acupuncture or moxibustion, or by the hands, fingers, or even the palms, elbows, knees and feet, depending on the treatment being administered.

Longevity is related to sufficiency of qi. If the qi is strong, life is long.

Wong Chong, *Essay on Balance* (400BC)

| A collection of herbs and equipment that can be used by a TCM practitioner include acupunture needles, moxa sticks and suction cups. || A consultation will involve a check on the body's meridians.

Treatments & Therapies

Acupuncture

The first recorded success of acupuncture (zhen fa) dates to roughly 400BC–300BC when a Chinese physician, Bian Que, revived a dying man from a coma.

When qi is disrupted the job of the acupuncturist is to nudge it back to equilibrium by inserting needles at specific points along the meridians and pulsing the body with a low electric current to free the blocked energy.

Acupuncture gained worldwide recognition in 1979 when the World Health Organization (WHO) issued a list of health conditions appropriate for acupuncture therapy including digestive complaints, gynaecological and respiratory ailments, headaches and migraines, tennis elbow, insomnia and muscular pain. While Western medicine remains unsure of exactly how acupuncture works, they know in certain situations that it does by producing measurable changes in the brain with the overall effect of numbing and comforting

There are approximately 365 acupoints along the body's main energy channels with many more on the lesser channels and, depending on the medical diagnosis, specific acupoints will be selected for treatment. Needles are inserted at acupoints in the area of pain or those on an associated meridian pathway. Insertion is usually quick with a slight sensation being felt and needles are normally kept in place for up to 30 minutes during which time various techniques are used to either sedate, disperse or tone the body's flow of qi.

Moxibustion

Moxibustion (jiu fa), the burning of the herb moxa (artemisia vulgaris) can be traced back to Chinese peasants who burnt herbs around parts of the body to relieve pain. While the ancients used heated rocks or hot sand wrapped in animal skin or tree bark in hot compresses to warm afflicted parts of the body, the most common form of moxa used today is the moxa stick. This is a compressed moxa leaf resembling a mini cigar which, when lit, is held or rotated above the skin of the affected area causing heat to enter the body. This stimulates the circulation of blood and qi.

Moxibustion can also be applied using cones of moxa directly on the skin, or indirectly via an insulating layer of other herbs (for example, ginger which releases warmth). For maximum effect acupuncture and moxibustion can be combined (zhen jiu) to restore harmony and balance in the body. When used in conjunction with acupuncture, the moxa cones are placed at the ends of inserted acupuncture needles and lit, allowing the heat and curative effects of the herb to be conducted into the body without scarring.

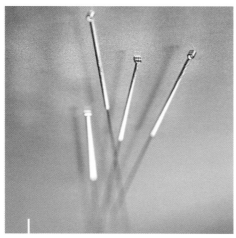

| Therapists can use up to nine types of acupuncture needles. Once inserted techniques such as vibration can be applied to stimulate the body's qi. || A moxa stick, the cigar-shaped implement used for moxibustion. ||| Dried herbs can be attached to the needle and lit. This warms the acupuncture point and strengthens the treatment. |||| Moxibustion on the navel helps to relieve abdominal pain and an upset stomach.

| With cupping, suction produces blood congestion at the targeted point thus stimulating it. This technique is used for lower back pain and sprains. | | In reflexology where the therapist concentrates on certian points which then releases blockages and restores the flow of qi to the whole body.

Acupressure

Acupressure is a term encompassing any number of massage techniques that use manual pressure to stimulate energy points in the face and body. Acu means care or precision and the acupressure system of therapy shares the same acupoints as acupuncture. However, instead of needles the therapist uses firm pressure with the hands and fingers to stimulate qi and enhance circulation through the meridians. The technique is highly effective for relieving constipation, diarrhoea, insomnia, back and muscle pain and poor digestion. Acupressure can also be used in conjunction with other massage techniques.

Cupping

An ancient form of therapeutic massage, cupping (ba guan) is an effective means of moving stagnant qi and invigorating the system. The technique involves the strategic fixing of small glass jars at various points on the skin using a pump to create a vacuum. The suction created increases the local circulation of qi and blood, and dispels cold and dampness from the body. Cupping is suitable for joint stiffness and pain and for relieving swelling and is often practised in conjunction with acupuncture and massage.

Tui Na

Literally translated as 'press and rub', tui na is the oldest and most common form of Chinese acupressure massage. It is believed to be the forefather of other bodywork techniques such as shiatsu (see page 33–34) and traditional Thai massage (see page 42–43).

There are over 20 different tui na techniques each involving deep digital stimulation of vital points along the meridians. But the most commonly practised include: tui (pushing), na (grasping), an

(pressing), mo (rubbing), gun (rolling), qian (pulling), da (beating) and dou (shaking). It is excellent for treating colds and headaches, insomnia, intestinal upsets, menstrual irregularities, lower back pain and stiff neck and can be applied to the whole body. Sensitive areas like the face and neck may require gentler movements. Oils generally act as lubricants but specific preparations can also be used to treat certain conditions. For example, ginger warms the stomach and spleen and is used to treat colds, vomiting and stomach pain (see recipe opposite) while whiskey or rice wine helps activate qi and blood flow.

Reflexology

As the feet (and to a lesser extent the hands) are regarded as a microcosm of the body in traditional Chinese thinking, reflexology uses pressure applied to reflex points in the feet to relieve stress and tension and improve circulation. Six major energy

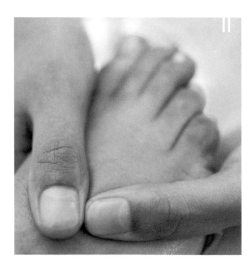

meridians terminate in the feet: that of the spleen, kidneys, liver, stomach, gallbladder and bladder—as do some of the major nerves. Using thumb pressure to press and deeply massage each of the tiny reflex zones in the feet a skilled reflexologist can stimulate the associated organs and glands thereby activating the body's natural healing mechanisms and correcting imbalances. The big toe for instance is connected to the head, and simply stimulating it through massage can help ease headaches.

Reflexology is suitable for all ages and has been proven to help improve circulation, ease pain, relax the body, and treat a wide range of acute and chronic illnesses ranging from post-natal depression to skin conditions.

Five Element Shiatsu

Based on the Japanese-inspired shiatsu technique (see page 33–34), five element shiatsu goes one step further by combining shiatsu with the physical and emotional energies of the five elements. This technique has been found to enhance energy flow through the body and relieve chronic conditions including back pain, insomnia, migraines, digestive problems, and asthma or can be enjoyed as pure and unadulterated relaxation.

Chi Nei Tsang

Developed by Chinese Taoist monks in mountain monasteries as a method of detoxifying and strengthening their bodies in preparation for attaining the highest level of spiritual practice, chi

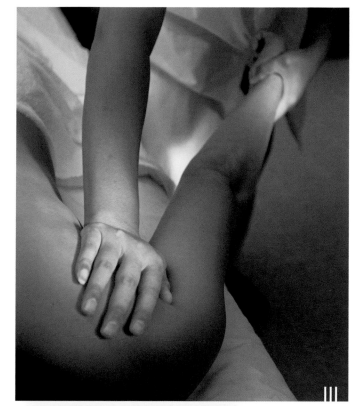

Tincture of Ginger and Spring Onion

30 g (1 oz) fresh ginger
30 g (1 oz) spring onion
250 ml (9 fl oz/1 cup) clear alcohol (vodka or white rum)

- For best results soak ginger and spring onion in alcohol for two weeks. Strain and store the solution in an airtight container and apply as needed.
- For a faster version, simmer ginger and spring onion in water for 15 minutes before applying to the skin.

| One of the fundamental techniques of tui na is qian, or pulling.
|| Another technique is na, or grasping.

Flowing water never stagnates. The hinges of an active door never rust. This is due to movement. The same applies to essence and energy. If the body does not move, qi does not flow and energy stagnates.

Spring and Autumn Annals (4th century BC)

nei tsang is a term loosely used to describe an internal organ massage of the abdominal area (or tan tien). Roughly translated into 'working the energy and programming of the internal organs', chi nei tsang is based on the belief that the abdominal area (specifically the lower abdomen around the navel) is the centre of energy in the body. It is also the centre for the metabolic processes of digestion, detoxification and energy dispensation, the structural centre of gravity and the area where stress, tension and negative emotions accumulate and congest, leading to a blockage in the flow of qi and a weakening of the internal organs. While other massage techniques work from the periphery inwards, chi nei tsang works from the centre of the body outwards cleansing and nourishing the internal organs. It helps to improve circulation, stimulate the lymphatic system and eliminate toxins. The massage also addresses visceral structures and is believed to help correct misalignment of the feet, legs and pelvis as well as relieve chronic pain in the back, neck and shoulders. Emotions become balanced too as negative emotion (stored in the digestive system) is cleared from the body.

Qi Gong and Tai Chi Chuan

Exercises that manipulate the flow of qi have been practised in a variety of forms for thousands of years. This is where movement becomes so closely intertwined with medicine as these therapies direct the flow of qi through the meridians to nourish and energize the body keeping in balance and health. If correctly executed on a regular basis, these exercises can help develop dynamic and powerful internal strength.

Qi Gong: The term qi gong, meaning energy work, was coined in the 1930s to cover an extensive system of therapeutic breathing, postural and moving exercises. Based primarily on manoeuvres learned by observing animals in nature, these flowing instinctive movements orchestrate balance and harmony between yin and yang, the five elements, the three treasures and the body, brain and electromagnetic forces of our internal and external environments.

Tai Chi Chuan (or Tai Chi): Literally translated as 'supreme ultimate reality', tai chi is meditation in movement and a gentler and more graceful art form than qi gong. It consists of a series of movements

| The ancient art of tai chi chuan focuses on the smooth movement through the joints and is based on relaxation rather than muscular tension. The slow and repetitive movements gently open the internal flow of qi causing long-term effects on stress relief.

that can take anything from five to 30 minutes to perform. Tai chi exercises help to regulate the body, the breath and the mind (through visualization and concentration techniques) and, with regular practice, stamina and strength are developed as well as grace and flexibility.

Herbal Medicine

In ancient China, large prosperous households often retained their own herbalists. These herbalists were paid when the household was healthy, and not when there was illness. Herbalists were thus concerned just as much with preventing as with curing disease. This dual function of Chinese herbal medicine still holds firm today.

Herbal medicine remains the prime orthodox medicine in China where hundreds of ingredients contribute to common cures. The term 'Chinese herbs' is not limited to plants; animal and mineral elements, for instance dried geckos and pearls, are also important sources. Chinese dispensaries stock herbs in their raw form as extracts and tinctures, oils and potions, as well as preparations ground to create ointments or poultices.

Herbs are classified according to their nature (hot, warm, cool or cold), taste (sour, bitter, sweet, pungent, salty and bland), effectiveness and preparation. Additionally their basic biochemical composition and medicinal effects are considered which together determine what herbalists call their 'natural affinities'. For example, herbs used for liver problems share an affinity with the liver meridian. When the herb is metabolized in the body, its energy enters the liver meridian and its therapeutic action targets the liver directly.

Herbal teas and tonics are used to complement physical treatments and are prescribed to re-establish the body's natural equilibrium. Chrysanthemum tea, for example has cooling properties and can help relieve fevers, sore throats and other heat-related illnesses. The properties in gingko tea can help to improve the memory and mental clarity. It is also known to increase blood circulation and metabolism.

| The herbal chest of traditional Chinese medicine contains all kinds of plants, animal and mineral elements. Herbs are processed in several ways before being administered. The processing is an important step as it modifies the herbs' therapeutic qualities. || Herbal tea will conclude most spa treatments.

Commonly Used Chinese Herbs

Ginseng (radix panax ginseng): Ginseng (Chinese or Korean) is an extraordinarily powerful tonic that stimulates the nervous and endocrine systems thereby increasing vital energy and treating a range of deficiency states including chronic fatigue, sleep problems, weakness and anxiety. Although ginseng extracts and powders are now widely available, a tea of top-quality ginseng should be taken monthly, during detox or at the beginning of the season to prepare the body for the months ahead.

Dandelion (herba taraxacum officinale or fisherman's herb): This is an excellent spring healer. The dandelion roots' bitterness cleanses and stimulates the glands that are involved with digestion, especially the liver. It is also used to treat mastitis, urinary infections, swollen eyes and as a lactation promoter. The diuretic properties, as well as the vitaman C, A, and iron content make dandelion leaves highly nutritious and are excellent in salads or taken as a tea. Since the plant is closely related to chicory, its roots are sometimes used as a coffee substitute. Both leaves and roots can be used in herbal preparations.

Bird's Nest (collocalia inexpectata or Asian swiftlets' nests): In Asia, bird's nest is a gastronomic delicacy. Literally a nest created by sea swallows native to South-East Asia who, rather than collecting twigs and debris, secrete a gelatinous saliva which hardens into a nest and sticks to the walls of the caves they make home. Medicinally, bird's nest is primarily indicated in convalescence-promoting digestion and absorption and helping delay the onset of ageing. It strengthens the lungs and is used to treat severe coughs, chronic bronchitis and emphysema.

Camomile (matricaria chamomilla): A herb for the stomach and spleen, camomile is one of the oldest and most popular Chinese herbs. Drunk as a tea it soothes and calms the stomach and is excellent for menstrual problems.

Externally, Camomile also relieves tiredness and irritation. Simply soak cotton-wool pads in cold camomile tea and place over the eyes. Lie down and relax and let the goodness of the herb soothe the delicate area.

Dang Gui (radix angelica sinensis or Chinese angelica): Considered the queen of women's herbs, dang gui is one of the most widely used herbs in China as a tonic for the blood, regulating the menstrual cycle and invigorating the entire system. As well as dilating the blood vessels, dang gui has anti-inflammatory, analgesic and antibacterial effects and is routinely prescribed for the relief of cramps and other menstrual symptoms as well as hot flushes which are associated with the menopause.

Dang gui can either be eaten raw or cooked, alone or combined with other herbs, in capsules or liquid form. Generally the whole root is cut into long slices and used either boiled with sweet dates (such as jujube) to make a sweet-tasting tea or used in a soup.

Ki

HOLDING THE JAPANESE HEALING BOWL

A visit to Japan is the perfect opportunity to experience something truly different. Unlike many other Asian countries the unique culture depicted in countless films still exists in daily life; be it in the meticulous preparation and presentation of traditional foods like sushi and sashimi, the takeaway bento boxes so beautifully packaged; the near absence of English being spoken on the streets; the spotless white gloves of the policeman; and the linen and lace seat covers in the taxis.

For a taste of authentic Japan a stay at a traditional inn or ryokan is a must. These Japanese inns hark back to medieval times and have become national treasures with many being located beside onsens or hot springs. What better way to become part of the rich history of this vast nation than by sleeping on a futon, bathing in the mineral-rich hot spring waters and eating cross-legged on wooden floors surrounded by paper screens, straw tatami mats and the gentle hospitality of the Japanese.

Purity is of utmost importance to the Japanese and spas are largely centred around bathing. Unlike most other spas, where the healing experience is essentially a private ritual involving only the therapist and recipient, onsens offer a communal atmosphere. Not your typical spa by any stretch of the imagination, but when in Japan onsens are the only way to go and the Japanese take this ritual as seriously as sipping their tea—it is done regularly, leisurely and sometimes with company. When bathing Japanese style the tub is used exclusively for soaking (the body is washed before getting into the bath) and a long soak at the end of the day stimulates circulation, relieves stress and leaves the body refreshingly clean.

Unlike this unique bathing ritual, many other Japanese therapies have their roots firmly grounded in Chinese, Korean and European disciplines. In fact, Japan's traditional medical system is the Japanese adaptation of traditional Chinese medicine.

| Beppu, on the Kyushu island of Japan, is famous for its nine onsen and is seen as Japan's onsen capital. || Traditional stone lanterns that decorate the parks and onsen. Some onsen have been made national treasures of Japan.

Go quickly to this river-mouth and wash your body with its water. Then take the pollen of the Kama grass of the river-mouth, sprinkle it around, and roll on it. If you do this your skin will certainly heal as before.

The Kojiki (712AD)

A Cultural Perspective

According to the Kojiki (Record of Ancient Matters), the Shinto deity Opo-namudi-no-kami outlined the above prescription for the white rabbit of Inaba who lost his fur to the sharks while attempting to return to his homeland across the ocean. The three native Japanese healing methods of exorcism, purification and herbal therapy are employed in this famous Japanese myth with Opo-namudi-no-kami, being the archetype of the ancient shamans or medicine men who performed exorcisms; the bath in the waters of the river-mouth purifying the white rabbit of Inaba; and the Kama grass pollen representing herbal therapy.

Traditional Japanese belief held that disease was the result of possession by vengeful spirits (kami), and the cure was purification rites (harai), or exorcism performed by shamans. Purification was seen to be important more for its preventive rather than its curative effects, and even today, bathing, purification rituals and careful attention to personal hygiene are an intrinsic part of Japanese culture.

The principles of the Japanese healing system as we know it derive primarily from TCM. Monks and travelling physicians were the original bearers of Chinese cures. A Korean physician, Kon-mu, who became the Japanese emperor's personal physician, first introduced Chinese medicine to the imperial court of Japan in the 5th century. Around 560AD, the Chinese physician Zhi Cong brought detailed medical documents, including texts on materia medica, acupuncture and moxibustion to Japan, which were studied avidly at court. From the 6th century, diplomatic exchanges between the two countries intensified as did the introduction of medical and scientific findings, and by the

| Bathing is a communal exercise in Japan. || The distinctive style of Japan is everywhere. ||| Japan's hot springs bear the importance of purification and personal hygiene.

7th century, Chinese medicine began to be systematically adopted by the Japanese.

The second half of the 16th century saw the introduction of Western medicine into the country and by the start of the Meiji period (1868-1912), all medical practitioners were required by law to study Western medicine. Medical licenses were issued only to those who passed the national examination in Western medicine. Traditional practices lost their status and became mainly the realm of blind practitioners. Some of the schools that were set up to train blind practitioners still exist, although sighted practitioners now outnumber the blind.

After the Meiji era, a classical revival began which saw the rise and establishment of Japanese medicine in modern Japan. The Japan Society of Oriental Medicine was established in 1950, and went on to become officially approved as one of the Japanese Associations of Medical Sciences in 1991.

Today, the Japanese adaptation of the Chinese system of healing still exists and is known as kanpo, although the term is now more commonly used when referring to herbal therapy. Although heavily influenced by Chinese ideology and methods, the Japanese have distinct features of their own, including the development of shiatsu and reiki therapies and distinctively Japanese diagnostic techniques, manipulative therapies and folk remedies.

While Western medicine still dominates, Japanese traditional medicine has retained a firm place in the country's modern health system. And despite immense scientific development—when it comes to healing—spiritual rituals and the use of talismans from temples and shrines remain the therapy of choice for many Japanese.

Treatments & Therapies

Ki

Qi, or the life force that sustains the body in TCM, is known as ki in Japan, and its manipulation is an essential component of most Japanese healing techniques. TCM's philosophy extends further with the yin and yang theory of balance (page 26–27) corresponding to the balance between in and yo in Japan, and Chinese medicine's network of meridians and 'extraordinary channels' being the same in the Japanese system.

Illness is believed to result when normal balance is disrupted due to either kyo (deficiency) or jitsu (excess) of ki. When ki is deficient, it is said to be in (or yin) in nature; when in excess, it is yo (or yang).

Bo-shin (observation diagnosis) and setsu-shin (palpation diagnosis) are the two primary ways a Japanese practitioner determines the state of the body's ki and overall health. In bo-shin, various visual indicators, including gait, skin, nails, hair, facial features, and body size and proportions are assessed, while setsu-shin is a diagnostic technique whereby the practitioner analyses the pulse readings at the wrist to determine the patterns of kyo and jitsu in the organs and meridians. Ampuku (abdominal diagnosis) is a further diagnostic tool, unique to the Japanese which is based on the premise that different areas of the abdomen correspond to specific organs. Through gentle pressure, the practitioner can detect conditions of kyo or jitsu, and, some believe, even life expectancy.

Once a practitioner has determined the status of ki in the organs and meridians, he can determine the root cause of imbalance and disease, and prescribe appropriate therapy. The primary aim of treatment, whether through acupuncture, massage or herbs, is kyo-jitsu-ho-sha, which means replenishing a ki deficiency or dispersing excess ki, to regain balance and harmony.

| Japanese acupunture will use finer needles and is more gentle than its Chinese counterpart. || Green tea is known for its detoxifying qualities. ||| An acupuncture model; traditional Japanese therapies are firmly rooted in traditional Chinese medicine. |||| Moxibustion, Japanese style, where the herb is placed closer to the skin.

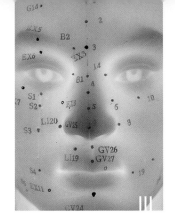

Acupuncture and Moxibustion

Acupuncture (hari) and moxibustion (kyu) have evolved directly from TCM with the same principles applying to both. However, the Japanese techniques are generally more subtle, using finer equipment. It is believed that the insertion of needles and the burning of moxa herbs at precise acupoints will stimulate the flow of ki, and replenish or disperse it.

With Japanese-style acupuncture the needles are generally finer and shorter than the Chinese with guide tubes being used to tap the needles into place. Unlike the Chinese treatment, where the needle sensation is felt both by the practitioner and recipient, Japanese acupuncture therapy is gentle and the needling is much more superficial, so the patient may not feel anything at all.

The use of moxibustion is widespread in Japan for the relief of pain and common ailments. Self-help packaged moxa is readily available. The most popular moxibustion technique involves direct contact with the skin. Tiny rice-sized moxa pieces are placed on appropriate acupoints and lit. They are then allowed to burn right down to the skin, or extinguished just before, with the process repeated until there is a feeling of warmth. Indirect moxibustion is also practiced with the techniques used being similar to those used in TCM.

Shiatsu

Shiatsu is a Japanese word literally translated as finger (shi) pressure (atsu). Often described as 'acupuncture without the needles', shiatsu is a marriage between Chinese acupressure and Western massage techniques and uses a variety of hands-on movements including holding, pressing

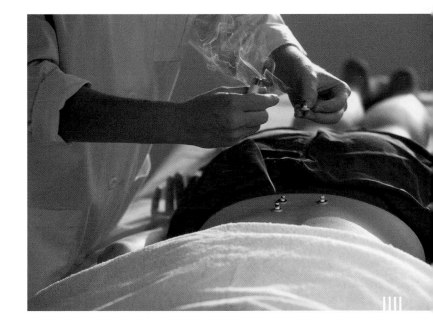

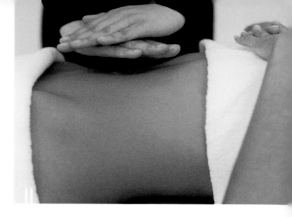

(with palms, thumbs, elbows, knees and feet) and, when appropriate, more dynamic rotations and stretches to improve the flow of ki through the body. It is a relatively modern system, popularized less than a century ago by the Japanese physician Tokujiro Namikoshi.

While based on massage, the one big difference between it and other physical therapies is that by manipulating the acupoints, shiatsu works on the body's energy system as a whole rather than localized areas and therapy is tailored to individual concerns whether it be back pain, migraine, neck and whiplash injuries, menstrual issues, sports injuries or rheumatic pain.

Regular shiatsu also helps boost stamina, improve digestion and concentration, relieve stress and calm both mind and body.

Kanpo

The Japanese system of kanpo (herbal medicine) is adapted directly from TCM. Some of the first kanpo recipes can be found in Japan's oldest medical text, the Ishinpo, compiled by Yasuyori Tanba in the 10th century. Today, kanpo medicine is fully integrated into the modern health care system and there are some 150 kanpo recipes listed on the Japanese National Health Insurance Drug Price Tariff. The recipes are generally gentler (but are just as effective) as the Chinese and differ in the finer and smaller quantities used.

The aim of the kanpo practitioner is simply to rebalance ki through herbs. Kanpo may not have any visible effects unless the body's natural equilibrium is disrupted; it then acts to re-balance and

strengthen the body by activating its self-healing potential. Kanpo medicine is highly individualized; the formula is tailored to the individual not the disease, and is designed not only to relieve the symptoms of disease, but to bring the person back to health and balance. Herbal remedies are available as teas, decoctions, or most commonly as pills or granules to be taken daily.

Kanpo ingredients are derived primarily from plants, with some mineral and animal ingredients. They are classified according to their side effects and toxicity: shang pin (upper-class) drugs generally have a weaker affect with no adverse side effects; zhong pin (middle-class) drugs have weak side effects in small doses or when taken over a period of time; and xia pin (lower-class) drugs have strong effects, often accompanied by adverse side effects. The drugs are carefully combined based on long-standing formulations with each ingredient acting synergistically.

The concept of balance in Japanese cuisine has been influenced by the principles of kanpo. The recipe below is recommended for those suffering

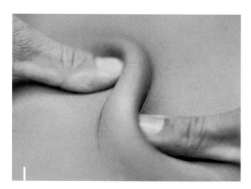

Steamed aubergines in sour sauce

3 tbsp soy sauce
2 tbsp sake
1 tbsp sugar
1 tbsp vinegar
3 tbsp hot water
½ spring onion, finely chopped
thumbsize piece fresh ginger, grated
pinch of finely chopped parsely
7 medium aubergines, peeled

To prepare seasoning, mix all ingredients apart from the aubergines, and chill in the refrigerator. Meanwhile, steam aubergines for 15 minutes and remove. While hot, squeeze out all liquid from aubergines using a rolling pin. With your hands, break them up into bite-size pieces and squeeze dry once more. Roll each piece into a ball and soak each in the seasoning. This must be done whilst the aubergine is still hot to increase absorption. Allow to cool and then place in the refrigerator. Serve aubergine balls chilled.

from high blood pressure or constipation and is easy to prepare at home. Traditionally, aubergines are said to be effective in eliminating fever or loss of appetite. Chilling and serving them with a slightly sour sauce helps to increase the appetite.

Reiki

Reiki is a Japanese word meaning 'universal life force' and is primarily perceived as a method of healing for body, mind and spirit. It is believed that the technique of reiki was rediscovered in ancient Tibetan Sanskrit sutras (Buddhist teachings) during the late 1880s by Dr Mikao Usui, who went on to practise reiki in Japan, introducing it to other masters. Today, it is one of the most popularly taught and practised therapies in the West.

Reiki is an extremely calming form of touch therapy with the practitioner harnessing his ability to control ki to heal others. Although ki is present in everyone, it is believed that a person needs to be attuned according to the ancient symbols before he

Just for today, do not worry.
Just for today, do not anger.
Honour your parents, teachers and elders.
Earn your living honestly.
Show gratitude to everything.

Dr Mikao Usui, from *The Five Ethical Principles of Reiki*.

| The finger pressure of shiatsu was discovered by Tokujiro Namikoshi. || Reiki works to clear, straighten and heal the energy pathways, thus allowing energy, or ki, to flow in a healthy and natural way. ||| An important part of reiki is that you take an active role in your treatment by drawing in energy as needed. An open and positive mind also helps to ensure that you will benefit from reiki.

can use it to heal others. Attunement is achieved after a few stages over a number of years.

During a reiki session, the practitioner transmits the energy from his body to the client by placing his hands over or on the areas requiring attention, starting with the head. When the practitioner channels this life force through his hands it is believed to rebalance and replenish areas where ki is depleted, and activate the client's innate healing ability. For instance, placing a hand over or on the abdomen is believed to cure a digestive problem or ease menstrual cramps. Treatment sessions generally last about one hour. Reiki is said to be effective in relieving many illnesses including arthritis, insomnia and migraine and apart from treating others, it is also considered an effective form of self-healing.

Baths

Cleansing the spirit and warding off disease are the main benefits thought to be derived from some 2,500 onsens or hot spring baths spotted throughout the islands of Japan. The term onsen can refer to a single bathing facility, or to an entire town or hot spring area. Onsens range in size from small tubs for one person to enormous pools that can accommodate over 100 bathers. Baths are traditionally measured in tatami mats, a traditional Japanese unit based on the size of the straw mats used in the home. There is a wide variety of springs throughout the whole of Japan, and these include uchi-buros (indoor baths), rotten-buros (outdoor baths) and mushi-yus (steam baths).

When bathing Japanese style, the body is washed and scrubbed clean before entering—soap should not get into the bath. Sitting on one of the small stools provided, the soap is rubbed into the tenugui (small towelling cloth) before being rubbed into the body. A quick rinse leaves the skin soft, smooth and invigorated as dead cells are removed and the blood circulation stimulated before immersing in the bath to enjoy a relaxing therapeutic soak. The extra-deep bathtub is filled to the top with very hot water, in which the person sits submerged to the neck. Most people in Japan spend about half an hour in the bath every night and it is a major part of the daily routine.

Many onsens are found close to areas of volcanic activity as bathing in mineral-rich waters is believed to cure a range of illnesses from nervous disorders and bad circulation to skin irritations, aches and fatigue. The seasons are important too as bathing washes off sweat during the hot summer months and warms the body during winter. Flavoured baths are popular. Mandarin orange peel features during the autumn, yuzu (an aromatic lemon) is traditionally used on the winter solstice in December, and ginger is used to warm the body during winter.

Autumn/Winter Bath
Place mandarin orange peel or freshly chopped ginger into muslin bags and toss them into your bath to infuse the water with their scent and healing properties. This aromatic bath aids digestion and clears catarrh.

| The deep rotten-buro, or outdoor bath is the concluding part to the bathing ritual. || The tenugui, or small cloth, ubiquitous at the Japanese onsen.

Thailand's Healing Legacy

HARMONY WITH NATURE

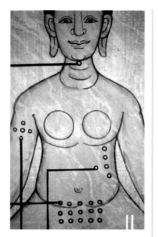

Thailand is the land of the wats (temples) and one of Asia's most desired holiday destinations. From the chaotic city of Bangkok and the hilly northern region of Chiang Mai to the southern beach paradise of Hua Hin and the pristine islands of Phuket and Koh Samui, there is no better place to escape and experience authentic Thai healing midst the tropical beaches, virgin forests of swaying palms and turquoise blue waters.

In a sense, the history of Bangkok is the history of the Chao Phraya river that runs through it, for it was on the east bank of the Chao Phraya that King Buddha Yodfa Chulaloke or Rama I, the first king of the Chakri Dynasty that still reigns today, established the new capital of Siam in 1782. The entire city is encircled by a network of khlongs (canals), which in those times allowed for quick and efficient troop transfer. Once the lifeblood of the city, most of the khlongs are now filled but it is still possible to catch a ferry along the remaining ones for just 7 baht (less than 20 US cents).

Of all the treatments offered in spas, the most popular and by far the most famous is traditional Thai massage or Nuat bo'rarn. No visitor to Thailand should leave without experiencing it and, when in Bangkok, Wat Pho, Thailand's oldest and largest temple is the place to loosen joints, soothe aches and pains, and ease muscle tension in the time-honoured spiritual Thai fashion.

| The spires of Wat Pho, the temple is known as the birthplace of Thai massage. Students can also learn the art of classic Thai massage at the temple complex. || Inscribed on stone slabs, in the walls of Wat Pho, are all that was known about Thai massage dating from the reign of King Rama III.

A Cultural Perspective

Buddhism is the dominant religion in Thailand with an estimated 95 per cent of the population being Theravada Buddhists. Temples can be found on almost every street all bearing testimony to the Thais' religious devotion.

Theravada Buddhism originated in India and spread through South-East Asia to Sri Lanka, Myanmar, Laos, Cambodia and Thailand. Not surprisingly, traditional Thai medicine began in the cultural and historical context of Theravada Buddhism, and like many other traditional medical systems, was deeply influenced by ayurveda (page 13–23) and TCM (page 25–35). The historical progenitor of Thai medicine, Jivaka Kumar Bhaccha (pronounced by Thais as 'Shivago Komarpaj') is revered by almost all practitioners as the 'Father Doctor' of Thai medicine. A contemporary of Buddha, he was personal physician to Buddha's order of monks and nuns over 2,500 years ago and was a renowned ayurvedic doctor considered by most to be the original teacher of Thai massage and the source of the country's complex herbal pharmacopoeia. Most herbalists, masseurs and traditional doctors maintain a shrine with statues of the Buddha and Father Doctor side-by-side and prayers are chanted daily to invoke the spirit of the Father Doctor to assist in healing.

Historically, monks were respected both for their religious authority and their ability to heal and

Buddhist temples were centres of learning, not only of religion, but also of worldly matters such as astrology and medicine. The meditation and prayer element of healing reflects how steeped the Thais were in their religious beliefs and even today, masseurs are encouraged to recite a prayer before beginning their work.

In 1836, the rising popularity of traditional Thai massage inspired King Rama III (1824-1851) to have all available knowledge on the subject carved on stone slabs. These slabs were later set into the walls of the Wat Pho temple in Bangkok. Today, the School for Traditional Medicine is located here as is the national headquarters for the teaching and preservation of traditional Thai medicine.

Energy

In Thai philosophy human life is holistically viewed as a combination of three essences: body which refers to the substance of which we are made; citta (translated as mind/heart) is understood to represent the thoughts, emotions and spirit that comprise our inner self; and energy (the equivalent of qi in TCM and the Indian concept of prana) is the force that sustains life, holding mind, heart and body together. This energy courses the body through a complex network of meridians called nadis which are believed to hold 72,000 acu or sên points, each with its own specific function.

Working with the essences Thai medicine is split into three disciplines: religious or spiritual healing, manipulative (Thai) massage and diet/herbal medicine. As many diseases are believed to flow from a troubled heart or mind, spiritual well-being is considered fundamental to overall health. To this end, healing is enveloped in a rich and intricate tradition of prayer, meditation, mantras and mythology that is based around Buddhist healing philosophy.

Traditional Thai massage is seen primarily as a therapy of energy. Applying appropriate pressure to sên points releases the body's natural healing energy, promotes blood and lymphatic circulation and eliminates toxins from within. Modern Thais fervently apply this belief and seek regular massage as a tool for both relaxation and for prevention of disease.

As herbs and food can affect the healing process at the physical and mental as well as energetic levels, they are therefore considered as therapies for the body essence. Herbal medicine is typically invoked only as a last resort, and when it is prescribed, it is always in conjunction with dietary recommendations.

As with other holistic Asian traditions Thai medicine believes in harmony, within the body and with nature, as being the key to health. The root cause of any disease is an imbalance or disharmony between body, citta and energy with the aim of therapy being to rebalance the essences thereby returning to health and harmony.

In modern Thailand the state-of-the-art hospitals and ancient traditions co-exist in harmony. Most modern and rural Thais utilize Thai massage, herbal and spiritual healing in addition to Western medical technology and the Thai government is one of the biggest supporters of this trend of rational and modern healing. In rural communities government-operated herbal clinics dispense traditional remedies alongside allopathic drugs.

| Thailand offers a range of spas. | | The classic Thai massage is now available at spas all over the world. | | | Thai herbs can be prescribed to rebalance the body's essences.

Treatments & Therapies

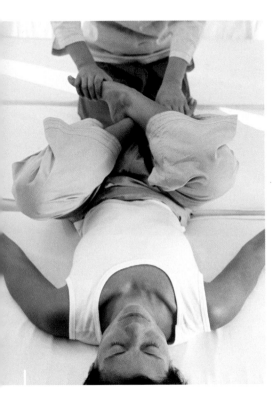

We pray for the one whom we touch,
That he will be happy and that any
illness will be released from him.

Part of the prayer recited by a therapist before a massage.

| Classic Thai massage is performed with loose clothing and no oil is applied, rather the therapist will use her own body for leverage. || Although Thai massage can be experienced anywhere, there is no better place than in Thailand itself.

Thai Massage

Thai massage or Nuat bo'rarn (meaning ancient massage) is primarily based on the acupressure system of Chinese and ayurvedic medicine with an added touch of yoga and was originally practised in Buddhist temples by monks who specialized in this 'manual manipulation' work. Today, it is no longer limited to monks and the temple setting but is a thriving therapy found in spas throughout Thailand and around the world.

To the uninitiated, Thai massage is associated with being contorted into all sorts of unimaginable body positions while being painfully kneaded by a therapist, but to the devoted, it is a healing, physically energizing and spiritual experience. While massage Thai-style does not necessarily seek to relax the body (unlike most Western massages), it remains popular among both Thais and visitors alike and integral to its effectiveness is correct breathing practice to induce a meditative state of mind.

A typical massage is performed on a floor mat with both therapist and massage recipient wearing loose and comfortable clothing. The therapist can then use his body as leverage to facilitate movements that would not be possible on a table. Massage begins with a meditative prayer called a puja, recited in the original Pali language which reminds the therapist of the 'Four Divine States of Mind' according to Buddhist teachings: compassion, loving kindness, vicarious joy and mental equanimity. When attained, these states of mind help the therapist provide a healing experience and their meditative state can then be imparted via touch to the recipient. It is only when a masseur performs his 'art' in a meditative mood that he can be considered a truly good practitioner of Thai massage.

Thai massage uses two primary techniques—use of gentle pressure with the hands and feet and a variety of passive stretching movements. The therapist uses his hands, forearms, knees and feet to apply pressure to the sên while also pulling, twisting and manipulating the body to encourage a smoother flow of energy.

When applied in a quiet, meditative atmosphere, the body begins to open and become more flexible while the mind returns to a state of calm alertness. Tension and toxic material is released from the joints, muscles and connective tissue and the body is revived and energized through the therapist's expert manipulation. A typical massage can last up to two hours, sometimes more, and its benefits include loosening of the joints, deep stretching and toning and, when performed correctly, a dynamic physical experience that integrates body mind and spirit.

Scrubs

Using only the most natural ingredients such as herbs and honey that are harvested in the northern part of Thailand, scrubs and masks exfoliate and nourish the skin while also improving the circulation of the whole body. Devarana Spa at The Dusit Thani Hotel in Bangkok offers the Wolfberry and Black Sesame Scrub to cleanse the body, stimulate circulation and promote silky smooth skin. Simple yet highly effective, it can be easily made and applied at home.

Wolfberry and Black Sesame Scrub

4 tbsp roasted and ground black sesame seed
2 tbsp ground wolfberry seed
1½ tbsp honey
1½ tbsp fresh milk
1 tbsp roasted and ground white sesame seed
1 tbsp sweet almond oil

Mix all the ingredients together thoroughly. Apply the scrub to wet skin, rub in a circlular motion and rinse off.
Black sesame has gentle exfoliating properties to help remove dead skin cells and protect skin from dryness. Wolfberry is an antioxidant herb that helps protect the skin from the harmful environment and wrinkles. The lactic acid in fresh milk is excellent for softening the skin.

Diet and Herbal Medicine

Like most other Asian medical traditions, Thai medicine is more about maintaining health and wellness than the curing of diseases. The emphasis is on prevention and not cure. Herbs are an essential ingredient and Thais believe that with an appropriate understanding of herbs, we can live in harmony with our lives and the changing seasons. By using traditional recipes the toxic effects of pollution and pesticides can be reduced, while energy, immunity and sexuality can be enhanced along with overall happiness and longevity.

The typical Thai kitchen is a treasure chest of herbs with each meal being considered therapeutic. Every food, drink and condiment—whether it be plant, animal or mineral based—can be classified by a predominance of one of 10 tastes and can therefore be used medicinally (see the chart above). Some foods can have a variety of different tastes. Thai curry for example is pungent, sweet and spicy all at once, while a dessert may be sweet and salty. It's this eclectic mix of flavours that has made Thai cuisine one of the tastiest and most popular around the world.

While many herbs (such as garlic, ginger and chilli) will help to preserve foods they also ward off illnesses especially in tropical climates where bacterial and viral infections are more prominent. Tom Yum Goong is a popular Thai soup that is excellent for treating colds, flu and intestinal problems. The key herbs used in the soup are lemongrass, kaffir lime leaves, chilli, garlic and galangal, all of which are effective decongestants and antibacterial agents.

Taste	Food/herb
Astringent	pomegranate, rhubarb
Oily/nutty	nuts, oils, seeds, butter
Salty	seafood, sea salt
Sweet	coconut, dairy, fruit, honey, sugar
Bitter	green tea, leafy greens, chrysanthemum
Sour	citrus fruits and juices
Hot/spicy	anise, basil, cayenne, cloves, garlic, ginger, lemongrass, peppermint, turmeric
Aromatic/cool	jasmine tea, edible flowers, lotus root
Bland	banana, pumpkin, squashes

Administering Herbs

Thai herbal remedies can be taken the following ways:

Tea or Infusion: Prepared by steeping herbs in hot (not boiling) water for 2–3 minutes. Generally teas are prepared from the more delicate parts of the plant such as flowers, leave, shoots or stems that can damage easily so therefore require just a short exposure to heat.

Decoction: Similar to tea, but the herbs are boiled for 10-15 minutes and more commonly used for thick and woody herbs like vegetables, barks and stalks that require cooking to release their therapeutic benefits.

Powder: Generally used for dried seeds, nuts or bark that are ground with a pestle and mortar (or coffee grinder). Prepared powders are typically taken dry with a mouthful of warm water.

Topical Application: Fresh or dried herbs can be mashed and pounded with a pestle and mortar and applied topically as a poultice or compress.

Steam Inhalation: Herbal remedies for the throat, lungs and eyes are usually delivered via steam. Alternatively herb bundles can be steamed and placed under the chest or nose of a patient.

Thai Herbal Wrap

Traditional Thai herbal wraps use mineral-rich mud to pamper and nourish even the most delicate of skins. The herbs used are chosen for their indigenous properties; for instance, turmeric is a natural antioxidant, while ginger moisturizes and warms the body. Ingredients are mixed into a paste and massaged over the body, paying extra attention to drier areas like the elbows, knees and feet. A plastic sheet can then be used to wrap the body for about 20 minutes. Alternatively, strips of cloth are soaked in a herbal solution and then used as a wrap, to encourage toxins to be expelled as the body perspires.

The Carrot and Pineapple Wrap recipe opposite is courtesy of the Six Senses Spa at The Evason Hua Hin. For convenience, when used at home it can be used as a mask rather than a wrap.

Thai Herbal Bolus Treatment

Herbs are routinely used in traditional Thai medicine as a complement to massage with most of the ingredients, for example lemongrass, kaffir lime, ginger and turmeric, taken from the traditional Thai kitchen. A herbal bolus (or pack) treatment uses herbs and spices that are then wrapped tightly in muslin or cotton and infused in hot water or steam. It is then used on the skin to rebalance the body and calm the mind.

The herbal-infused pack is both inhaled and absorbed by the skin. To treat muscular aches and pain, the therapist uses the hot bolus as a medium for body massage. Alternatively, the hot bolus can be placed on selected body areas to relieve sore muscles, stimulate circulation and refresh the skin. This therapy is especially popular for women who have recently given birth as the hot bolus soothes and calms the muscles while the herbal steam gently eases the mind.

Carrot and Pineapple Wrap

1 carrot, grated
½ pineapple
3–5 tbsp white clay
1 tsp turmeric powder

Mix all ingredients together, apply on the body and leave it to dry, for about 5-10 minutes. Rub off using yoghurt and carrot juice. Shower to get rid of the excess. This mask leaves the skin supple and radiant. Pineapple helps to whiten and brighten the skin, carrot will moisturize and turmeric is an excellent astringent and cleanser.

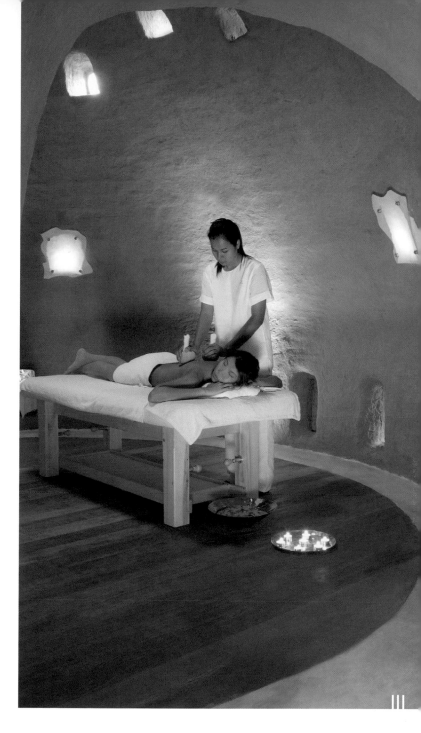

| Traditional Thai herbs that make up the natural pharmacy. || A herbal bolus (or pack) contains dried herbs that are infused in hot water or steam to stimulate the healing properties. ||| The packs can be used to massage oil onto the body. |||| A bolus can also be applied to selected areas of the body to relieve aches and pains.

Jamu

INDONESIA'S HEALING ELIXIR

A tropical paradise comprising some 17,000 islands and populated by an estimated 200 million people, Indonesia is home to possibly the most beautiful holiday destinations imaginable. The national motto 'unity in diversity' holds true for this exotic tropical archipelago where each region retains its own individuality and character.

Synonymous with spas in Asia is the geographically and spiritually unique island of Bali. Blessed with volcanic mountains, mineral rich waters, lush tropical forests and sandy beaches, Bali is also the only Hindu island in the world's most populous Islamic nation. Home to the majestic Ayung river, spirituality in Bali is a lifestyle firmly grounded in the Balinese village where the people strictly adhere to tradition. Fastidious about their culture and appearance, every shrine no matter how small, benefits from intense personal attention be it food, colourful clothing and song.

The vast majority of spas in Indonesia are located in Bali, with its myriad of tempting treatments from scrubs and baths to massages, wraps and full body rituals guaranteed to nurture both body and soul. Despite the range of treatments, they all share the same fundamental belief in the importance of maintaining balance and equilibrium as does ayurveda (page 13–23) and traditional Chinese medicine (page 25–35).

| Swaying palms and calming waves of the ocean make this a true tropical paradise. || Jamu, the traditional tonics of Indonesia, are a part of ordinary life.

A Cultural Perspective

Although the use of herbs for healing is as old as Javanese civilization itself, sourcing the roots of ancient healing has proved a mighty task. While written records of traditional medicine are extremely rare, evidence of the use of herbal remedies and body massages can be found etched on the walls of Borobudur, the famed Buddhist monument in central Java dating from circa 800-900AD. In these carvings the kalpataruh leaf (from the mythological 'tree that never dies') and other ingredients can be seen being pounded to make health and beauty potions.

Dating written material was not easy as, in the absence of the modern printing press, hand-copying texts was the only way of making these manuscripts available to a wider audience. Arguably the best references on Indonesia's traditional and herbal medicine (or jamu) are *Serat Kawruh bab Jampi-Jampi* (*A Treatise On All Manner of Cures*) and *Serat Centhini* (*Book of Centhini*) both of which can be found at the Surakarta Palace library. The former comprises a total of 1,734 formulae made from natural ingredients, many of which are still in use today. For example, spots on the skin can be cleared up with a preparation of pucung paste made from the fruit of the kluwak tree (pangium edule) mixed with urip

(euphorbia tirucalli; milk bush) and widuri (calotropis gigantea; mudar plant) which has been boiled with the fruit. The paste is applied to the spots while still warm and kept in place for at least one day. The instructions suggest completing the cure by grinding elung ubi jalar (the young leaves of sweet potato or Ipomoea batatas) with powdered lime and rubbing onto the affected area. A further 244 entries in the treatise are in the form of prayers or symbolic figures used as powerful amulets or talismans to cure specific diseases and protect the owners from black magic.

Although these manuscripts were generally in the realms of royalty and the rich, the contents were usually written in verse and sung or intoned as part of regular public performances. It is in this way that Javanese knowledge and philosophy spread to all levels of society.

Indonesia's medical profession only started to recognize the value of its vast natural apothecary in the early 1940s when, at the Second Congress of the Indonesian Physicians Association, a motion was passed recommending an in-depth study of traditional medicine and its applications. During the Japanese Occupation (1942–1944) the Dai Nippon government further supported herbal medicine by setting up the Indonesian Traditional Medicines Committee and more and more people began to turn to traditional medicine to heal and prevent disease.

Within Indonesia itself, healing traditions differ from region to region. However, one tradition that has remained constant is the use of jamu. From the days when it was first used, jamu has permeated all levels of society and today it is fast gaining popularity around the world.

| Ancient baths in Java. || Javanese style is inspired by the surrounding culture of central Java including the historic monument of Borobudur.

Jamu

Jamu is touted as the ancient elixir of life and despite the lack of scientific proof supporting its benefits, many Indonesians swear by its effectiveness with up to 80 per cent of the population believed to drink a glass of jamu daily after reciting a prayer.

Jamu is believed to have originated during the 17th century, when princesses in the Central Javanese courts of Surakarta and Yogyakarta began experimenting with plants, herbs and spices to concoct beauty potions. Since then, the use of jamu has expanded considerably and an entire beauty regime can be created just on jamu alone, from facial masks to hair conditioners and hand creams.

Although spanning an eclectic mix of drinks, brews, pills and powders, jamu has four basic functions: to cure illness; to prevent disease and maintain good health (by promoting blood circulation and increasing metabolism); to relieve aches and pains (by reducing inflammation and aiding digestion); and to correct malfunctions (such as infertility and menstrual irregularity). It can also be multi-functional for example, a jamu can be taken as a general tonic while also acting as an antiseptic to prevent stomach infection. Jamu is used in body wraps, as a facial mask or massage ointment. Its use depends very much on the complaint or need. It can be a herbal drink taken to prevent illness, the answer to chronic illness or indeed taken as an infusion, distillation, brew or as a paste to treat lifeless hair. Its advantage is that when correctly administered it has no side effects. Results may take a while and are not seen overnight and it is the job of the herbalist to ensure that the jamu created is a powerful and curative medicine.

Up to 150 ingredients are used to produce jamu, although only a few are used at any one time. Raw ingredients include the leaves, bark and roots of spices such as ginger, tamarind, turmeric and cinnamon with natural sweeteners like palm sugar often added for flavour. If the jamu drink is too bitter, a sweet drink will be offered to counter the unpleasant flavour.

Both males and females are introduced to jamu from birth as recipes pass through generations. Throughout a woman's life, jamu is her support; it guarantees harmony in the home and through life. The first real lesson for a girl is when she starts menstruating and her female relatives and friends sprinkle her with perfumed water as their blessing. The girl is then given jamu gadis (virgin jamu) made with a little earth she picks up from the garden and adds to other ingredients, which are then steamed. The ceremony symbolizes her entry to womanhood,

| A jamu gendong delivering the traditional elixir of life to the villagers. || Jamu is widely used across Indonesia.

her fertility, future resilience to and recovery from childbirth and her eternal love for family and friends. Traditionally at weddings, the mother of the bride presents the newly married couple with a box containing several kinds of seeds, rhizomes, spices and dried cuttings of traditional medicinal plants which are to be used on the first day of marriage, and more importantly, to be planted in the garden of the couple's home as a symbol of the mother's ongoing interest in her daughter's good health.

Today, jamu gendong (ladies selling jamu) can be seen throughout the country. With bottles of jamu in a basket slung over their shoulders with a slendang (carry cloth), they go from door to door in the villages, keeping the age-old tradition alive.

Below is a recipe for a traditional jamu drink courtesy of the Four Seasons Resort, Bali. Kunyit Asam is a Balinese herbal remedy, believed to remove heat from the body and cleanse the blood.

JAMU KUNYIT ASAM

100 g (3½ oz) fresh turmeric, peeled and sliced
1.2 L (2 pints/5 cups) water
130 ml (4 fl oz/½ cup) honey
25 g (1 oz) tamarind pulp, diluted in 1–2 tbsp water and strained
4 tbsp lime juice

Blend water and turmeric in a blender until smooth. Strain, transfer to a saucepan, add honey and bring to a boil. Remove from heat, add lime juice and tamarind and mix thoroughly. Strain again with a fine strainer. Cool and refrigerate. The jamu is best served chilled.

Treatments & Therapies

Crème Bath

Before commercial shampoo was readily available, Indonesian women used gel from crushed hibiscus leaves and coconuts to keep their hair healthy and strong. The heavier milk from the coconut is ideal for conditioning, washing, and massaging, while its lighter milk is used for rinsing and conditioning. In a mandi kepala (crème bath hair treatment) conditioner is applied liberally before massaging the hair section by section. Ingredients are chosen to suit individual hair condition—for instance, henna is used to nourish dry or treated hair, avocado for dry strands, and candlenut to achieve glossy locks. The shampoo treatment may sometimes include a stress-relieving head and neck massage to stimulate the scalp and soothe sore shoulders. A mixture of aloe vera, vitamin E moisturizer, jasmine and camomile essential oils is particularly suitable for dry hair. The crème bath should be applied to the hair and wrapped in a warm towel for 15 minutes before rinsing off. The result is shiny, softer and stronger hair.

Cupping

As with the TCM cupping technique (page 30), small glass jars are strategically fixed at various points on the skin and a pump is used to create a vacuum effect. The suction created increases the local circulation of blood and is useful for treating joint stiffness and pain as well as relieving swelling.

With the traditional Javanese style of cupping, which still remains popular amongst the older generation, a small amount of coconut oil is poured onto a ceramic saucer, which is placed directly onto the stomach or back. A piece of cotton cloth is then set alight on the oil creating a candle effect. A larger upturned glass or cup is placed completely over the saucer where the lack of oxygen makes it stick to the skin creating a vacuum. Left in place for about 15 minutes the tell-tale red ring appears on the skin and indicates a boost in circulation.

Traditional Lulur

The lulur (Javanese word for 'coating the skin') is most often associated with the luxurious pre-wedding ritual of Indonesian women. The treatment traditionally lasts for over 40 days, during which the bride-to-be is kept in confinement. Today's modern brides opt for a seven-day ritual without confinement.

A truly pampering ritual, the lulur is a treat for everyone. It generally comprises an aromatic massage, exfoliating body scrub and relaxing floral bath. The typical treatment varies slightly between spas, with some opting for added massage to moisturize, soften and hydrate the skin, while others choose an energizing shower before the floral bath. The following lulur recipe from the Ritz-Carlton, Bali Thalasso Resort & Spa moisturizes the skin restoring its natural balance.

TRADITIONAL LULUR

2 tsp rice powder
2 tsp turmeric
½ tsp sandalwood, ground
3 drops essential jasmine oil
500 ml (1 pint/2 cups) youghurt mixed with a little water

To make lulur paste, combine rice powder, turmeric, sandalwood and jasmine oil. Massage the body with massage oil, then generously apply lulur paste. Once dried gently rub off the paste to exfoliate. Apply yoghurt to the skin to moisturize, rinse off and soak in a floral bath.

| The crème bath will strengthen and revitalize your hair. || The floral bath, the conclusion to the traditional lulur, is common in spas and can easily be done home. ||| An ingredient in the traditional lulur is turmeric, which is great for treating skin disorders.

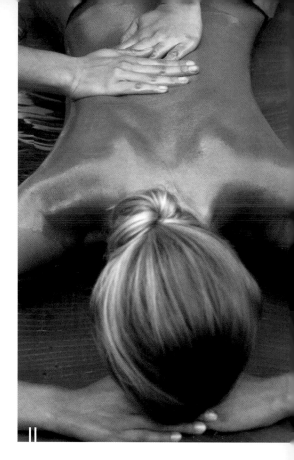

Mandi (Baths)

Mandi Susu: Cleopatra's legendary smooth skin has long been attributed to her fondness for bathing in milk. In Indonesia, Javanese princesses were also known to indulge in milk baths, especially goat's, sheep's or cow's milk. A mandi (bath) susu (milk) is one of the treatments available in spas for softer, smoother skin. It is believed that the lactic acid in milk naturally dissolves the 'glue' that holds dead skin cells together. So in effect, a mandi susu removes dead skin to reveal the new skin below.

This mandi susu recipe from Maya Ubud Resort and Spa in Bali can be performed in the comfort of your own home:

Drop 5 teaspoons of yogurt-based milk into the bath. Soak for bout 20 minutes before rinsing with warm to cool water. The best time for a soak is before a meal.

Floral Bath: A long soak amid fragrant blooms brings about a sense of tranquillity at any time but especially after body massages, wraps and other treatments. At the Maya Ubud Resort and Spa, a floral bath also includes the use of fragrant bath salts.

Dissolve aromatherapy bath salts in the bath-try orange rosehips or bergamot lime salts-add your favourite fresh flowers and soak in your flower bath for 10-15 minutes. Rinse with cool or warm water.

Indonesian Massage

Massage is an integral part of the Indonesian approach to inner and outer health and beauty and is often complemented by herbal brews and other traditional healing therapies. Traditional Indonesian massage can be classified into two main types: urut (the Indonesian word for massage) and pijat (the Javanese word for massage).

Urut Massage: The urut style is based on the meridians and acupoints of TCM (page 27–28). Using indigenous oils as lubricants, the skilled therapist uses the fingers, palms, knuckles and sometimes the whole body (which can be quite painful but highly effective) to manipulate muscles and energy pathways thereby improving blood circulation and eliminating toxic build up. This intense massage technique is most frequently used to treat specific medical complaints like bone fractures and chronic backaches. As the pressure applied by the therapist is quite strong some find it uncomfortable, even unbearably painful, but the end results make it all worthwhile.

| Flowers abound on the tropical islands of Indonesia. | | For Indonesian massages, natural oils are used. | | | The spring water of Sebatu provides the village with public baths.

Pijat Massage: Pijat-style massage is far gentler and comprises simple repetitive squeezing and kneading movements of the fingers and palms to relax tense muscles and calm the body. Generally the fingers hold the area being worked on while the thumb produces a pressured squeeze. Pijat massage does not require the same depth of knowledge as urut and is widely practised in villages across Indonesia.

Money Massage: Called kerokan, this style of massage involves a coin being dragged diagonally across the skin of the back, neck, shoulders, stomach and sometimes the feet, leaving strong red lines as if the person has been attacked. When it is correctly administered kerokan is painless and according to local custom this form of massage helps alleviate colds, colic and weak, aching bones by expelling bad wind from the body. If a medical doctor diagnoses gas or wind in the abdomen then kerokan can be prescribed to relieve the nausea and discomfort.

Scrubs

The Indonesian kitchen is a treasure trove of pampering and nourishing goodness for the face and body. From the local herbs and spices, to other kitchen items such as coffee, coconut, honey and avocado, local women don't have to travel far for their beauty needs. Body scrubs work by removing the dead layers of skin, revealing the soft, supple skin beneath. There are scrubs for all skin types but certain ingredients are not suitable for those suffering from rashes, acne, sunburn or women during their pregnancy.

Bali Coffee Scrub: As its name suggests, this scrub is based on finely ground local coffee beans. Balinese beans are preferable but if they cannot be found you can substitute with others. This scrub is a real treat for all coffee-lovers, who will undoubtedly savour the rich aroma while their skin is both cleansed and refreshed.

Balinese Boreh Masque: This traditional village remedy was originally used by rice farmers in Bali. It is believed that the boreh would warm the body and relieve aching muscles and joints especially during the rainy season.

Hand-crushed spices were applied to the farmer's legs after a hard day's work in the padi fields. Because it promotes warmth, the boreh masque is also used to relieve fevers and headaches, as well as prevent colds. It is not recommended for pregnant or nursing women, or for those with sun-damaged skin.

Opposite is a Balinese boreh recipe courtesy of the Ritz-Carlton Bali, Thalasso Resort & Spa. It can be used at home as an alternative deep heat treatment for those cold winter nights.

BALI COFFEE SCRUB

200 g (7 oz/2 cups) coffee beans
3 tbsp kaolin clay or cosmetic clay
a pinch of ground pumice stone
220 g (8 oz) carrots, blended
1 tsp gelatin, already set

Ground the coffee beans finely and mix with the kaolin clay and pumice stone. Add a little water so that the mixture becomes a paste. Rub the paste all over your body, taking time to thoroughly exfoliate the skin. Remove the excess scrub with a damp cloth. Mix the carrot with the gelatin. Apply to your body and leave it on for a short while. Rinse off and moisturize.

BALINESE BOREH

4 tsp ground sandalwood
2 tsp ginger, finely chopped
2 tsp whole cloves
1 tsp coriander seeds
1–2 tsp rice powder (fine ground rice)
1 tsp ground cinnamon
1 tsp turmeric, finely chopped
1 tsp ground nutmeg
1 tsp spice-blended oil

Blend all the ingredients with water to make a thick paste.
Spread the paste over your body. If the masque feels too hot
add more rice powder to cool down the herbal ingredients.
Leave the paste on until it dries then exfoliate your skin by
rubbing the paste off. Then rinse off.

Indonesian Wrap

Indonesian women are famed for regaining their
slender figure shortly after childbirth, which is widely
attributed to the bengkung (herbal wrap) treatment.
Akin to an adult form of swaddling, a long, hard
cotton sash (measuring 8–15 metres (26–50) is very
tightly bound around the abdomen and hip areas,
The traditional treatment takes about one month and
is usually carried out by an ibu pijat (female masseur)
who visits the new mother's home each morning for
her daily hot bath and herbal oil massage. A herbal
paste comprising, among other ingredients, betel
leaves (for their antiseptic properties and ability to
combat odour), lime juice (to flush toxins),
eucalyptus (to aid digestion) and crushed coral (for
its high mineral content and ability to keep the body
warm) is applied before the body is wrapped in the
sash. This paste is also believed to 'cleanse' the
womb while firming and shrinking the stomach.

The bengkung is tightly wound to increase its
effectiveness in contouring the figure and reducing
the excess flab and is believed to help rid the body of
excess wind, restore muscle tone, flush toxins and
strengthen the new mother. It is also said to stimulate
the lymphatic system, thus quickening the process by
which the new mother sheds her excess weight.

PAPAYA, KEMIRI, MINT BODY WRAP

1 medium papaya, mashed
20 kemiri nuts, grated
10 peppermint leaves
water as required
banana leaves as required

Blend all the ingredients until you get a fine paste. Apply
the paste generously over your body, especially over the
drier areas. Wrap the body with banana leaves and secure
with a sarong.
Allow sufficient time for the body to soak in the paste,
then remove the leaves and gently rinse off the ingredients
with warm water.

In the modern spa environment the body wrap is
far less complex. As with bengkung, a herbal paste
comprising indigenous ingredients such as aloe and
lavender is applied which is usually followed by a
relaxing floral bath. This traditional Papaya, Kemiri,
Mint Body Wrap recipe above can be applied after a
traditional massage.

| The Balinese coffee scrub for coffee lovers is a real
treat and will work to exfoliate and nourish the skin.
|| Traditionally, bengkung is wrapped tightly around
the body to help contour the figure.

Philippine Tradition

THE NATURAL FIILIPINO SPA

An archipelago of about 7,000 tropical islands, many of which are uninhabited, the Philippines is home to a multitude of remote pockets of land separated by vast stretches of sea and the almost complete absence of infrastructure.

With its history of Spanish and American colonialism and blend of some of the great medical traditions of China, India and Yunani-Tibb (or Greek-Persia) this nation is culturally unique and by virtue of its indigenous healing knowledge, attitudes and practices truly stands apart. With information on ancient healing therapies only starting to be made known, the spa world is certain to see more of the Philippines' ancient healing therapies in the future.

| A tropical paradise, the Philippine islands and sand banks are the perfect backdrop to the pursuit of well-being. || Spas across the archipelago are referring back to the indigenous therapies.

Use all the natural power to heal because all of us come from God. One can overpower illnesses and cure oneself using this natural healing power.

Traditional healer in Camarines Sur, Philippines.

A Cultural Perspective

Traditional Filipino medicine is believed to have been first recorded in the annals of Asian travellers starting circa the 8th century. Even before the Spanish colonial era, traders from China, India and Persia had been visiting the islands of South-East Asia and imparting their healing therapies and traditions. Hence the influence of Traditional Chinese Medicine (page 25-35), ayurveda (page 13-23) and Unani-Tibb medicine (a healing culture practised in Southern India) in indigenous Philippine therapies.

During the Spanish colonial era (1521-1898) much of the Hispanic literature in the Philippines documents indigenous healing practices and the botanical descriptions of medicinal plants and trees. The advent of Catholic Christianity led to the suppression of many of these traditional healing practices which were labelled as pagan and 'works of the devil'. Hispanic medicine was greatly influenced by the Unani-Tibb (as Spain was under the Moors of Persia and Arabia during the first centenaries of the second millennium) with traces still in existence today. For example, the technique of bentosa (cupping) to clear heat from the body (similar to TCM page 30) was a Moorish-derived therapy. Also certain herbs, fruits and flowers like mint (yerba buena), avocado (guacate), and chrysanthemum (manzanilla) originally came to the Philippines from Spain and are now an integral part of the country's herbal pharmacopoeia.

With North American health and medical systems deeply imbedded in government and society during the American colonial era (1898-1946), traditional Filipino medicine was sidelined and mostly ignored. North American influences are still in evidence today with some traditional healers (especially around the Southern Luzon region) using synthetic medicines and injections in their practice.

As with TCM, Aboriginal and other forms of indigenous therapies, Filipino healers believe that the universe (macrocosm or kalawakan) and humankind (microcosm or sangkatauhan) are intricately interlinked and any fluctuations occurring within the body are a direct consequence of environmental change and vice versa. Therefore, healers respect their environment, be it the far off universe with its constellation, stars and planets or the immediate surrounds of the atmosphere, forests, rivers, oceans, animals and other living creatures and people. They believe that nature, whether seen or unseen, is one and should exist in harmony and peace.

Of equal significance are the four elements of earth (kalikasan ng lupa), wind (kalikasan ng hangin), fire (kalikasan ng init) and water (kalikasan ng tubig). Each element is interrelated and must remain in harmony and balance to achieve peace (kapayapaan), calm (katahimikan) and serenity (kaginhawahan) in the body and the greater world.

Following the Chinese tradition of yin and the yang, traditional medicine labels every object on earth from people to plants, foods, aromas and daily activities as either cold (lamig) or hot (init) with balance between both being the key to health and harmony. A dominance of one humour will result in disease. To restore balance and health in the body, a

hot type disease will be treated with a cold medicinal plant. Finally, the theory of energy (kisig) and balance (patas) states that for ultimate health and well-being the opposite forces of humankind and the environment, hot and cold and the four elements must exist in balance and harmony (or patas-patas).

Traditional Healers

Traditional healers are an indigenous part of Philippine culture and tradition and are present in all 42,000 villages countrywide. Most villages normally have at least two or three healers (usually a traditional birth attendant, a herb healer and a bone setter/massage therapist), while others may also have a spiritual and/or a psychic healer and an energy (or biomagnetic) healer.

Pre-Spanish Filipinos were spiritual in nature believing in an almighty supreme being called Bathala, with the advent of Spanish colonialism spiritual beliefs and religious practices were supplanted by Catholic Christian prayers and rituals. Even today, traditional healers pray in Latin or consider a number of Latin phrases as powerful mantras and almost all healing is performed through the intercession of Christ and Catholic Christian saints.

Generally healers in rural Philippines are home based. However, in Metro Manila and other major urban areas (like Cebu, Davao, Cagayan de Oro, Iloilo, Baguio), many have their own clinics or are part of Complementary and Alternative Medicine (CAM) Clinics along with medical doctors and other integrative medical specialists. With the recent upsurge in all things spa, healers specializing in traditional massage or bone setters can now be found working alongside massage and facial therapists.

| A holistic approach to health and wellness is adopted at The Farm, one of Philippines' leading spas. || Massage is a common technique in traditional Filipino therapy.

Treatments & Therapies

The hand is the source of human electrical energy and this energy is transmitted by the hand (of the healer) to all parts of the body.

A traditional healer in Talamban, Cebu, Philipines.

The Filipino Hilot

An eclectic blend of indigenous massage techniques, the Filipino hilot is the oldest and most popular traditional healing therapy still practised everyday in villages throughout the country. While there are many forms of indigenous massage (generically known as hilot sa pilay) The Filipino hilot, as it exists today, represents the fusion of techniques from seven major ethno-linguistic cultural areas of the Philippines.

The focus of therapy goes far beyond a typical body massage harnessing the bio-energies of the universe (cosmic, spiritual and ethereal), botanicals (leaves, flowers, essential oils, herbal poultices and teas) and the hilot therapist himself who becomes the medium for harvesting these energies and restoring balance, harmony, health and wellness.

A distinctive feature of hilot is the use of warm strips of banana leaves minimally laced with extra virgin coconut oil, which are applied to the body at the beginning and end of the massage. As the banana leaves are naturally ionized (and cleansing) they act on the molecular and bio-energetic fields on the skin and body to determine which areas are most in need of the therapist's healing energy.

The Hilot Haplos with Coco-Cocoa Scrub therapy at The Farm At Saint Benito combines the hilot experience with a luxurious coconut cream and cocoa body scrub and warm coconut milk bath to truly pamper both body and soul. See the coco-cacao body scrub recipe courtesy of The Farm below.

The Paligo

Literally meaning bath, paligo therapy uses warm decoctions of air-dried tropical and indigenous aromatic leaves and flowers that have medicinal properties which, when added to a bath, help relieve a whole range of problems. For example, availing of the antiseptic properties of guava, boiled guava leaves are commonly used to hasten healing for mothers who have just given birth. Also, boiled tanglad (or lemongrass) helps boost overall health, ampalaya (momordica charantia or bitter gourd) is a known fertility regulator and sambong (blumea balsamifera or camphor) and lagundi (vitex negundo or horseshoe vitex) help to relieve colds and lethargy.

The paligo or baths are broadly classified into hot-cold balancing, earth-wind-fire-water balancing, and a binat regulator, or stress regulator, bath. In traditional Filipino healing, the term binat is used to describe a state of disease or severe discomfort that has arisen from severe stress, childbirth or grief.

| Banana leaves play a major role in the Filipino hilot, the leaves are known for their cleansing properties. || Baths, paglio, can be drawn with flowers or herbs.

Coco-Cacao Scrub

225 ml (8 fl oz/1 cup) coconut milk
3 pieces tabliya (Batangas chocolate)

Using a blender, mix milk and chocolate together. Scrub over the body and rinse with warm water to leave your skin feeling smooth and revitalized. After exfoliation, soak in the bathtub with 1 cup of coconut milk.

The Oslob

The Oslob is a traditional form of steam inhalation generally used to treat people with excess cold or wind energy. The patient lies under a small cotton tent and infusions of boiling water poured into a mixture of aromatic medicinal plants and herbs are slowly administered for about 20 minutes inducing the patient into a state of deep calm, easy breathing and relaxation.

The herbs used for the oslob are mostly hot in nature and include: premna odorata, yerba buena (mentha cord folia or mint leaves), sambong (blumea balsamiferous or blumea camphor), balanoy (ocimum basilicum or sweet basil) and lagundi (vitex negundo or horseshoe vitex).

The Dinalisay

Dinalisay are decoctions of indigenous medicinal foods and herbs grown in certified organic farms throughout the country. They are classified into hot, cold, earth, wind, fire and water and are used to treat specific conditions related to the elements and humours with the aim of restoring balance in the body. Dinalisay is normally prepared using three handfuls of fresh chopped leaves (or plant parts depending on requirements) mixed with 240 ml (9 fl oz/1 cup) of water. The mixture is placed in an open earthen pot and left to simmer on a low heat until the mixture reduces by half (usually about 15 minutes). The decoction is strained, cooled and taken throughout the day with a glass in the morning, noon and early evening.

Hot Dinalisay: This type of dinalisay uses hot foods and herbs for example, ginger, tamarind, capsicum, citrus, mango and jackfruit.

Cold Dinalisay: The cold variation uses cold foods and herbs like avocado, guava, anonas and banana.
Earth Dinalisay: Earth foods and herbs for example, radish, sampaguita (jasminum sambac or Arabian jasmine) are used.
Wind Dinalisay: This variety uses wind foods and herbs such as coconut and lagundi (vitex negundo or horseshoe vitex).
Fire Dinalisay: Here, fire foods and herbs like garlic, turmeric, ginger and capsicum are used.
Water Dinalisay: Water foods and herbs include corn hair, cat's whiskers and cogon grass.

Kisig Galing

This implies the use of biomagnetic energy healing from naturally gifted traditional healers. Using their hands as vehicles for the transfer of positive biomagnetic energy (kisig) from both themselves and the environment to the person in disease, they are able to heal (galing) and rebalance the body.

The Tapik Kawayan

The tapik kawayan, or bamboo tap, is a massage technique using a one-centimetre-thick (½-inch), five-centimetre-long (2-inch) bamboo stick (kawayan) to tap specific areas of the body that are believed to have energy blocks or a predominance of cold humours. The technique is generally applied on the back and gluteus, the upper and lower arms, thighs and legs freeing blocked energy and rebalancing the body. The head, chest, abdominal and groin areas remain untouched. Tapik Kawayan was traditionally performed in the village homes of traditional healers but is now starting to appear on therapy menus of city spas.

| The oslob entails a herbal steam infusion under a cotton tent. || Natural ingredients of the traditional Filipino therapies. ||| Bamboo tap uses a small stick of bamboo to gently tap any blocked humours, and stimulate the flow of energy. |||| Dagdagay, a foot massage with a Filipino twist, clay is used to cleanse and bamboo stimulates the soles.

Moxa Ventoza

Derived from the ancient Chinese therapy, moxibustion, (page 28) with evidence of elements of Unani-Tibb medicine, moxa ventoza has been practised by ancestral Filipino traditional healers for centuries. Using heat resistant circular glass vacuums that, after being warmed, are applied to the meridians primarily on the back to create a vacuum that draws out toxins and excess cold energy from within. A relaxing massage then follows with the application of virgin coconut oil that soothes and calms the skin.

Dagdagay

Meaning foot massage, this authentic tribal massage uses herbal clay to cleanse and purify the feet, bamboo sticks to stimulate the soles of the feet (as with the tapik kawayan or bamboo tap technique) and a soothing leg and foot massage to calm and restore a sense of complete balance and harmony in the body.

The Unang Lana

Unang lana or Filipino virgin coconut oil holds a special place in healing. Only the flesh of freshly picked 90-day old coconuts are used, which is cold pressed to extract the first coconut oil or unang lana. The clear colourless virgin oil with its distinctive sweet aroma is rich in lauric acid, vitamin E and other anti-oxidants. It is directly metabolized by the liver and converted immediately into energy. It is widely used in different facets of healing from being a total body rub, hair tonic, massage liniment, facial mask to a daily jigger drink for health, harmony and body wellness.

Australian Wisdom

TRADITIONS OF THE ABORIGINAL DREAMTIME

Native Australian Aboriginals live and survive in harmony with nature and their relationship with the environment commands the utmost of respect. So deeply connected to the essence and energy locked within their land, they recognize that earth sustains all life and believe that they are merely custodians of this land and live to ensure its vitality.

To most indigenous Aboriginals health is not simply a matter of good diet or a prudent lifestyle. It is viewed holistically and is the outcome of a complex relationship between body, land and spirit. The Aboriginal concept of therapy is preventive; its purpose being to maintain equilibrium and health utilizing the produce of their environment such as native Australian plants, ochres and salts. Taking care of the land is ultimately, taking care of oneself. In a world that is fast losing its indigenous traditions, some Australian Aboriginal customs and techniques for well-being are still alive.

| The rainforests of Australia, include Daintree, the oldest living rainforest in the world. || Face painting of an Aboriginal tribesman.

We had our own medicine. We had
doctors of our own-doctors who used to
give a man life again.

Magarruminya, a Mardarrpa (Yolngu) man.

The Aboriginal Dreamtime

For more than 40,000 years, the indigenous
Aboriginal people of Australia have held the world's
oldest continuous living tradition of sacred
knowledge, known as the 'Dreamtime'. It is from
this that all aspects of Aboriginal life are derived,
including an innate wisdom of the relationship
between humankind and nature and a unique
understanding of the workings and spiritual
dimensions of the world.

According to this Dreamtime tradition or lore,
everybody, everything and all time and space is
intimately linked to the sacred seed of creation,
from which life has grown and continues to grow.
Every thought, footprint, gust of wind, plant or
animal that lives, has lived or is yet to live, is seen
to impart its unique vibration upon the earth, which
in turn resounds through eternity as part of the
ongoing wheel of life. Living in harmony with this
understanding, Aboriginals view their lives as being
custodians of the physical and spiritual dimensions
of the earth. Their philosophy is to tread lightly and
with the utmost of respect, for it is through the
Dreaming that the potential for creative perfection
is ultimately determined by the unseen vibration of
all around it.

The Healing Elements

As with ancient Chinese, Indian and Japanese
traditions amongst others, traditional Aboriginal
culture recognizes the significance of the natural
elements in terms of their physical, emotional,
spiritual and environmental energies and their place
in maintaining balance and harmony in both the
body and in life. The five elements of air, earth, fire,
water and wood are essential to life and a key part
of indigenous healing therapies in Australia.
Achieving balance is the main objective and
traditional techniques draw upon the power of
these elements through the use of native flora,
muds and clays, minerals and salts to cleanse,
nourish and harmonize body, mind and spirit.

Many traditional treatments use an extensive
range of native plants or aromatherapy oils which

when infused through the air (element) bring a sense of peace and calm to both body and mind. Earth represents the centre of grounding. Earth is our mother and we are her protectors. To reconnect the body with earth's healing and balancing energy peat, clays and desert salts are used directly on the skin to cleanse and nurture the body in the earth's warmth. The fire element is represented as much today as ever before with fire rituals where a collection of bark and leaves is burned in a small handheld coolamon—a traditional Aboriginal wooden vessel—to create a soft smoke that clears energy and calls upon earth's healing powers to enter the sacred space. Known for its healing, cleansing, purifying and emotionally restorative properties, water clears blocked energy and awakens a sense of vitality (as in Yanko Jindalee or warm water massage therapy). Wood's grounding energy comes alive with the coolamons. These unique Aboriginal mallee wood vessels, semi-circular in shape, are widely used for storage and in traditional smoking rituals. Carved by hand and exclusively by women, coolamons are decorated with images from the Dreamtime stories by burning lengths of wire into the outside of the vessel.

A Spiritual Perspective

The ancient Aboriginals shared a unique view on life. Often referred to as the four basic tenets or foundations on how to live, this holistic approach considers a person's mental and physical relationship with the world in terms of their spiritual, environmental and social health and well-being. The four tenets of the Ya'-idt'midtung tribespeople are as follows:

Aildt (pronounced 'ail-t'): Meaning everything is one. Everything and every person is seen as inextricably linked and as part of one creative force or universal soul which is known as Aildt.

Adtomon (pronounced 'ad-omon'): Meaning truth is the path. By living in harmony with our own truth and being true to the universe and one another, we are 'one' and will discover the true path of nature and real health and well-being. Failing to live one's own truth (or observe Adtomon) can result in illness and disease.

Dtwongdtyen (pronounced 'dt-won-tienne'): Meaning a varied perspective is the key to perception. In other words, Dtwongdtyen suggests looking at things from different perspectives. Each person's trust is equally valid with acceptance of varied perspectives being the key to perception.

Linj'dta (pronounced 'linj-ta'): Meaning that now is the moment. This fourth tenet focuses on the importance of living in the now, where life's energy is. Being distracted from the present by looking too much into the future or past is viewed as pointless as it takes the energy from today and cheats us of our present lives. To be healthy and balanced we must focus on what is now and let the future take care of itself.

| Tradtional Aboriginal art. || O'yarrarng and lemon myrtle are burnt in the coolamon to create a calming space. ||| Muds from the rainforest are an essential ingredient and are used to cleanse and nourish the body. |||| The coolamons can be used for storage as well as for applying mud or oil to the body.

Treatments & Therapies

Tread lightly.
When most people look at the rainforest they
see a complex wall of green. But for traditional
Aboriginal families, the rainforest is a kitchen,
medicine chest, tool shed and a church.

Daintree Eco Lodge & Spa, KuKu Yalanji Rainforest Guides.

For the ultimate native Aboriginal journey the earthly delights of invigorating desert salts, nourishing plant actives and clarifying earth ochres are comprehensively packed into The Dreaming—or 'the unseen vibration of creation'. It entails pure therapy for the whole body, from the roots of the hair to the feet. It restores clarity by awakening the mind and spirit and leaving the body energized, revitalized and positively glowing.

Commonly Used Aboriginal Ingredients

Macadamia: Known as bopple nut by indigenous Australians, the macadamia nut kernel is rich in mono-unsaturated oils and vitamins A and E it is readily absorbed onto the skin and acts as a superb natural skin nourisher.

Mapi Pure Earth Clays: Sourced from ancient riverbeds and streams, earth clays draw out impurities from the skin thereby refining its texture and imparting deeply enriching nutrients to the skin through their indigenous trace elements that give them their vibrant colours. Red clay is believed to be associated with initiation and grounding, yellow clay with joy and welcoming and white clay is used at traditional ceremonies to purify the spirit.

Munthari Berry: Replete with essential minerals, vitamins and fruit acids the munthari (or muntrie) berry has a high wax content which provides a

natural protective barrier and facilitates deeper penetration into the skin. It is most commonly found in the coastal regions of southern Australia and western Victoria.

Lemon Myrtle: The world's purest source of citral, lemon myrtle is a powerful antiseptic that works wonders for sebum control in problem skin. It stimulates circulation and is believed to relieve stress. Dried leaves and essential oils are used.

| Some of the native plants, flowers, nuts and leaves, that make up the Aboriginal medicine chest, are stored in a coolamon. || Ochres of the rainforest. ||| Natural ingredients of the forest can be used for facial treatments. |||| The body draws nutrients from the ochre which draws impurities from the skin and refines texture.

Lillypilly: This small pink berry most commonly found in eastern Australia, is rich in vitamin C and skin rejuvenating fruit acids. Although traditionally eaten as a fruit it makes an excellent revitalizing cleanser.

Quandong Extract: Quandong, a native peach to Australia, is a berry-shaped fruit traditionally used for adding density, lustre and shine to hair and relieving dry, itchy scalp.

Tasmanian Kelp: Harvested from the Australian Bass Straight this brown hued kelp is rich in iodine, calcium, sulphur, iron and vitamins. It is naturally detoxifying and an ideal replenisher that will restore natural moisture and balance to sluggish skin.

Wattle Seed: Found countrywide, the protein-rich seeds from this native Australian Acacia tree make a perfect facial exfoliant, as by virtue of their circular shape they will not damage delicate facial capillaries.

Wild Lime: Sourced from the arid inland regions this tiny citrus fruit (about 1-2 cm (½ inch) long) is rich in vitamin C and delivers a refreshing zingy aroma.

Wild Rosella: The coastal and rainforest regions of northern Australia are home to this bright red flower that has a deliciously sweet fragrance. Wild rosella is a protein-rich member of the Hibiscus family and soothes and heals the skin.

Each individual Aboriginal tribe possesses intimate knowledge of native plants and healing modalities that have over time evolved into their own unique methodologies and techniques. The following therapies and plant wisdoms are based mainly on the Aboriginal teachings from elders of the Ya'idt-midtung tribe (near Northern Victoria and Southern New South Wales) who through the years have shared their expertise with the spa company Li'Tya, who mindfully bring these native therapies to life.

Many of the following therapies are available at Daintree Eco Lodge & Spa in Queensland although some have been modified (in technique and the local produce used) while also using different treatment names, all out of respect for the local Kuku Yalanji rainforest people with whom the spa works closely.

Kodo

Meaning melody, kodo is an indigenous massage technique using a combination of pressure point therapy, rhythmical spiralling movements, native essential oils (rejuvenating, harmonizing or detoxifying) and body stroking with a traditional coolamon vessel. This wonderfully revitalizing therapy helps unleash blockages, realign the body's energy fields and relieve physical and emotional tension.

Lowanna

Meaning beautiful, this sensual and nurturing journey recharges the body's energy and essence. Using plant actives, native essential oils and extracts, this facial, hand and foot treatment cleans, purifies and conditions the whole body.

Mala Mayi

Mala mayi, meaning clan food, works to harness the combined powers of a kodo massage and mud and water therapy to relax the mind, purify the body and ground the senses.

Therapy comprises an aromatic body massage followed by a gentle buffing with native desert salts to increase circulation and purify the skin. Then after a warm water wash, the body is cocooned in silky soft mapi body mud to draw out impurities and refine the skin's texture. After a calming scalp massage and water therapy boost, mala mayi concludes with an energizing and spiritually uplifting rhythmic kodo massage.

Miji Jina

Miji jina, or little footprint, therapy begins with a soothing aromatic jiga jina (native bath blend for feet) soak to wash away any anxiety. Then the feet are exfoliated and reflex points stimulated with desert salts to reconnect the body with the earth's healing element. A skin-nourishing pepperberry foot mask then follows, before a final smothering with munthari lotion and massage to replenish feet, nails and cuticles.

Miji Polama

Miji polama, or little hand/fingers, therapy is designed to soothe, strengthen and wash away tiredness. Therapy starts with a relaxing jiga polama (native blend for hands) soak, followed by an invigorating exfoliation with native wattle seed protein polish. Hands and cuticles are then nourished by a Tasmanian kelp hydrating mask and massaged with a vitamin rich munthari lotion.

Mikiri

Mikiri, meaning deep, facial therapy combines powerful plant actives (such as wattle seeds) and native essential oils (for example desert lime, lemon myrtle, sandalwood and mandarin) with indigenous massage techniques to deeply cleanse, nourish and refine the skin, renewing vitality and restoring a smoother texture and look.

Paudi

Paudi, or scalp, massage harnesses the power of Aboriginal pressure point massage to penetrate the 21 acupressure points on the face and scalp to relieve stress and calm the mind while nourishing the hair with the soothing and conditioning qualities of quandong (native peach) mask.

Yanko

Using the healing and purifying energy of water, yanko (song of running water) therapy involves the body being smothered in native aromatic oils, before being purified and cleansed with a desert salt scrub harvested from local river beds and soothed by a warm water massage.

The extended yanko Jindalee (song of running water on skin) treatment combines yanko with a hydrating facial, soothing paudi scalp massage and nourishing quandong hair mask.

| The coolamons, an integral part of Aboriginal therapies, are decorated with images of the Dreamtime. || Part of the mala mayi treatment is the warm mapi body mud mask which delivers essential nutrients to the skin. |||The Australian rainforests are home to a natural pharmacy.

Contemporary Cosmopolitan

A KALEIDOSCOPE OF CURES

The word spa, which literally means sanus per aquam or health by water, is taken from the town of Spa in Belgium, which was one of the first places to recognize the healing properties of mineral-rich water. The benefits of water and massage in strengthening the constitution and treating disease date back to Hippocrates (c. 460-377BC, best known as the father of Western medicine), and the ancient Egyptians, who believed that water had both physical and sacred properties. Similarly in both ayurveda (page 13-23) and TCM (page 25-35), water—being the medium through which the life force of qi or prana travels within the body—is central to restoring health and harmony.

While many of the more modern therapies appearing in spa menus worldwide have their roots firmly grounded in traditional Oriental medicine, they also avail of the more Western scientifically-based tools to enhance and restore health. The founders of these more modern techniques are often trained in traditional Oriental healing methods which they later modify to suit their needs. Not surprising then is the emergence of a new style of therapy—contemporary cosmopolitan, or a fusion of East and West—and treatments that are firmly grounded in the ancient principles of balance and harmony yet add an extra dimension to enhance the overall spa experience and therapeutic benefits.

Given that an estimated 85 per cent of all illness is stress related, massage is increasingly used both preventively and therapeutically to combat the effects of stress and promote relaxation. And the beauty of massage as we know it today is that the recipient can benefit from a number of healing traditions within a single treatment. So wherever in the world we may be, from Bombay to Bali, New York and London, we can benefit from ancient time-honoured traditions combined with modern scientific techniques to de-stress, heal and truly calm body, mind and spirit.

| Natural, mineral-rich water is as an essential ingredient in the cosmopolitan style therapy. || Water and massage are key to promoting health and vitality.

Treatments & Therapies

Aromatherapy

The Egyptians have a rich history of using aromatic plants as perfumes to embalm their dead. Imhotep, the Egyptian god of medicine, is said to have recommended fragrant oils for bathing and massage. However, credit for aromatherapy as we know it today belongs to the French chemist René-Maurice Gattefossé. In 1910, a laboratory explosion badly burnt his hands. After immersing them in lavender oil, they quickly healed without scarring or infection. Thereafter his life was devoted to the study of essential oils. It was later, during World War II, that a French doctor, Dr Jean Valnet used the healing properties of essential oils for treating injured soldiers. His findings were documented in his book, *Aromathérapie*. The use of aromatics in massages was introduced by Madame Marguerite Maury in the 1950s, who, although trained as a biochemist, was unable to dispense essential oils as medicine and discovered their therapeutic and cosmetic benefits via massage.

Essential oils are the aromatic essences extracted from plants, flowers, trees, fruit, bark, grasses and seeds. Each essential oil may contain up to 100 chemical components, which when combined together, exert powerful effects on the body, mind and emotions. Over 150 essential oils have been identified to date which can be used alone or as a blend to treat specific complaints, without any recognized side effects. A maximum of three oils in a blend is recommended otherwise the individual qualities of the oils be lost.

Because essential oils are highly concentrated and extremely volatile, they are usually diluted with base oils (e.g. almond, walnut or evening primrose oil) to inhibit the evaporation of the essential oil and encourage better absorption into the skin. While it takes a skilled aromatherapist to truly understand their properties, it is generally possible to treat common ailments with some of the more commonly used essential oils (see table below).

Essential oils are easily absorbed into the blood stream via the lungs, nose and skin. The vapour travels to the limbic system of the brain which is the area responsible for the integration and expression of feelings, learning, memory, and physical drives. Used for physical ailments, the relief of congested sinuses or throat and chest infections for instance, the oils can be inhaled through a tissue or via steam by simply

Essential Oil	Uses
Lavender	For stress related disorders such as anxiety, insomnia, depression and various skin complaints.
Tea Tree	Has anti-viral, antiseptic, fungicidal and immune stimulant properties. Tea tree is also good for skin complaints such as acne, rashes, dandruff as well as respiratory disorders such as asthma, bronchitis and sinusitis.
Rosemary	Has stimulant properties, particularly to the central nervous system, helps strengthen mental clarity and aid concentration. It is also an expectorant and a tonic for the whole system.
Roman Camomile	A mild relaxant and anti-inflammatory agent, it is good for the stomach, intestinal or menstrual problems and headaches. Camomile is especially suitable for children.
Peppermint	For digestive complaints such as nausea or indigestion, for respiratory problems and for treating colds, flu and fevers.

adding a few drops of oil (for example, eucalyptus mixed with lavender or camomile) to a shallow tub of hot water. Place a towel over the head, lean over the steam, take a few deep breaths and feel the nasal passages and head quickly clear. Also a few drops of lavender on the pillow before going to bed helps aid sounder sleep. For the face, try jojoba oil mixed with a small amount of wheatgerm oil. For children suffering with colic, try 1 drop of Roman camomile with 1 drop of sweet fennel in an aroma lamp.

When used in massage, essential oils are absorbed through the skin and carried to the muscle tissue, joints and organs. While more concentrated oils can be used for the relief of physical complaints such as muscle aches and skin lesions (for example, lavender helps relieve burns and scarring), the essential oil is best diluted with a base oil before using especially when used on sensitive skin or during pregnancy.

Cranio-Sacral Therapy

Cranio-sacral therapy (or CST) can be described as a gentle hands-on method of enhancing the functioning of the body's cranio-sacral system which comprises the membranes and cerebrospinal fluid that surrounds the brain and spinal cord. By gently manipulating the central nervous system, CST improves overall health as well as effectively treating a range of medical problems from chronic neck and back pain, migraines, scoliosis, temporomandibular joint syndrome (TMJ) and post-surgical problems in adults to post-birth traumas, colic and learning difficulties in babies and young children. The response to therapy varies as will the number of sessions required from just one to up to three a week for several weeks.

| There are over 150 essential oils used in aromatherapy.
|| Lavender can be used to relieve stress and anxiety as well as depression. For the skin, lavender deodorizes, and stimulates, which aids acne and fluid retention. ||| The oils' healing properties are absorbed into the bloodstream via the skin.

Equilibropathy

Equilibropathy (dullayaphap bumbud) combines the principles of traditional Oriental healing with modern medical science and was devised by Dr Taworn Kasomson to help rebalance body, mind and spirit.

A diagnosis is first made after examination of the spine and associated muscle groups. By looking and touching, the practitioner detects both symptomatic and asymptomatic problems and determines their cause and effects. The therapist then uses a combination of acupuncture and breathing, balancing and stretching exercises to ease muscle tension and, more importantly, clear any energy blockages within the body which are believed to improve circulation and nerve signal transmission. Recommendations on maintaining proper posture are also given, as it is believed that correct posture helps maintain balance within the body. Regular practice of these movements is advised in order to maintain health and improve the body's natural healing abilities.

Flotation Therapy

The first flotation tank was designed in the 1950s by Dr John C. Lilly, an American neuro-physiologist and psychoanalyst who discovered that when the body was submerged in a tank in the absence of external stimuli the brain functioned at a much higher level than normal.

Flotation involves floating in an enclosed tank or pool of water about 25 centimetres (10 inches deep) and saturated with Epsom salts to keep the body buoyant. Two hours of floating effortlessly with the eyes and ears deprived of light and sound is said to be equivalent to eight hours of deep sleep.

Today flotation tanks can be found in spas, bio-fitness institutes and hospitals. The Epsom salt laden water is heated to an average skin temperature of 34°C (93.5°F) to reduce the sensation between body and water. Fresh air circulates inside the tank and, for those who are uncomfortable in absolute silence, soft soothing music or guided meditation tapes can be played. As digestive discomforts can interfere with the floating experience light meals are only advised before therapy and stimulants such as caffeine and alcohol are best avoided. As Epsom salts are strong detoxifiers essential fluids must be replaced after floating.

Flotation therapy helps relieve chronic pain such as arthritis, headache and back pain, and is also often used to enhance meditation. The effects can last from a few hours to a few days, and are prolonged with subsequent sessions. It is not recommended for those suffering from epilepsy, schizophrenia, kidney conditions or skin disorders.

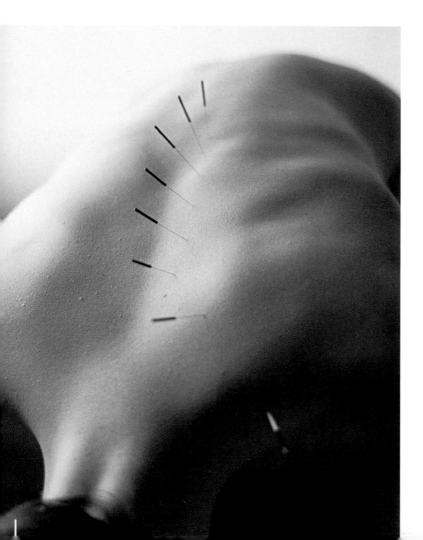

| Equilibropathy can be used to treat medical conditions such as asthma, migraine, sinus congestion and any other where there is lowered immunity. || Just two hours of flotation therapy is said to equate an eight-hour sleep. ||| The popular four hand massage is a sensual massage experience.

Dry Flotation

A variant on the wet flotation tank, the dry tank resembles a rectangular waterbed with upholstered sides. Lying on a raised platform the body is lowered and suspended (yet protected from the heated water by the upholstered vinyl sheet) and left to float for about 40 minutes. For added benefit, the body can be smothered in skin-nourishing milk or warm oil during the treatment. The sensation is akin to that of floating on air and it helps relieve tension and calm both body and mind.

Four Hands Massage

The overall effect of a four hands massage, when correctly performed by two therapists in perfect tandem, is a deeply sensual massage experience by one therapist with two pairs of hands. To help achieve this, many spas try to partner therapists who match each other in terms of both physique and disposition. The first therapist is the lead or 'mother' while the second acts as a 'mirror'. The second therapist is discreet—he or she usually enters the room only after the first has invited you to lie face down on the bed.

Modern four-handed massages are a blend of Eastern (ayurveda's abhyanga, page 16) and Western therapies. For instance, the Mandara Massage, is a rich blend of aromatherapy oils with shiatsu (page 41–42), Thai (page 50–51), Indonesian (page 62–64), Swedish (page 89) and Hawaiian Lomi Lomi (opposite) techniques.

During the massage treatment, the therapists stand on either side of the body and begin by simultaneously placing their palms over the client to balance and synchronize energies. Next, each therapist places one hand below the shoulder blade and the other above the hipbone and they simultaneously stretch the upper body. They do the same with the lower body, with one hand at the heel and the other below the hipbone. After these stretching movements, the massage begins and their smooth movements along the length of the body are focused on creating the illusion of four hands and one therapist.

Lomi Lomi

Originally performed in temples, lomi lomi is more than just massage, it's healing, with its roots firmly anchored in ancient Hawaiian traditions. Traditionally a lomi lomi session comprises prayer, fasting and massage but today the emphasis rests very much on essential oil-based massage using rhythmic dance–like movements of the palms, knuckles and forearms of one or two therapists in perfect synchrony. Lomi lomi helps disperse stagnant energy, improve circulation, stimulate the lymphatic system and instil a positive sense of being.

Lymphatic Drainage Massage

Likened to a state-of-the-art waste disposal system the body's lymphatic system is vital to ongoing health. Lymphatic drainage massage uses subtle manual manoeuvres to stimulate gentle wave-like movements through the lymphatic system to remove toxic build up and enhance the flow of lymph (the milky fluid in which the organs and muscles are

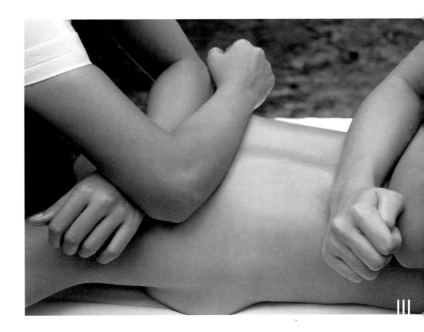

bathed) through the body. Working in tandem with the immune system, lymphatic drainage massage helps reduce fluid retention and clear toxic build up, making it an ideal adjunct to slimming while also helping relieve sports injuries, body strains, and other orthopaedic problems.

Sports Massage

A relative newcomer to the massage portfolio, sports massage is essentially a form of Swedish massage catering specifically to athletes. It is used before, during or after events to enhance athletic performance, as part of an athlete's training regime or to speed up recovery from injuries. Generally, a sports massage is slow and thorough; the therapist begins with superficial strokes to identify potential problem areas and detect overused muscles, which are a very common cause of injuries. These muscles are hard and tense compared to the surrounding tissues. A sports massage is usually given through clothing and lasts from 30 minutes to one hour.

Swedish Massage

Swedish massage is the most popular of all traditional European massage styles. Developed by Per Henrik Ling in the 1700s, who merged Western and Eastern healing techniques, it was the first organized and systematic method of modern therapeutic massage in the Western world.

Using oil or lotion as a lubricant Swedish massage incorporates the following five strokes, all of which are done on the more superficial layers of the muscles and towards the heart:

Effleurage: Meaning touching lightly, effleurage comprises long gliding strokes from the neck to the base of the spine, or from the shoulder to the fingertips. Done with the entire hand or the pads of the thumb, it helps relax the muscles while also enabling the therapist to examine the texture and quality of the muscle tissue.

Pétrissage: Meaning kneading, pétrissage involves the kneading, rolling or squeezing of the muscles to encourage deeper circulation through the veins and lymph vessels. This stroke is also believed to help clear toxins from the muscles.

Friction or rubbing: This consists of deep circular or transverse movements of the thumb pads or fingertips around the joints and other bony areas to break down adhesions (or knots of muscle fibre which develop in response to muscular trauma or strain).

Tapotement or tapping: Here the therapist taps the muscles with the edge of the hand, tips of the fingers or with a closed fist to release tension and cramping and stimulate circulation in an area of atrophy. When performed correctly this technique invigorates the muscles, before relaxing them.

Vibration or shaking: This is performed at the end of the massage when the therapist presses his hands on the back or limbs and rapidly shakes them for a few seconds. This stroke is particularly helpful for relieving lower-back pain.

Stone Therapy

The Hawaiians are thought to have been the first to use lava stones in a lomi lomi-style massage to warm the body, relax the muscles and soothe the soul. In stone therapy, ultra-smooth stones are placed on strategic energy points of the body and are handheld by the therapist who glides them over the body using long, flowing strokes. As the stones are better able to retain heat and cold (than hands), when used in conjunction with Swedish, lomi lomi or other massage techniques they have a deeper, more powerful effect on the body. The most commonly used stones are basalt, which are derived from lava and shaped and smoothened by nature.

| Hot and cold stones can be applied to the body in various ways to relieve stiff and sore muscles, the result is an alleviation of chronic and acute problems. || A lymphatic drainage massage helps stimulate the lymphatic flow, aiding weight-loss and body strains and injuries.

Smaller stones can be used in a variety of ways from facial treatments to reflexology, as well as for manicures and pedicures.

Modern stone therapy is attributed to the American massage therapist Mary Nelson who first used heated stones to help relieve an existing shoulder injury. A variation of the warm stone massage, LaStone® therapy uses combines hot and chilled basalt and marble stones with Swedish massage techniques. The alternation of hot with cold is believed to boost circulation and help the body to heal itself.

Thalassotherapy

The word thalassa is Greek for sea and what distinguishes thalassotherapy from other forms of hydrotherapy is its emphasis on seawater and seaweed ingredients. To the ancient Greeks hot seawater was an all purpose cure, with both physicians and philosophers alike—from Hippocrates and Galen to Plato and Aristotle—advocating warm seawater bathing as an adjunct to health. The French living on the Atlantic coast have also long advocated the benefits of thalassotherapy.

| Becoming more and more common in spas across the region is watsu therapy, a shiatsu-style treatment that is administered in water. || Thalassotherapy and hydrotherapy make use of the benefits of the sea to heal and promote overall wellness.

The restorative power of thalassotherapy stems from the similarity between seawater's mineral composition and that of human blood plasma. Minerals and trace elements found in seawater are believed to have innate healing properties that when heated to body temperature are easily absorbed through the skin. Water with a high concentration of salt is used to treat muscular, skeletal and skin complaints while the buoyancy effect of the water itself protects the joints from injury and eases the pressure on the spine.

Packed with minerals, vitamins, trace elements and amino acids, seaweed has traditionally been used to treat a range of ailments including constipation, rheumatism, arthritis and fluid retention. Applied externally in the form of body wraps, (kelp) baths and poultices it cleanses and tones the skin, soothe aches and pains and helps relieve rheumatic complaints. Even the sea air is said to be beneficial, as it is richer in negative ions than the air over land.

According to the authoritative French Fédération Internationale de Thalassothérapie, a true thalassotherapy centre should be located on the coast, operated under medical supervision and must use fresh (or live) seawater and marine derived substances like seaweed, algae, sea mud, salts scrubs and sand to enhance health and treat ailments. Using baths, jet massages and large heated pools with massage jets, the benefits of this ancient healing tradition come to life restoring and soothing the body and mind. Home thalassotherapy in the form of bath salts and oils, seaweed wraps and kelp extract formulae is growing in popularity.

Watsu

Watsu is derived from the words water and shiatsu and was developed by Harold Dull in 1980, who after training in the techniques of shiatsu in Japan, returned to his California home where he began conducting the first watsu sessions in hot springs. Conducted in chest-high warm water, it is a form of shiatsu (page 41–42) that also involves gentle cradling and rocking of the body to loosen the spine. When immersed in water, the body is immediately more flexible while the buoyancy effect of the water protects the joints from injury and eases pressure on the spine. Watsu helps release stress and anxiety while also improving flexibility and strength of the spine as the resistance created by the water pressure makes the muscles work harder. Therapy is particularly suited to pregnant women and those suffering from muscular dysfunction and joint problems such as arthritis.

Spa Cuisine

The passion for food in Asia and the attention devoted to well-being come together in spa cuisine. Meals are kept low in fat, low in salt and as much raw food as possible plays a major part in the following recipes. Spa cuisine is well balanced and designed to be easily digested while giving the body more energy and encouraging a change in lifestyle. Many spas tailor to specific needs, some use organic produce, often with herbs and vegetables from their own gardens.

The following recipes have been shared by the chefs of top spas and restaurants in the Asia-Pacific region.

The Indian Kitchen

SPICE HEAVEN

Indian cuisine is well known, and loved around the world, for its rich curries, dals, breads and especially known for its generous use of spices. Ayurvedic texts dating back some 3,000 years recorded the use of spices for their curative properties. For instance, garlic is believed to lower cholesterol levels and hypertension, turmeric provides relief from stomach ulcers and ginger aids digestion.

Ananda – In the Himalayas has its own herb garden to ensure a steady supply of rare herbs and spices and its spa cuisine is centred around locally available fresh organic produce. Organic brown rice, baby potatoes or whole wheat pastas are served as staples. Also, a wide range of soya products such as soya yoghurt and tofu, along with organic mountain lentils fulfil the protein requirements of vegetarians.

The following recipes are served at Ananda's restaurant where the chefs draw inspiration from traditional Indian dishes as well as international favourites and these are included here.

Parinda Kebab

Serves 4
Kilocalories 318 kcal > Protein 45 g > Carbohydrate 8 g > Total Fat 11 g

4 chicken breasts, skinned
120 g (4¼ oz) chicken, minced
2 tsp chopped mint
1 tsp minced ginger
½ tsp chopped garlic
½ tsp mace powder
salt and white pepper

Marinade:
½ cup yoghurt cheese
1 tsp minced ginger
½ tsp minced garlic
1 tsp garam masala
1 tbsp chana powder (chickpea flour)
1 tbsp mustard oil
salt and white pepper

Slice into the chicken breast from the top to create a flap and keep aside. Mix minced chicken with mint, ginger, garlic, mace powder, and salt and pepper. Fill this mixture in the chicken breast and seal the top end. To prepare marinade, mix all ingredients well. Coat the chicken breast with marinade. Transfer to a tray, cover and leave for two hours. Cook the chicken on a high heat for 15 minutes until cooked and serve hot.

Mushroom Galouti Kebab

Serves 4
Kilocalories 140 kcal > Protein 1 g > Carbohydrate 4 g > Total Fat 14 g

200 g (7 oz) mushrooms, blanched
50 g (1¾ oz) paneer (a variety of cheese)
50 g (1¾ oz) potatoes, boiled and grated
80 g (3 oz) onion, chopped
2 tbsp ghee
½ tsp cardamom powder
1 tsp black cardamom powder
½ tsp mace powder
2 tsp saffron
2 tsp kewra (essence of pandanus flowers)
1 tbsp roasted chana powder (chickpea flour)
2 tbsp ghee to grease the pan

Combine mushroom, paneer and potato. Next, sauté onion in ghee and
add cardamom powder, black cardamom powder, mace, saffron and
kewara water and mix with mushroom mixture. Grind mixture to a fine
paste. Add roasted chana powder and mix well. Divide the mixture into
16 balls to make small patties. Grease a non-stick pan with ghee and
cook patties on gentle heat until golden on both sides.

Goat's Cheese Quiche with Beetroot Reduction

Serves 4
Kilocalories 546 kcal > Protein 12 g > Carbohydrate 21 g > Total Fat 53 g

Beetroot Reduction:
½ medium beetroot
1 tbsp raspberry vinegar
½ tsp sugar
pinch of salt

Pastry:
100 g (3½ oz) all-purpose flour
pinch of salt
4 tbsp sweet butter
2 tbsp freshly grated parmesan cheese
1 egg yolk
1–2 tbsp cold water

Filling:
1 egg
115 g (4 oz) goat's cheese
1 tbsp grated parmesan cheese
2 tbsp thick cream
225 ml (8 fl oz/1 cup) milk
salt fresh ground pepper
15 g (½ oz) sun-dried tomatoes, diced
½ tbsp chopped fresh basil

To prepare beetroot reduction, peel and purée beetroot to extract the juice. Transfer to a pan, and add raspberry vinegar, sugar and salt and simmer until thickened. Strain through a muslin cloth and store in an airtight container.

To make pastry, sieve the flour and salt into a bowl and rub in the butter by hand until the mixture resembles fine bread crumbs. Stir in cheese, egg yolk and water to form a smooth, soft dough. Add the extra tablespoon of water if the dough is too firm. Wrap and refrigerate for 30 minutes. Preheat the oven to 200°C (400°F). Roll out the dough and line a deep fluted tart pan. Prick the bottom to keep the pastry from puffing. Chill for 10 minutes. Bake blind for 20 minutes, or until the pastry is lightly golden and crisp. Once cooked, remove from the oven and allow to cool. Reduce the oven temperature to 190°C (375°F).

To prepare filling, beat egg, goat's cheese, parmesan, cream, milk, salt and pepper together. Pour the cheese mixture into the pastry case. Sprinkle the sun-dried tomatoes on top of the cheese mixture and bake for 25–30 minutes, or until golden and firm to the touch. Remove tart from the oven and serve hot, warm, or cold, with a crisp green salad, beetroot reduction and basil.

Steamed Trout With Oriental Greens, Light Soy Sauce & Sesame Oil

Serves 4

Kilocalories 331 kcal > Protein 42 g > Carbohydrate 8 g > Total Fat 14 g

4 whole trout fish
a pinch of salt
3 tbsp lemon juice
1 garlic clove, sliced
30 g (1 oz) spring onions, diced
20 g (¾ oz) ginger
1 tbsp light soy sauce
1 tbsp sesame oil
4 tbsp leafy herbs

To prepare the fish, slit open the stomach, clean and wash thoroughly. Slice fish at 2.5 cm (1 inch) intervals on both sides. Season with salt and lemon juice. Insert sliced garlic in the slits and fill the trout stomach with leftover garlic, spring onions and ginger. Leave for 30 minutes. Steam trout for 4 minutes on a medium heat and transfer to 4 plates. Sprinkle light soy sauce over fish and top with herbs. Heat sesame oil to smoking temperature, remove from heat and pour over fish. Serve with vegetables.

Brown Rice Rasiya

Serves 4

Kilocalories 151 kcal > Protein 4g > Carbohydrate 25 g > Total Fat 5 g

80 g (3 oz) brown rice
425 ml (15 fl oz/2 cups) water
180 g (6 oz) jaggery (dark unprocessed sugar), scraped and dissolved in 100ml warm water
3 cardamom pods, crushed
20 g (¾ oz) cashew nuts
20 g (¾ oz) raisins
50 ml (2 fl oz/¼ cup) low fat milk
1 tbsp pistachio nuts, blanched and chopped

Wash and soak rice for 30 minutes, boil until almost cooked. Add the dissolved jaggery and crushed cardamom and simmer for another 5 minutes. Then add cashew nuts and raisins. Before serving, add milk and mix well to give a smooth consistency. Garnish with chopped pistachio nuts and serve warm.

Braised Boneless Mandarin Fish with Tomato & Celery

Serves 4
Kilocalories 150 kcal > Protein 27 g > Carbohydrate 2 g > Total Fat 3 g

1 x 500 g (1 lb 2 oz) Mandarin fish (a meaty, freshwater fish found in China, sea bass or perch may be used as a substitute)
1 tsp salt
1/2 tsp sugar
3 tbsp light soy sauce
2 slices fresh ginger, julienned
120 g (4 1/4 oz) tomato, peeled and diced
40 g (1 1/2 oz) celery, peeled and diced
salt, to taste

To prepare fish, remove gills and scales, and gut fish. Rub inside and outside with salt and sugar and place on a shallow heatproof dish, pour over light soy sauce and scatter over julienned ginger. Steam over medium heat for 10–20 minutes until fish is cooked and meat flakes off easily. When cool enough to handle, de-bone fish, keeping the flesh in as large pieces as possible. In a small pot, pour reserved juices from the steamed fish and bring to a boil. Add tomato, lower heat and simmer for 3–5 minutes until cooked but not mushy. Lift out with a slotted spoon and place in centre of plate. Bring juices back to a boil, add celery, lower heat and simmer for 5 minutes until tender but not mushy. Remove celery with a slotted spoon and set aside. Strain cooking liquid through a fine mesh strainer, season to taste and keep warm. Arrange de-boned fish meat on top of the bed of tomato dice and scatter the celery over. Moisten with strained cooking liquid and serve.

Bird's Nest
with Steamed Egg White

Serves 4
Kilocalories 105 kcal > Protein 18 g > Carbohydrate 2 g > Total Fat 2 g

40 g (1 1/2 oz) dried bird's nest
1.5 L (2 3/4 pt/5 2/3 cups) stock
12 egg whites
salt to taste

Soak bird's nest in warm water for 1 hour. Remove any feathers and other impurities with a pair of tweezers and drain. Heat 1 litre (1 3/4 pint/ 4 1/2 cups) stock until hot and put into double boiler with soaked and cleaned bird's nest. Cover and double boil over a low heat for 3 hours. To prepare steamed egg white, combine whites with remaining stock and season to taste. Pour into shallow heatproof dish and steam over high heat for 2 minutes. Then lower heat and continue steaming for further 10–15 minutes until custard is just set but not hard. Top steamed egg with cooked bird's nest and serve hot.

Sweetened Pumpkin with Fresh Lily Bulbs

Serves 4
Kilocalories 135 kcal > Protein 1 g > Carbohydrate 34 g > Total Fat 0 g

500 g (1 lb 2 oz) pumpkin
100 g (3½ oz) rock sugar
50 g (1¾ oz) fresh lily bulbs (starchy,
ivory-coloured, petal shaped bulbs)
1.2 L (2 pt/5 cups) water

Clean, skin and de-seed pumpkin. Cut into 3 cm (1½ inch) cubes.
Rinse rock sugar. Clean lily bulbs by separating petals and soaking in
water for 10 minutes. In a saucepan, bring water to a boil and add
pumpkin and boil for 10 minutes. Lower heat and simmer for about
30 minutes or until pumpkin is soft but not mushy. Add rock sugar and
fresh lily bulbs to the pan and continue to simmer on lowest heat for a
further 20–30 minutes. Serve warm.

The Vietnamese Kitchen

DELECTABLE INDO-CHINESE

Like others in Indo-China, Vietnamese cuisine has been deeply influenced by China, India, and France.

The Vietnamese use chopsticks and eat from bowls rather than plates, they stir-fry their food and regard rice and noodles as staples in their diet. Northern Vietnamese cuisine bears the most resemblance to Chinese cuisine, where soy sauce is preferred over fish sauce, and black peppers rather than chillies are used to spice up a dish. In contrast, Southern Vietnamese cuisine features fish sauce,

chillies, coconut and spices; ingredients that are more commonly found in Thai or Indian cuisines.

During their presence in Vietnam, the French philosophy of food and eating was appropriated and ingredients such as asparagus and avocado, as well as techniques such as sautéing, were introduced into Vietnamese cuisine.

These authentic Vietnamese recipes, with typical flavours of mint, coriander, lemongrass and other fresh herbs, come from the Ana Mandara Resort.

Crispy Rice Flour Pancakes with Seafood

Makes 8 pancakes
Kilocalories 397 kcal > Protein 12 g > Carbohydrate 42 g > Total Fat 21 g

Batter:
400 g (14 oz) rice flour
5 g turmeric
750 ml (1 ¼ pt/3 cups) coconut milk or water (or mixture of both in equal volumes)
1 egg

Filling:
100 g (3½ oz) peeled prawns, squid, sea bass or grouper
50 g (1¾ oz) fatty pork, cut into strips
50 g (1¾ oz) straw mushrooms
½ onion, sliced thinly
30 g (1 oz) bean sprouts
30 g (1 oz) spring onions
15 g (½ oz) green beans, soaked and pre-cooked
500 ml (18 fl oz/2¼ cups) vegetable oil

To accompany:
500 ml (18 fl oz/2¼ cups) fish sauce dip
(see Seafood Simmered in Claypot page 108)
mixed herbs (basil, mint, perilla) and lettuce leaves

To prepare batter, combine rice flour, turmeric, coconut milk or water and egg and mix well. Strain through a fine sieve. To prepare pancakes, fry seafood and pork in a non-stick pan with a little oil. Add mushrooms and onion and continue to cook over medium heat until seafood and pork are medium- to well-done. Pour a ladleful of batter into a separate pan, tilting it so that the batter is evenly distributed.

Once set sprinkle over seafood filling, bean sprouts, spring onions and green beans. When the base of the pancake has become brown and crispy, fold the pancake in half, enclosing the filling. (If necessary, add more oil so the pancake browns and caramelizes properly). Lift pancake out of the pan with as little of the oil as possible. Scatter over fresh herbs and serve immediately with fish sauce dip to accompany.

Hot & Sour Fish Soup

Serves 4
Kilocalories 99 kcal > Protein 12 g > Carbohydrate 5 g > Total Fat 3 g

Tamarind essence:
500 ml (18 fl oz/2¼ cups) tamarind juice
3 tsp fish sauce
2 tsp lime juice
1 tsp sugar

Soup:
500 ml (18 fl oz/2¼ cups) pork stock*
85 g (3 oz) pineapple, sliced
2 tomatoes, de-seeded and cut into wedges
2 pods okra, sliced
1 large red chilli
150 g (5½ oz) grouper, sea bass or other seafood
2–4 tbsp tamarind essence
fish sauce, sugar and salt, to season
1 tsp chilli oil

To garnish and accompany:
50 g (1¾ oz) mint stalks, sliced
50 g (1¾ oz) bean sprouts, chopped
coriander leaves
saw-leaf herb
20 g (¾ oz) shallots, sliced and deep-fried

To prepare essence, combine all ingredients and mix well. To
prepare soup, put stock (see below) in a pan and bring to a boil.
Add pineapple, tomato, okra and chilli. Bring back to a boil and
add fish and tamarind essence. Lower heat and simmer a few
minutes until fish is cooked through. If necessary, adjust
seasoning and balance of flavours with fish sauce, sugar and salt
and add chilli oil. Put mint stalks and bean sprouts in a serving
bowl and pour in boiling soup. Garnish with herbs and deep-fried
shallots and serve immediately.

*To make pork stock, boil pork bones, skin or feet in water in the
pork to water ratio of 1:3. Add some chopped carrots, onions,
celery and the white part of a leek and bring back to a boil.
Reduce heat and let it simmer for 10 minutes. Remove from heat,
allow to cool and strain.

The Indonesian Kitchen

SELAMAT MAKAN

Indonesian cuisine was influenced by traders in the 1500s who brought spices such as nutmeg, clove and pepper with them. Satay, for example, is said to be a reinterpretation of the Arab traders' kebab. Stir-fried dishes, and the use of the wok as a kitchen utensil, are no doubt the result of Chinese influence. Similar to Indian cuisine, Indonesian cuisine also involves the use of the pestle and mortar to grind spices into a fine paste which is then fried to release their aroma and flavour.

Many of the spices used in Indonesian cooking are common to other cuisines. For instance, shrimp paste is used across Asia, in Thailand, Vietnam and the Philippines. Turmeric, ginger and cumin are common in Indian cuisine, while lemongrass and coriander are frequently used in Thai dishes.

Despite the amalgam of influences, Indonesian cuisine is distinctive with its chillies, coconut milk and spices. The following authentic recipes are from the Four Seasons Resorts Bali.

Prawn Summer Rolls

Serves 4
Kilocalories 219 kcal > Protein 4 g > Carbohydrate 52 g > Total Fat 1 g

Stuffing for rolls:
8 prawns, blanched and halved
100 g (3½ oz) fresh rice noodles
40 g (1½ oz) shredded carrot
40 g (1½ oz) shredded daikon
20 g (¾ oz) bean sprouts
20 mint leaves
20 coriander leaves
10 g (¼ oz) chopped chives
4 tbsp lime juice
2 tbsp fish sauce
20 g (¾ oz) sugar

Wrappers:
8 sheets rice paper
8 leaves butter lettuce

Dipping sauce:
6 tbsp grated palm sugar
9 tbsp fresh lime juice
6 tsp fish sauce
4 chillies, finely sliced
6 small cloves of garlic, finely sliced
4 tbsp water

To prepare stuffing, marinate prawns, rice noodles, carrot, daikon, bean sprouts, mint, coriander and chives in lime juice, fish sauce and sugar. To prepare wrappers, soak rice paper in water until soft (be careful as paper softens rapidly) and place on a dry cloth. To assemble each roll, first place 2 coriander leaves on sheet of rice paper sheet, followed by 2 prawn halves and some of the other mixed ingredients. Add butter lettuce leaf and roll up. Repeat process to obtain 8 rolls. To prepare sauce, dissolve palm sugar in lime juice. Add fish sauce, chilli, garlic and water. Pour into small dipping bowl and let stand to develop the flavours, and then serve.

Spiced Tomato Soup with Crabmeat

Serves 4
Kilocalories 629 kcal > Protein 42 g > Carbohydrate 57 g > Total Fat 31 g

Soup:
6 tbsp extra virgin olive oil
180 g (6 oz) chopped celery
1 large onion
225 g (8 oz) chopped carrot
7.5 cm (3 inch) long piece fresh ginger, peeled and chopped
6 cloves garlic, chopped
450 g (1 lb) chopped red pepper
210 g (7¼ oz) chopped fresh fennel
1.35 kg (3 lb) plum tomatoes, diced
1.2 L (2 pt/5 cups) vegetable broth
2 tsp hot pepper sauce
450 g (1 lb) fresh crabmeat
thinly sliced radishes, to garnish
chopped fresh chives, to garnish

Spice mix:
1 tbsp coriander seeds
1 tbsp cumin seeds
1 tbsp fennel seeds
1 tsp black peppercorns
1 tsp yellow mustard seeds

To prepare spice mix, toast all ingredients in heavy-based frying-pan over a medium heat, stirring occasionally, for about 7 minutes, until spices darken slightly in colour and start to pop. Turn off heat and allow to cool in pan. Transfer to spice mill and grind finely. To prepare soup, heat oil in a large heavy pot over medium-high heat. Add celery, onion and carrot. Sauté until vegetables soften slightly. Add ginger and garlic and sauté for 3 minutes. Add pepper and fennel. Stir-fry for a further 2 minutes. Add tomatoes and cook for 8 minutes, until softened and broken down. Add broth and bring soup to a boil. Reduce heat to medium, simmer for 25 minutes until all vegetables are tender. Add ground spice mix; return soup to boil, remove from heat; cover and leave to infuse for 20 minutes. Place coarse sieve over a large bowl. Strain soup, 450 ml (16 fl oz/2 cups) at a time, into the bowls, pressing liquid and most of solids through sieve. Season soup to taste with hot pepper sauce, salt and pepper. Refrigerate soup until cold (it can be made 1 day ahead, covered and kept chilled). Ladle soup into 4 serving bowls. Divide crabmeat among bowls. Garnish with radish and chives and serve.

Braised Leek & Black Cod with Spicy Rose Apple Salad

Serves 4
Kilocalories 190 kcal > Protein 13 g > Carbohydrate 24 g > Total Fat 4 g

Braised cod:
250 g (9 oz) black cod fillet, sliced
3 tbsp white wine
1 tsp extra virgin olive oil
4 tsp chicken stock
4 cloves garlic, crushed

Rose apple salad:
325 g (11 ½ oz) rose apple
4 stalks lemongrass, sliced

Braised leeks:
400 g (14 oz) leeks

Dressing:
2 tsp lime juice
2 tsp olive oil
1 tsp fish sauce
small bunch fresh coriander
1 tsp chopped red chilli
1 tsp chopped kaffir lime leaves
salt and pepper to season

To prepare cod, place in an oven proof dish with white wine, extra virgin olive oil, chicken stock and crushed garlic and braise in a pre-heated oven at 175°C (350°F) for 15 minutes. To prepare rose apple salad, slice rose apple thinly and place in a bowl with lemongrass. Reserve. To prepare leeks, cut off and discard green part of leeks, keeping the white sections and wash carefully. Braise in a pre-heated oven at 175°C (350°F) for 15 minutes until tender and allow to cool. To prepare the dressing, combine lime juice, olive oil, fish sauce, coriander, chilli, kaffir lime leaves and season to taste. Toss rose apple and lemongrass salad with dressing and set on serving plates. Add remaining ingredients and decorate with coriander leaves.

Tofu Pumpkin Custard with Mediterranean Sea Bass, Acacia Leaves & Almonds

Serves 4
Kilocalories 343 kcal > Protein 27 g > Carbohydrate 13 g > Total Fat 20 g

Pumpkin and tofu custard:
400 g (14 oz) pumpkin, peeled and diced
40 g (1 ½ oz) chopped shallots
20 g (¾ oz) galangal
160 ml (5 fl oz/⅔ cup) fish stock
1 tbsp olive oil
4 egg whites
200 g (7 oz) fresh tofu

Mediterranean sea bass:
325 g (11 ½ oz) Mediterranean sea bass fillet
8 tsp extra virgin olive oil
4 cloves garlic
3 tbsp dry white wine
160 g (5 ½ oz) acacia leaves
40 g (1 ½ oz) sliced almonds
salt white pepper, to season

To prepare custard, place diced pumpkin, shallots, galangal, fish stock and olive oil in an oven-proof dish and braise in a pre-heated oven at 220°C (425°F) for 20 minutes, or until soft. Allow to cool completely. Blend cooled pumpkin with egg white and tofu. Season to taste. Divide the mixture between 4 soup plates, cover each with cling film and steam for 12 minutes at 80°C (176°F). To prepare sea bass, cut fillets into slices. Place olive oil, garlic and white wine in a saucepan and season to taste. Bring to a boil, add fish and lower the heat. Cover the pan and simmer gently for 3 minutes, add acacia leaves and cook for 1 more minute. Remove soup plates from steamer, set the fish on top of the custard and use acacia leaves to decorate rims of plates. Sprinkle sliced almonds over fish, drizzle a little olive oil over and serve.

3 Detox Granites: Beetroot, Carrot and Celery

Each granite serves 4
Kilocalories 384 kcal > Protein 0 g > Carbohydrate 99 g > Total Fat 0 g

Beetroot granite:
4 fresh beetroots
400 g (14 oz) sugar
juice of 4 freshly squeezed limes
1 tsp salt

Carrot granite:
4 fresh carrots
400 g (14 oz) sugar
juice of 4 freshly squeezed limes
1 tsp salt

Celery granite:
4 stalks fresh celery
1 kg (2 lb 4 oz) sugar
juice of 4 freshly squeezed limes
1 tsp salt

Juice beetroot, carrot, celery and separately in a juicer and reserve juices in separate containers. Each granite should be prepared separately. Place sugar, salt and lime juice in a pot and warm until the sugar and salt dissolve. Remove from the heat and allow to cool. Add the lime mixture to each of the vegetable juices and place in freezer overnight until frozen. Spoon granite into suitable glasses and serve immediately.

Spa Digest

The Asia-Pacific region provides a range of dramatic backdrops for a spa experience to suite every taste, from the beaches of Thailand and the Philippines to the rainforests of Australia and Indonesia, from mountain retreats in India and Japan to the city centres of Singapore and Kuala Lumpur. In these sensuous and luxurious surroundings, the spas offer a tranquil retreat from the daily grind with therapies drawn from both East and West.

Many of the following spas offer high-touch therapies, which are inspired by the healing cultures from the region, alongside the latest high-tech treatments from the rest of the world. A spa experience can be enhanced with complementary therapies from acupuncture to visualization; physical activities from tai chi to yoga; and cultural experiences such as Vietnamese cooking classes or story-telling from the Aboriginal Dreamtime. The Spa Digest introduces you to Asia-Pacific's best and most stylish spas, and whatever you choose, your spa journey will rejuvenate body, mind and spirit.

Ananda – In The Himalayas

INDIA

In Sanskrit, the word Ananda means happiness and self-contentment. An apt name indeed for a sanctuary set on the foothills of the Himalayas in Rishikesh. This is the birthplace of yoga and ayurvedic medicine, where for centuries, those in search of enlightenment—including the Beatles in the 1960s—have come to spend time in its numerous ashrams. Ringo Starr, it is rumoured, arrived with a suitcase full of baked beans, just in case his stomach fought against the region's back-to-nature diet.

Today, enlightenment can be attained in the more sumptuous setting of Ananda – In The Himalayas. This opulent, Raj-inspired destination spa was created to address the international crowd who want to dip their toes in the river of knowledge without having to spend the night on a charpoy.

The Spa occupies 40 hectares (100 acres) in the turn-of-the-century Moorish-style palace and estates of the Maharaja of Tehri-Garhwal. In his time, these palaces resounded with the footsteps of political and spiritual personalities, including the last British Viceroy of India, Lord Louis Mountbatten, and the late former Prime Minister of India, Indira Gandhi.

70 rooms and five suites offer guests unparalleled views of the Ganges River, Rishikesh town or the Viceregal palace. Complementing these exquisite accommodations is the Spa, with its extensive menu of over 79 body and beauty

treatments. There are extensive recreational facilities like an outdoor lap pool, a 16-station life-cycle gym and a squash court. But it is, of course, the languorous spa rituals and therapies that are Ananda's main draw.

Integrating the traditional systems of ayurveda with the more contemporary Western spa approach, Ananda strives to achieve complete harmony between the physical and the mental realms of each individual. Arriving guests are invited to meet with Ananda's spa director and ayurvedic doctor to plan a menu of treatments and exercise. This personalized therapy and activities programme was designed to meet individual needs and health goals. Guidance on nutrition, exercise, stress management, detoxification and deep relaxation complements the spa experience for a truly holistic approach.

On the other hand, those who prefer to breeze into the spa for a few days to lounge by the pool, take in a massage or two, or sup on endless helpings of spicy food and chilled beers, are welcome as well. The calming combination of verdant greenery, fresh mountain air and Himalayan spring water are themselves enough to rejuvenate any frazzled soul.

Guests can choose from a range of individual treatments or participate in the full experience which sees each day beginning with a rejuvenating sunrise meditation. Throughout the day, yoga and pranayama

| The grounds at Ananda are vast and provide many opportunities for peaceful walks. || The resort is set in a Moorish-style palace and, with many important residents over the past, it has a rich and interesting history. ||| Yoga is an integral part to a stay at Ananda. Staff inform their guests of the extensive yoga sessions that are on offer that day. |||| Drawing from across Asia, Thai massage has a presence at the spa. ||||| Ayurvedic therapy is the spa's speciality, this is a traditional ayurvedic treatment bed where therapies are administered.

(breathing) sessions are conducted by Ananda's resident gurus, with elegant spa cuisine served at every meal. The early evenings signal an hour of Quiet Time, while night brings cultural programmes and workshop activities to stimulate the mind.

Of course, each day comes with its own collection of healing treatments such as the Ahyanga. This synchronized body massage is performed by two therapists using specific herbal oils prescribed according to individual body types or dosha. It promises to improve eyesight, promote better sleep and bestow a refreshing glow to the skin.

To relieve stress is the Thakradhara, during which warm, unctuous buttermilk is gently poured onto the forehead for 45 minutes. Equally restorative is Gandusa, during which guests hold a decoction of medical oils in their mouths for several minutes. Almost magically, it lends radiance to the complexion, improves lines and wrinkles, and assists with mouth, voice or teeth disorders, all while cleansing the ear, nose and throat pathways too. Certainly a good all-in-one method to looking and feeling better without any pain.

Eastern philosophies of chakras and aura cleansing are incorporated into all Ananda's treatments. It is a special thing indeed when a masseuse administers energy rebalancing during a Swedish massage, or as one writer put it, "(listening to) a pedicurist describe his favourite Hindu goddess as he scrapes the calluses of your feet".

All other elements of rejuvenation are well in place at Ananda. The morning wake-up call is a gentle knock on your door, which follows with a serving of detoxifying tea with lemon, ginger and honey. Each evening, the spa's attentive staff deliver a note bearing details of the next day's complimentary yoga, aerobics and meditation sessions.

Yoga is taken very seriously here. Amongst its five yoga venues set amongst the lush Himalayan Sal Forest is one dedicated to the world famous spiritual leader, Ma Anandamayi. Legend has it that this renowned propitiator of universal love blessed this palace with her divine presence and her aura still lingers in Ananda's premises today.

Beginners and experienced participants are supported to experience the true spirit of yoga. Sessions begin with a detail consultation with Ananda's resident instructors and gurus to define each guest's physiology, philosophical and theoretical yoga goals. These are then explored with recommended yogic activities.

At the spa's signature restaurant, the finest Indian, Asian and Western cuisine awaits. Based on the fundamental values of traditional cooking, the Restaurant offers meals enriched with the vivid flavours of organic vegetables and herbs grown in a nearby grove of old Sal trees. There are two spa choices—vegetarian or non-vegetarian—which add up to a mere 1,200 to 1,400 calories a day. A third menu option—an ayurvedic plan tailored to the individual doshas—is also on offer.

In the hot season, wander the cool hills above the boiling cauldron that is Rishikesh or play a round of golf on an interestingly vertical course nearby. On balmier days, traipse into town to take in the vibrant garlands that hang all over Rishikesh and pick up souvenirs of cultural paraphernalia. Meanwhile, wind, water and trekking encounters are a safe yet adventurous way to explore the Himalayan wilderness. Whatever guests choose to do, it is returning to Ananda that is the true reward—good food, divine spa treatments and a plush, stylish palace setting to sink back into. Indeed, at this palace in the Himalayas, there is want for nothing.

| The various treatments can be delivered both outside and in. || Traditional lotions and oils are used in this Himalayan setting. ||| The spa lobby stands grandly and leads onto the 20 therapy rooms. |||| The surroundings are truly stunning. ||||| Herbal pouches are used to administer oil-based massages.

Spa Statistics

SPA AREA
1,950 sq m (21,000 sq ft)

FACILITIES
20 therapy rooms, Kama Suite for couples; 4 consultation rooms ayurvedic section, oriental therapy room; 4 relaxation rooms; western and hydrotherapy areas; 1 outdoor Jacuzzi; 5 yoga venues, fitness centre; 1 outdoor swimming pool; 1 spa boutique

SIGNATURE TREATMENT
Ayurveda treatments

OTHER TREATMENTS AND THERAPIES
Aromatherapy, ayurvedic consultations and treatments, baths, body scrubs, body wraps, facial treatments, hair treatments, hydrotherapy, manicures/pedicures, massages, reflexology, waxing, wellness consultations

PROVISIONS FOR COUPLES
Kama suite, Romance Package

SPA CUISINE
Available

ACTIVITIES
Aerobics, ashram visits, cave excursions, fitness consultations, hiking, kayaking, lifestyle consultations, make-up classes, meditation, nature walks, spa cuisine demonstrations, Rishikesh Ashram excursions, river angling, wellness lectures and workshops, white water rafting, visiting master sessions, yoga

CONTACT
The Palace Estate
Narendra Nagar
Tehri-Garhwal
Uttaranchal 249175
T +91 1378 227 500
F +91 1378 227 550
E sales@anandaspa.com
W www.anandaspa.com

Mandara Spa at JW Marriott Hotel

SHANGHAI, CHINA

A slice of old Shanghai has been brought to bear at China's first Mandara Spa. Located at the JW Marriott Hotel Shanghai, it is a sanctum of sumptuous ancient comforts juxtaposed against the hotel's supremely modern architecture. The Mandara Spa echoes the elegance of a bygone era with intricate wooden panels, unpolished old bricks and exposed wooden beams, typical of the old Shanghainese Shikumen houses. These old world touches are accented with Thai and Chinese elements such as Oriental ceramics and colourful silks to render a spa setting that is as indulgent as its menu of treatments.

Each sumptuous spa suite features bright orange lounge chairs, vibrant wall recesses showcasing a beautiful collection of local artwork, and blue ceramic sinks that blend tastefully with sea green mosaic glass wall tiles. In these suites, an array of treatments that are drawn from traditional Asian healing rituals and modern spa techniques await both male and female guests.

Its signature treatment, Yin and Yang, restores the balance and harmony between face and body through simultaneous treatments on the face and feet. While the complexion is pampered with a scrub, massage and mask, the feet enjoy a relaxing massage. If that's not enough, throw in a Chinese Herbal Back Treatment, which comprises an exfoliating scrub of herbs and spices to cleanse and revitalize the skin; a deep tissue massage, and a warm compress of Chinese herbs offer added relief to those stressed muscles.

Men also get special treatment here. Mandara Spa's popular men's packages were designed to energize and relieve stress through deep cleansing scrubs, deep tissue massages and facial treatments

tailored to fight the rigours of urban life. The spa's prime location also means that businessmen can take advantage of these services before significant events such as an important business meeting, a date, or a special occasion.

Mandara Spa offers treatments that are suited to the seasons. During the summer, the Javanese Lulur, is a blissful and reviving luxury as it softens, nourishes and refreshes by using a blend of spices, sweet woods and cool yoghurt. The Mandarin Spice Aromatherapy massage uses a blend of ginger, cloves and mandarin and is a sensual way to warm the body and soothe aching bones from the cold.

Yet another aspect of the Mandara Spa Shanghai that is unique to China is its romantic Celebration Packages that hold all the trappings of serious romance. Soak in an exquisite aromatic bath by candlelight while sipping on Veuve Cliquot Champagne and nibbling fine chocolates and fruit. Or give each other a sensuous rubdown with Mandara's specially created salt and honey scrub in the privacy of your own herbal steam bath. And that's just the beginning. Follow with a deep tissue or aromatherapy massage, or with the Yin and Yang treatment for the ultimate indulgence. Then lie back and spend quiet time together taking in the bliss and onchantment in this oasis of well-being in the heart of China's most modern city.

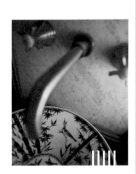

Spa Statistics

SPA AREA
1,000 sq m (10,765 sq ft)

FACILITIES
2 single indoor treatment suites, 6 double indoor treatment suites; 3 plunge pools; 7 private steam rooms; hair salon, waxing room; spa boutique

SIGNATURE TREATMENT
Yin and Yang, Chinese Herbal Back Treatment

OTHER TREATMENTS AND THERAPIES
Anti-cellulite treatments, anti-ageing treatments, aromatherapy, baths, body scrubs, body wraps, Chinese therapies, eye treatments, facial treatments, firming and slimming treatments, hair treatments, hand and foot treatments, hot stone therapies, Indonesian therapies, jet-lag treatments, manicures/pedicures, massages, purifying back treatments, reflexology, salon services, Thai therapies, waxing

PROVISIONS FOR COUPLES
Celebration packages, Couples packages

SPA CUISINE
Available upon request

SERVICES
Corporate programmes, private spa parties

MEMBERSHIP/ADMISSION
Available, but not required

CONTACT
JW Marriott Hotel Shanghai
6th Floor, 399 Nanjing West Road
Shanghai, China 200003
T +86 21 5359 4969 ext 6798, 6799
F +86 21 5852 1155
E infochina@minornet.com
W www.mspa-international.com

| Old-world charm creates a welcoming ambience, and contrasts with the modernity of the hotel outside. || Reminscent of the old Shikumen houses, the treatment rooms display the quintessential Shanghai style. ||| Tones of blue intermingle with the warm reds to create a serene atmosphere. |||| A flower bath offers the chance to unwind and relax before and after treatment. ||||| Traditional touches are everywhere in the spa.

Chuan Spa at Langham Place Hotel

HONG KONG

The Chuan journey begins the moment guests step through the Moon Gate on the 41st storey of the luxury Langham Place Hotel, Hong Kong. As you enter, the hectic pace of city-life gives way to the soothing sound of flowing water, conveying an overall sense of peace and tranquillity. Indeed, Chuan means 'flowing water' in Chinese. And true to its name, water forms an essential component of the spa's décor and ambience.

In keeping with its Oriental heritage, the spa is designed in a contemporary yet modern Chinese architectural style. Hints of Chinese culture are interpreted in splashes of colour, carefully chosen furniture and the use of oriental fabrics that appear all around the spa. Designed in thoughtful consultation with a feng shui master, Chuan is harmoniously laid out so that guests are ensured they will have a divine experience.

All elements of Chuan Spa have been guided by the tenets of Traditional Chinese Medicine (TCM). The focus is on supporting the three treasures of

Jing (our life force), Qi (our vital energy) and Shen (our mind and spirit) to promote rest and relaxation, as well as mental well-being. Chuan treatments are all a nod to the TCM pillars of Wu Xing (the Five Elements), Yin and Yang, and Jing Luo (the Meridian System). Each visit begins as Chuan's qualified therapists take guests through a Five Elements questionnaire in order to determine which elements are out of balance and to custom-design each individual package or treatment.

As a prelude to the Chuan experience, guests are welcome to enjoy the delights of a sauna, steam and Oriental hot tub before descending along the candlelit stairway to the spa's beautiful treatment rooms. Within these havens of relaxation, a choice of five teas—each reflecting an element—is served. Relax and unwind to the strains of gentle music before one of 60 holistic treatments is administered to restore your tired soul.

Chuan's signature treatment, Serenity Shen, is the ideal way to sample the best its extensive menu

| An overall sense of peace and tranquillity pervail as soon as guests step through the door. || Flowing water abounds at Chuan Spa and plays a key role in affirming the ambience. ||| The heated swimming pool offers the chance to take in Hong Kong's breathtaking skyline. |||| Feng shui principles have guided the decoration at Chuan and this includes the gorgeous treatment rooms. ||||| A relaxation lounge, where guests can rebalance their body after treatment. |||||| The moon gate entrance.

has to offer. This three-hour treatment begins with a stone therapy massage, followed by a long soak in the private hot tub. Next, an indulgent facial treatment, which encompasses blended essential oils and a marine algae mask, is administered before a Chinese-inspired spa snack and herbal tea is served in the private suite.

Like all spas of repute, Chuan boasts its own range of exclusive products that was created with the help of a Chinese healthcare expert. These include massage oils, aroma mists, mud and hair masks that are used in all Chuan's signature treatments and available as luxury retail items that guests can take home.

Couples may share their spa experience in complete privacy in the Chuan Suite. This can be booked in advance for any package or treatment and is best known for its oversized twin tub that overlooks the Hong Kong skyline. Chuan occupies the top three floors of the Langham Place Hotel and recently opened its heated rooftop outdoor swimming pool. Also part of the spa is a state-of-the-art fitness studio so those of more active persuasion may burn some energy before surrendering themselves to the experienced hands of Chuan's therapists and enjoying some exquisite pampering.

Spa Statistics

SPA AREA
1,675 sq m (18,017 sq ft)

FACILITIES
8 double indoor treatment rooms; 1 consultation room; 2 relaxation rooms; 1 hydrotherapy room, 1 Jacuzzi, 2 oriental hot tubs; 2 saunas, 2 steam rooms; 3 nail salons; 1 fitness studio with cardio machines; 1 rooftop heated swimming pool; 1 spa boutique, reading corner

SIGNATURE TREATMENT
Serenity Shen

OTHER TREATMENTS AND THERAPIES
Anti-ageing treatments, anti-cellulite treatments, baths, body scrubs, body wraps, Chinese therapies, eye treatments, facial treatments, firming and slimming treatments, hair treatments, hand and foot treatments, holistic treatments, hot stone therapies, hydrotherapy, jet-lag treatments, manicures/pedicures, massages, pre- and post-natal treatments, salon services, waxing

PROVISIONS FOR COUPLES
Spirit Room, with private bathroom and Jacuzzi

SPA CUISINE
Available
Provision for dietary requirements available upon request

ACTIVITIES
Aerobics, aquaerobics, martial arts, tai chi, yoga

SERVICES
General healthcare consultations, body composition analysis, gift certificates, nutrition consultation, personal training, skincare consultations

MEMBERSHIP/ADMISSION
Available but not required

CONTACT
Level 41, 555 Shanghai Street
Mongkok, Kowloon
Hong Kong
T +852 3552 3510
F +852 3552 3529
E hkg.lph.info@chuanspa.com
W www.chuanspa.com

I-Spa at InterContinental

HONG KONG

While the bustling city of Hong Kong throbs below, I-Spa, situated on the 3rd floor of the luxury InterContinental Hong Kong, awaits its guests quietly like an exclusive sanctum of calm. This peaceful retreat was the city's first feng shui-inspired spa and was thoughtfully built around the principle of inner and outer harmony, as the Chinese call it: the yin and yang.

Feng shui is the highly respected ancient art of achieving this perfect balance and does so through the five basic elements of water, wood, fire, earth and metal. As such, by following the qualified recommendations of the renowned feng shui master Jackie Chan, I-Spa has cleverly incorporated these five elements to create an utterly harmonious, serene and stress-free environment where mind, body and spirit become completely relaxed and rejuvenated. For starters, each spa suite and room has been named after an auspicious Chinese quality to enhance its positive energy flow or Qi. Each room also represents one of the five basic elements, which are portrayed by a decorative accessory that's been embedded in its décor.

Lavish private suites clad from floor to ceiling in polished green granite are perfect for those seeking the full spa experience and each room comes with its own sauna, steam-shower, whirlpool bath and massage facilities. Meanwhile, I-Spa rooms are equally elegant, with teak floors and rich sycamore, blackwood, South African wenge walls and their own Japanese-style garden.

While the I-Spa is renowned for its state of the art treatments and equipment, it is its Jet Lag Relief and Oriental Healing treatments that have proven

the most popular. The Ancient Rituals of the Orient brings together the various traditions and healing disciplines of the East, resulting in a ritual that harmonizes the body's energies beautifully. This journey begins with a ceremonial Thai Foot Bath that is adminstered as guests sip graciously on a detoxifying infusion. To enhance the circulation and ease the flow of energy, a Japanese green tea and ginger exfoliation is applied to the body. After a warm shower, hot stones, rich unctuous oils and Chinese acupressure points are used to massage the back and rebalance yin with yang. Finally in order to calm the mind, a continuous stream of warm Indian Ayurvedic oil is poured onto the forehead, on the third eye, and through the scalp, while the hands and feet are indulgently massaged at the same time. All this culminates with an Oriental Head Massage that leaves guests feeling entirely restored and nourished.

Already the spa is highly acclaimed and has won numerous international awards. Notably, it was voted the Top Spa in Hong Kong by *SpaFinder* magazine in 2004, and the Best Spa of Hong Kong by *SpaAsia* magazine in 2005. It's easy to see why—in a city as bustling as Hong Kong, finding an oasis of calm right in its very heart is itself a magical thing.

| I-Spa's treatments use innovative products alongside traditional Oriental techniques. || The infinity-edged spa pools afford a magnificent view of Hong Kong's skyline. ||| Each treatment suite comes complete with a whirlpool bath that can be used before and after treatment. |||| Ayurvedic treatments make up I-Spa's Ancient Rituals of the Orient package where guests are taken on a sublime journey of traditional healing. ||||| A body scrub, part of the Men's Ritual.

Spa Statistics

SPA AREA
500 sq m (5,381 sq ft)

FACILITIES
3 single indoor spa suites, 2 double indoor spa suites, 2 dry treatment rooms, 1 manicure/pedicure room, 1 outdoor spa pavilion; 1 relaxation area; 3 temperature outdoor infinity-edged spa pools, 1 outdoor swimming pool; 1 spa boutique

SIGNATURE TREATMENT
Ancient Rituals of the Orient, Chinese Herbal Wrap, Five Elements Stone Therapy

OTHER TREATMENTS AND THERAPIES
Anti-ageing treatments, anti-cellulite treatments, aromatherapy, ayurveda, baths, body scrubs, body wraps, Chinese therapies, eye treatments, facial treatments, firming and slimming treatments, hand and foot treatments, holistic treatments, hot stone therapies, jet lag treatments, lymphatic drainage massages, Anastasia brow treatments, manicures/pedicures, purifying back treatments, reflexology, scalp treatments, waxing

PROVISIONS FOR COUPLES
2 double indoor spa suites

SPA CUISINE
Available at Pool Terrace, Harbourside café and in-room dining (for hotel guests)

ACTIVITIES
Personal trainer (upon request), and complimentary tai chi and yoga classes

SERVICES
Babysitting, corporate programmes, gift certificates, personal butler service, personal training, private spa parties, skincare consultation

MEMBERSHIP/ADMISSION
I-Spa club membership is available but not required

CONTACT
18 Salisbury Road
3rd floor, InterContinental Hong Kong
Kowloon, Hong Kong
T +852 2721 1211
F +852 2739 4546
E hongkong@interconti.com
W www.hongkong-ic.intercontinental.com

The Oriental Spa
at The Landmark Mandarin Oriental

HONG KONG

Opened in late 2005, The Landmark Mandarin Oriental promises to offer the ultimate spa experience in Asia. This new hotel is home to the 1,950-square-metre (21,000-square-foot) Oriental Spa and Wellness Centre that serves as the group's global urban spa flagship. It took two years to design and conceptualize the spa, which features spaces for Zen tranquillity and holistic exercises. Much care and attention to detail was brought to bear to ensure a space that is the perfect environment in which to relax and restore a harmonious balance between mind, body and spirit.

Spread over two storeys, the spa offers the most comprehensive range of wellness facilities and beauty and body treatments in the Asia-Pacific region. Its selection of exclusive signature spa treatments include the Oriental Harmony, where four hands work in perfect unison to provide a warm scrub that smoothes and replenishes the skin. Later, a synchronized massage that is nothing short of sublime is performed and culminates in a simultaneous head and foot massage, which energizes the body and uplifts the mind.

Another treatment unique to the spa is A Taste Of Traditions. Over 110 minutes, the spa's therapist guides you to various parts of the world to experience each country's traditional therapeutic remedies. The treatment begins in the Orient, which honours the ancient Chinese massage technique known as Tui Na to stimulate the meridians of the body and increase the flow of energy and vitality. This is followed by the Mediterranean, where fluid and relaxing movements are inspired by the ocean and its waves. The brisk, energetic strokes that

represent India then balance the energy before the soothing movements of Arabia (think smooth, undulating sand dunes) allow your senses to be calmed and grounded.

True to the authentic meaning of the word 'spa', which connotes health through the use of water, The Oriental Spa boasts vitality pools, amethyst crystal steam rooms, 'experience showers', hamam, one of Asia's first authentic rasul chambers, and a Roman Laconium. Spa treatments can be taken in one of the spa's 15 deluxe treatment rooms, as well as a 65-square-metre (700-square-foot) deluxe VIP Sanctuary Suite designed specially for couples. Soothing water features plays an important part in the spa's décor, which also uses bamboo, natural stone and gold leaf to add to the peaceful and luxurious experience.

The spa café and relaxation lounge are the ideal spots for guests to relax before or after using the extensive wellness facilities. Here, health food takes on a new meaning as its culinary concept is based on the Cretan diet pyramid. Essentially this low-caloric cuisine is rich in fruit, vegetables, cereals and olive oil, which are then supplemented by beautifully cooked fish. Complement your meal with a glass of fresh juice or a cup of herbal tea. After lunch, fitness buffs might like to use the high-tech fitness centre, complete with yoga and pilates studios.

Indeed, the Oriental Spa experience is a holistic one, where every aspect of feeling good and being well is matched by the Mandarin Oriental's legendary service. With a mix like that, there is no doubt that this upcoming wellness centre will be one of the hottest spots on discerning spa goers' list.

| One of Asia's first authentic rasul chambers, guests can enjoy spa traditions from all over the world. || Whilst relaxing, the vitality pool offers an alternative way to unwind. ||| Chakras are rebalanced in one of the spa's traditional treatments. |||| The Landmark caters for all; the yoga and pilates studios are just part of the services that promote health and well-being.

Spa Statistics

SPA AREA
1,950 sq m (21,000 sq ft)

FACILITIES
14 single indoor treatment rooms, 1 double indoor treatment room; 1 relaxation room; 1 rasul room, dry sauna and tropical rain sauna for gentlemen, amethyst crystal steam room for ladies, tepidarium chairs, ice fountain, vitality pools, laconium for ladies, hamam and private scrub room for gentlemen, Experience showers; 1 fitness centre, pilates studio, yoga studio; outdoor/indoor swimming pool (from Summer 2006); spa boutique

SIGNATURE TREATMENT
A Taste of Tradition, Oriental Harmony, Time Rituals

OTHER TREATMENTS AND THERAPIES
Anti-ageing treatments, anti-cellulite treatments, aromatherapy, body scrubs, body wraps, facial treatments, firming and slimming treatments, hand and foot treatments, holistic treatments, hot stone therapies, jet-lag treatments, manicures/pedicures, massages, pre- and post-natal treatments, purifying back treatments, Thai therapies, reflexology, waxing

PROVISIONS FOR COUPLES
Couples packages and VIP Sanctuary with steam shower with amethyst crystal and vitality tub and flat screen TV

SPA CUISINE
Available at Spa Café
Provisions for dietary requirements available upon request

ACTIVITIES
Meditation classes, pilates, sports instruction, personal training and assessments, talks by visiting consultants and yoga

SERVICES
Comprehensive range of spa services, gift certificates, personal training and skincare consultations

MEMBERSHIP/ADMISSION
Membership is available for fitness centre and also available for hotel guests. Spa services are open to outside guests.

CONTACT
The Landmark Mandarin Oriental
15 Queen's Road Central
The Landmark
Central, Hong Kong
T +852 2132 0011
F +852 3127 8011
E lmhkg-spa@mohg.com
W www.mandarinoriental.com/landmark

Plateau at The Grand Hyatt

HONG KONG

On the 11th floor of the prestigious Grand Hyatt Hong Kong sits a world where Fitness, Aesthetics and Relaxation awaits. Spread over 7,430 square metres (80,000 square feet), it boasts a range of facilities, services and experiences that promise to deliver a sense of well-being and luxury. Aptly called Plateau, its name conveys its location as a high, open and flat area, as well as its objective of offering services for discerning individuals.

Inside the spa is a series of spacious, state-of-the-art fitness and exercise studios and an expansive set of outdoor spaces, among which are an idyllic tree-lined courtyard and a garden with a 50-metre (164-foot) swimming pool. Venture further into Plateau's premises and discover a range of spa treatments and residential accommodations in 23 well-appointed guestrooms and suites.

Plateau Relaxation is a residential spa, where a team of carefully selected staff ensure discreet service and keen attention to detail. Specialists are available by appointment for a variety of spa treatments which can be enjoyed in a treatment room or in the comfort of a Plateau spa guestroom.

Among Plateau's signature treatments is the Plateau Massage, a combination of Shiatsu, Thai, and Swedish techniques that uses essential oils to relieve tired muscles and soothe the mind. Depending on mood or goal of the treatment, guests can choose from various aromatherapy balms including Relax, Tonic, Flow or Detox.

Unique to Plateau Relaxation is the Vichy Hydro Massage. This luxurious water treatment detoxifies, hydrates and deeply relaxes with its specially designed shower bar complete with pressure point

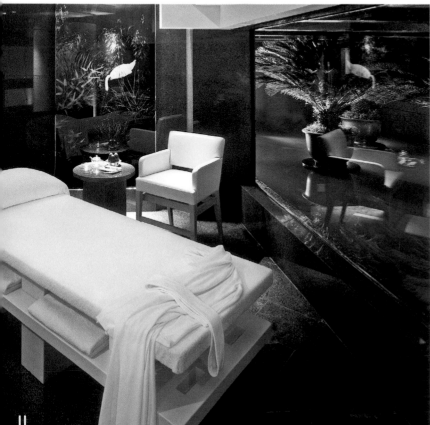

Spa Statistics

SPA AREA
7,430 sq m (80,000 sq ft)

FACILITIES
23 single indoor treatment rooms; 1 relaxation room;
14 spa guestrooms and suites; 3 Jacuzzis; 2 saunas;
2 steam rooms; 1 gymnasium; 1 outdoor swimming pool;
1 golf driving range, 2 tennis courts, 2 squash courts

SIGNATURE TREATMENT
Carita Pro Lifting Facial Treatment, Collagen Facial,
Mother-to-be Massage, Plateau Body Treatment, Plateau
Massage, Plateau Scrub, Vichy Hydro Massage

OTHER TREATMENTS AND THERAPIES
Anti-ageing treatments, anti-cellulite treatments, aqua
therapy, aromatherapy, body scrubs, body wraps, eye
treatments, facial treatments, firming and slimming
treatments, hand and foot treatments, holistic treatments,
hot stone therapies, jet-lag treatments, lymphatic drainage
massage, manicures/pedicures, massages, reflexology,
Thai therapies, Vichy shower, waxing

PROVISIONS FOR COUPLES
Indulge Spa Programme, Plateau Harbourview Deluxe
Treatment Room, Water Garden Treatment Room

SPA CUISINE
Available
Provisions for vegetarian diet available

SERVICES
Day use rooms, gift certificates, personal training, private
spa parties, skin care consultations

MEMBERSHIP/ADMISSION
Not required

CONTACT
11th floor Grand Hyatt Hong Kong
1 Harbour Road
Hong Kong
T +852 2584 7688
F +852 2584 7738
E plateau@grandhyatt.com.hk
W www.plateau.com.hk

massage jets. When targeted across the body, it
stimulates the lymphatic system, which then releases
the body's toxins. At the same time, a therapist
performs a full body massage using a custom
blended aromatherapy oil containing the essences of
lavender, lemon and pepper to soothe and relax.

At Plateau Aesthetics, another part of the spa, a
wide range of therapeutic and grooming services is
available with treatment rooms that come with
private en-suite facilities. Its signature treatments
include the brilliant Carita Pro Lifting Facial
Treatment, which has been described as a non-
surgical facelift. Combining an exclusive product
called Renovateur with technology created by French
beauty company Carita. The treatment liquefies
impurities in the pores and lifts and firms the skin.

Also available is the Plateau Face Treatment,
which uses Decléor products, created specially for
the spa. In it, a vitamin C serum is used to even out
skin tone, brighten the complexion and protect the
skin against environmental assaults.

To celebrate your new sense of well-being, you
can enjoy a healthy meal at Plateau. Besides
breakfast, all-day snacks and cocktails in the
courtyard, guests can dine at the impressive outdoor
grill restaurant or order a Plateau speciality in the
privacy of their rooms or in one of Plateau's private
dining venues. Indeed, with so much choice and
luxurious pampering, life at the top can be so good.

| Based on the 11th floor, the view of Hong Kong harbour from the Plateau
spa is outstanding. || This treatment room overlooks the beautiful water
garden, part of Plateau's impressive complex. ||| The sauna, complete
with floor-to-ceiling windows, provides a unique experience. |||| Part of
Plateau's charm is that you can actually stay in the spa. This is one of the
luxurious, yet minimalist spa suites. ||||| Spa cuisine is available at
Plateau, which serves meals either in outdoors or in suite.

The Spa at Mandarin Oriental

MACAU

The former Portuguese enclave of Macau is today a city of contrasts, where centuries-old buildings exist alongside glitzy casinos, and where Asian culture collides with Western ideals. It is an exciting city, to say the least, with attractions galore and entertainment everywhere you turn.

Situated at the Outer Harbour, minutes from the Macau Ferry Terminal and Cultural Centre, is Mandarin Oriental, Macau. This elegant city-centre resort hotel boasts some of Macau's most spacious rooms, all tastefully appointed in Portuguese fabrics and teak furnishings. At the heart of the resort hotel is The Spa. Here, the focus is on calming and indulging guests through the spa's exquisite treatments, comfortable surrounds and fabulous service.

By harnessing the healing properties of essential oils, aromatic herbs and exotic spices, The Spa's experienced therapists deftly ease away the effects of modern day living. Ask for a custom treatment tailored to your personal needs, or choose from a range of signature treatments that were designed to gently comfort and soothe the body and mind as well as restore the body's energy after a long and exhausting day.

One of these signature treatments is the 50-minute Natural Glow. Guests can choose from a selection of three blends, namely Rice Fields, Ocean Glow or Almond Renewal, which are combined with a Vichy shower treatment that will cleanse and lightly massage the whole body.

In Rice Fields, ground rice—known traditionally for its whitening powers—is ground and blended with orange and grapefruit to reveal smooth silky skin that tingles with a refreshing citrus fragrance. Ocean Glow uses pure sea salt, seaweed and mint to boost and revitalize the skin while removing toxins from the body. Meanwhile, Almond Renewal, a smooth buffer of ground almonds and avocado paste, is applied to deliver moisture and hydration to the skin, leaving it soft and velvety smooth. Great for skin that has been ravaged by the harshness of the sun's rays.

Special packages for couples are also available, including the Romantic Couple's Delight, which comprises a Natural Glow, Hot Stone Massage and

Vital Scalp treatment. These therapies combine to send you into a state of sublime bliss, where staying horizontal for as long as possible is the best option.

Before or after treatments, guests can make use of The Spa's excellent facilities, which include a temperature controlled swimming pool, an outdoor garden Jacuzzi, sauna, steam rooms and whirlpool, as well as a relaxation lounge. Separate male and female facilities make guests completely comfortable, while a VIP suite can be booked for romantic encounters complete with your own steam shower. All treatment rooms are equipped with outdoor Jacuzzis and private gardens to ensure uninterrupted bliss.

Yoga aficionados can participate in The Spa's complimentary group yoga classes including asana, sun salutation and pranayama. Private sessions for guests who prefer their yoga instruction to be a one-on-one affair can also be arranged.

If however, you prefer to just lay back and be pampered with state-of-the-art spa treatments, then choose from The Spa's selection of over 30 health and beauty therapies that could keep you blissfully occupied for days.

The Spa recently introduced a new range of Comfort Zone products that guests can purchase through its well-stocked spa boutique. That means the magic of The Spa's treatments can also be enjoyed in the comfort of your own home. Such experiences certainly are memorable.

Spa Statistics

SPA AREA
805 sq m (8,665 sq ft)

FACILITIES
5 single indoor treatment rooms, 2 double indoor treatment suites; 2 relaxation rooms; 2 indoor Jacuzzis, 1 outdoor Jacuzzi; 2 saunas, 2 steam rooms; 1 gymnasium, 1 aerobics studio; 1 outdoor swimming pool, 1 multi-purpose court (for football, basketball or volleyball), 2 tennis courts, 1 squash court; spa boutique

SIGNATURE TREATMENT
Natural Glow, Oriental Harmony, Romantic Couple's Delight

OTHER TREATMENTS AND THERAPIES
Anti-cellulite treatments, anti-ageing treatments, aqua therapy, aromatherapy, baths, body scrubs, body wraps, Chinese therapies, eye treatments, facial treatments, firming and slimming treatments, hand and foot treatments, holistic treatments, hot stone therapies, hydrotherapy, jet-lag treatments, lymphatic drainage massage, manicures/pedicures, massages, pre- and post-natal treatments, purifying back treatments, reflexology, scalp treatments, Thai therapies, waxing

PROVISIONS FOR COUPLES
Romantic Couple's Delight, Jasmine Suite, Palmarosa Suite

SPA CUISINE
Provision for dietary requirements available upon request

ACTIVITIES
Aerobics, biking, meditation classes, rock-climbing, stretching classes, tennis, yoga

SERVICES
Babysitting and childcare, free transfers to ferry terminal, personal training, gift certificates, private spa parties

MEMBERSHIP/ADMISSION
Available but not required

CONTACT
Mandarin Oriental, Macau
956-1110 Avenida da Amizade
Macau
T +853 793 4824
F +853 713 168
E momfm-spa@mohg.com
W www.mandarinoriental.com/macau

| Asian artefacts decorate the spa throughout. || With its rich design the partially outdoor Jacuzzis provide the perfect end to a day at the spa. ||| Guests can unwind in the indoor Jacuzzi before their treatments begin. |||| The spa boutique means guests can take their experience home with them. |||| Simple and stylish, the treatment room décor is carefully considered.

Banyan Tree Spa

GORA, HAKONE, JAPAN

Just 90 kilometres (56 miles) southwest of Tokyo, the Japanese town of Gora in the Hakone district is famed for its pristine quality hot springs, or 'onsen' as they are known in Japanese. Easily accessible by car or train, Gora has quietly made a name for itself as one of the highest-end hot spring resorts in Japan—comparable to its better-known counterparts such as Beppu, Minakami and Atami—and offers sublime bathing opportunities that are so popular with the Japanese.

It is here, within the serene natural beauty of Gora, that the renowned Banyan Tree Spa has chosen to open its legendary spa in the Land of the Rising Sun. Drawing on the five elements in Chinese philosophy, as well as other Asian traditions that date back hundreds of years, Banyan Tree Spa Gora Hakone offers stimulating therapies that centre on the characteristics of Earth, Gold, Water, Wood and Fire. These time-honoured therapies feature more

than 73 traditional Chinese herbs and natural ingredients such as ginseng, pearl, sandalwood, lotus, black sesame seed and winter melon.

Enter the spa and your senses immediately warm to the comforting scent of flowers and the wafting aroma of essential oils, herbs and spices. With touches of traditional Japanese décor including tatami flooring, the spa's fluid combination of contemporary interior design and charming Asian artwork inspires guests to lay back, relax and surrender themselves to the intuitive hands of its professionally trained therapists.

There are, of course, a myriad of exquisite treatments to choose from—massages, body wraps, body conditioners, scrubs, facials and other beauty therapies. A good way to sample a range of these therapies is to opt for a Spa Package like the Onsen Indulgence. Spread over 90 minutes, the Indulgence begins with a calming and oil-free yoga massage to

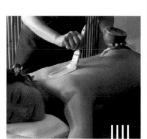

clear the mind of all thoughts. It isn't long before your body is relieved of any tension. As you unwind, your therapist will prepare your choice of body scrub which the therapists skilfully apply. Choose from the Apple and Green Tea Polisher, Azuki Scrub, Turmeric and Honey Cleanser, Seaweed Scrub, or Melon and Black Sesame Scrub. Using only natural products that are gentle on skin, these body scrubs not only cleanse, but moisturize and nourish at the same time. To complete this languorous treatment, enjoy a soak in the steaming and rejuvenating onsen before emerging renewed, refreshed and ready to face the world with newfound vigour.

The spa also offers five Yin and Yang packages that reflect the characteristics of the Five Elements to induce equilibrium and relaxation. Earth, which represents balance, was designed to regulate and promote even energy distribution throughout the body. Gold symbolizes purification and its treatment cleanses the body's energies, eliminates toxins and relieves tension. Naturally, Water is a nod to constant, gentle flow and accordingly, its treatment is meditative, gentle and refreshing. Meanwhile, Wood represents spring with a treatment that regenerates and stimulates growth. Finally, Fire is a symbol of energy and its Yin Yang treatment serves to counter excessive bodily heat.

The end of each treatment is signalled by the delicate ringing of the Tibetan bells. This gentle sound softly awakens the senses as guests emerge from their treatments to a cup of ginger or soba tea. Outside, the serene world of Gora awaits, the perfect surroundings to continue the quiet and peaceful sensation of Banyan Tree Spa bliss.

| A Shiatsu Massage is carried out on traditional tatami flooring. || Therapists use calming Tibetan bells to awaken your senses, once treatment is over. ||| Private onsens are filled with the natural spring water from Gora. |||| The Honey and Tofu Body Conditioner is a unique Japanese-influenced treatment. ||||| Japanese décor is evident throughout.

Spa Statistics

SPA AREA
850 sq m (9,150 sq ft)

FACILITIES
8 double indoor treatment rooms; 1 relaxation room; 1 Rainmist room, 1 private onsen with treatment space, 1 onsen (natural hot spring); Banyan Tree Gallery

SIGNATURE TREATMENT
Onsen Retreat

OTHER TREATMENTS AND THERAPIES
Baths, body scrubs, body wraps, facial treatments, hand and foot treatments, manicures/pedicures, massages

PROVISIONS FOR COUPLES
4 double rooms with bathtub and shower, 4 double rooms with shower

SPA CUISINE
Available with Banyan Day Package, only for guests staying at the Granforet Villa Gora Club.

MEMBERSHIP/ADMISSION
Not required

CONTACT
Level 2 Granforet Villa Gora Club
1320-123 Aza-Mukoyama, Gora, Hakone-machi
Ashigarashimo-gun, Kanagawam
250-0408
Japan
T +81 460 2 7790
F +81 460 2 7791
E spa-gorahakone@banyantree.com
W www.banyantreespa.com

Mizuki Spa at Conrad Tokyo

JAPAN

Located in the heart of Tokyo's Shiodome media-entertainment complex, the Conrad Tokyo has plenty to boast about. Two restaurants by British celebrity chef Gordon Ramsay, views of the 17th-century Hamarikyu Gardens and, of course, the largest hotel spa in the city are some of the hotel's main claims. The Mizuki Spa, is a Zen-calm refuge at the top of the tower, which has won arduous fans since its inception. By far the most exclusive spa in the city, it features the 10 largest treatment rooms in any Tokyo city hotel spa, awash in soothing tones and moon and water motifs.

Guests are greeted at Mizuki's entrance with the quiet calm of a clear blue carpet that mirrors a full moon over an ocean blue surface. Tranquillity is further evoked through its ultra-modern Japanese design and the healing strains of soft music that float through its space.

Treatments here range from the traditional (Hinoki bath) to the nouveau (Napa Valley grape seed facial treatments), reflecting the spa's fusion of time-honoured rituals with modern day sensibilities. Its signature spa package, the Mizuki Spirit exemplifies this philosophy, borrowing from the soul of Japanese spa culture and blending it with the needs of the modern day spa-goer. The package begins with a relaxing soak in a hinoki cypress-wood tub before the body is prepared with a gentle foot massage. An Essence Massage follows, using pure essential oil blends to calm the mind, detoxify the body and rejuvenate the spirit. This massage is touted as an effective jet lag or travel stress reliever and is a favourite treatment for overseas guests who come here. Next an Express Facial refreshes and cleanses

your visage before the Mizuki Spirit culminates with a traditional Japanese tea ceremony.

Yet another exquisitely indulgent treatment is the Spa Suite Ritual. Taken in the sumptuousness of a Mizuki Spa suite, the 150-minute-long treatment includes an invigorating scrub, a deep, uplifting soak in the bath, a body wrap of your choice and a massage. Designed to return to your body and soul a little of what everyday life takes out, the Spa Suite Ritual rejuvenates, nurtures and revives the senses.

At the heart of each treatment is Mizukis Spa's signature range of products that are made from Napa Valley grape seeds, renowned for their antioxidant and anti-ageing properties. Additionally, the spa uses the Dr Spiller range of products from Germany, all of which are made entirely of natural ingredients and combined with advanced technology to refresh the skin and create a beautiful bodyline.

Fitness facilities are also available. The spa boasts a fully-equipped gym and aerobics studio, a 25-metre (82-foot) 'Sumie' style indoor lap pool and sauna and steam rooms, plus a dedicated relaxation zone.

To end your Mizuki Spa experience, head to the renowned modern French restaurant, Gordon Ramsay at Conrad Tokyo, and enjoy a spa menu that includes champagne and caviar. Once the mind, body and belly are satiated, the soul relaxes too.

| The serene swimming pool evokes utter calm as you swim and take in the surroundings. || Ultra-modern and Japanese in style, the Conrad Tokyo is a feast for the senses. ||| The fully-equipped treatment rooms come complete with bath and stunning views. |||| The stylish and minimalist bedrooms offer the perfect sanctuary during your stay in busy Tokyo.

Spa Statistics

SPA AREA
1,400 sq m (15,000 sq ft)

FACILITIES
8 single indoor treatment rooms, 2 double indoor treatment rooms; 1 relaxation room; 4 Jacuzzis; 2 saunas, 2 steam rooms; 1 nail salon station; 1 gymnasium, 1 aerobics studio; 1 indoor swimming pool

SIGNATURE TREATMENT
Mizuki Spirit

OTHER TREATMENTS AND THERAPIES
Anti-ageing treatments, aromatherapy, body scrubs, body wraps, facial treatments, hot stone therapies, jet-lag treatments, manicures/pedicures, massages, pre- and post-natal treatments

PROVISIONS FOR COUPLES
Marine Caviar Deluxe, Mizuki Spirit, 2 double indoor treatments rooms

SPA CUISINE
Available at Gordon Ramsay At Conrad Tokyo
Provision for various dietary requirements available upon request

MEMBERSHIP/ADMISSION
Available but not required

CONTACT
Tokyo Shiodome Building 29F
1-9-1 Higashi Shinbashi,
Minato-ku, Tokyo 105-7337
Japan
T +81 3 6388 8620
F +81 3 388 8001
E mizuki.conradtokyo@hilton.com
W www.conradhotels.jp

The Spa at Mandarin Oriental

TOKYO, JAPAN

Newly opened, at the end of 2005, the Mandarin Oriental, Tokyo, promises to be a prestigious landmark in the heart of Japan's main financial district. Bringing a sense of contemporary luxury to Nihonbashi, the historical and cultural centre of Tokyo commerce, the hotel offers views of the Imperial Palace to the west and Tokyo Bay to the east.

Guests that arrive at the Mandarin Oriental, Tokyo are ushered through a private entrance and led, via spacious high-tech elevators, directly to the 38th-storey Sky Lobby. Here, gasp at the dramatic views of the impeccably laid out cityscape and then train your sights on Tokyo's newest luxury spa.

Located on the top two floors of the hotel, The Spa at Mandarin Oriental, Tokyo is the perfect space in this efficiently run city to breathe a sigh of relaxation and throw your cares to the wind. High above it all, The Spa merges healing therapies and philosophies from around the world to offer an exotic blend of holistic treatments.

Within its nine serene rooms and exclusive suites, guests are guided through a personal journey to deliver an exceptional awareness of true well-being. This is achieved through The Spa at Mandarin Oriental concept of Time Rituals which are blocks of time set aside to restore your natural state of equilibrium and to attend to your body's needs with a specially tailored ritual. Each Time Ritual begins with a welcoming foot ritual. Signature treatments include Oriental Harmony and A Taste of Traditions. The former features a luxurious four-hand treatment, which sees two therapists working in complete harmony, first providing a warm scrub to smooth and replenish the skin, then performing a massage to balance the body. The treatment culminates in the sublime experience of both head and feet being massaged simultaneously, using their own branded Mandarin Oriental signature products.

A Taste of Traditions offers a choice of four traditionally inspired treatments guiding you to the

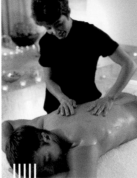

different corners of the world through varying massage techniques combined with The Spa's line of Comfort Zone products.

Given The Spa's Oriental origins, it is only natural that its décor is nothing short of inspirational. To reflect its natural theme, the five elements are subtly represented, with a focus on the feeling of lightness amidst the grandeur of its spectacular views.

Marble walls line the wet areas, while slate walls and floors bestow a sense of urban luxury to communal spaces. Treatment suites feature raised wooden floors with floor-to-ceiling glass windows, while the spa reception and lounge boast unique, wall fabrics by famed textile designer Reiko Sudo.

In true Japanese style, everything within the spa has been planned and executed flawlessly. From the soft lighting to the careful selection of music, the resulting experience is one that removes you from the rigours of the outside world and places you within a comforting space with experts trained to ease away any tension. Indeed, The Spa at Mandarin Oriental, Tokyo is set to live up to its unrivalled location at the top of the world.

| The Mandarin Oriental, Tokyo, stands tall and affords stunning views of the vast city below. || Rooms provide the ultimate luxury. ||| As expected, spa treatments are given in impeccably styled treatment rooms. |||| Asian-based treatments and holistic therapies are expertly administered. ||||| As are body wraps. |||||| As part of the spa experience, guests may enjoy a relaxing foot ritual. ||||||| Dining in style at the Hotel.

Spa Statistics

SPA AREA
975 sq m (10,500 sq ft)

FACILITIES
4 single treatment rooms, 5 luxurious spa suites with extensive views of Tokyo; 2 relaxation rooms; 1 rasul room, 2 saunas, 2 crystal steam rooms, separate male and female heat experiences: waterbeds, vitality pools, ice fountain, experience shower; 1 state of the art gymnasium featuring Peak Pilates equipment; spa lifestyle store

SIGNATURE TREATMENT
A Taste of Traditions, Oriental Harmony, Time Rituals

OTHER TREATMENTS AND THERAPIES
Anti-ageing treatments, anti-cellulite treatments, aqua therapy, aromatherapy, body scrubs, body wraps, eye treatments, facial treatments, firming and slimming treatments, hand and foot treatments, holistic treatments, hot stone therapies, manicures/pedicures, massages, pre- and post-natal treatments, purifying back treatments, reflexology, Thai therapies, waxing

PROVISIONS FOR COUPLES
2 double spa suites with views of the Imperial Palace gardens, Mount Fuji and Tokyo Bay

ACTIVITIES
Pilates, talks by visiting consultants, yoga

SERVICES
Body composition analysis, gift certificates, personal training, private spa parties

MEMBERSHIP/ADMISSION
Available but not required

CONTACT
2-1-1 Nihonbashi Muromachi
Chuo-ku, Tokyo 103-8328
Japan
T +81 3 3270 8800
F +81 3 3270 8308
W www.mandarinoriental.com

Six Senses Spa at
Ana Mandara Evason Resort

NHA TRANG, VIETNAM

Reminiscent of an old Vietnamese village, the Ana Mandara—which means 'beautiful home for guests'—is situated directly on the beach off the famous Tran Phu Boulevard thoroughfare. Resting beautifully on 26,000 square metres (280,000 square feet) of private tropical gardens, this spectacular resort is furnished with native woods and rattan to reflect the authentic image of Vietnam.

The usual Evason warm hospitality and peaceful surroundings ensure an unforgettable experience at Ana Mandara resort. From the moment guests set foot on this stunning slice of paradise, refined hospitality takes over and the stresses of the everyday seem to dissolve.

Set alongside the beach on a coconut plantation is the holistic Six Senses Spa. By using a palette of natural colours, traditional Vietnamese styles and water features as accents, Six Senses has set new standards in spa design in the region.

Pools and miniature waterfalls surround three sunken outdoor treatments salas so guests can relax to the therapeutic sounds of falling water. Inside the spa, treatment rooms for singles and couples come with sunken Jacuzzi baths, a Vichy shower and a Japanese style bath.

Even its changing areas are bestowed with a 'back to nature' feel, surrounded by glassy ponds and lush vegetation. Among these naturalistic

comforts are saunas and steams to gently coax
hydration back into the skin. Private consultations
prior to each treatment take place in the restful
Vietnamese style salas, raised on stilts and
surrounded by coconut trees. Take your cue from the
spa's qualified therapists or choose from a spa menu
that boasts a range of treatment techniques that hail
from both the east and west.

A wide range of massages sees to it that there
is one to suit every guest's needs. The Holistic
massage is a free-style full body and scalp massage
for those seeking a gentler soothing treatment. To
stimulate circulation and eliminate toxins, the
Swedish massage is particularly effective and helps
to relax aching muscles at the same time. The
Energizer massage is a reviving upper body
treatment that focuses on key areas to relieve
tension and ease the muscles, while the Oriental
massage, which uses acupressure, is best suited for
those who want an uplifting ritual.

Mind and body balancing activities like tai chi
and aikido are taught by masters and guests are
welcome to participate in the classes. Six Senses'
range of Sodashi products—all made of 100 per cent
plant extracts-are also on sale for those who want to
take home a piece of their special experience here.

At the end of the day, stroll to the nearby
shopping and entertainment area to take in the
sights and sounds. Then return to this tranquil resort
and spa for a sumptuous meal at its beachside
restaurant before retiring to bed for what will no
doubt be an excellent night's sleep.

| Coconut Beach, where the resort is situated, offers
numerous activities and relaxing opportunities. | | A large
infinity-edge swimming pool stretches out to the even larger
South China Sea. | | | Décor is classic, simple and Vietnamese-
inspired throughout. | | | | The relaxation area is the perfect
spot to readjust and take in the atmosphere. | | | | | Just one of
the skin-nourishing treatments available at the spa.

Spa Statistics

SPA AREA
1,920 sq m (20,670 sq ft)

FACILITIES
3 double indoor treatment rooms, 2 sunken outdoor
treatment pavilions; 2 relaxation rooms; 2 Jacuzzis;
1 sauna, 1 male and 1 female steam room; 1 beauty
room; gymnasium, yoga platform; 2 swimming pools;
1 tennis court, 1 spa boutique

SIGNATURE TREATMENT
Energizer Massage, Holistic Treatment, Jetlag Recovery,
Oriental Massage, Swedish massage

OTHER TREATMENTS AND THERAPIES
Anti-cellulite treatments, body scrubs, body wraps,
facial treatments, firming and slimming treatments,
hair treatments, holistic treatments, jet-lag treatments,
manicures/pedicures, massages, reflexology, scalp
treatments, waxing

PROVISIONS FOR COUPLES
Available

SPA CUISINE
Available

ACTIVITIES
Biking, cooking classes, hiking, martial arts, massage
classes, sailing, scuba diving, snorkelling, tai chi, tennis

SERVICES
Babysitting

MEMBERSHIP/ADMISSION
Not required

CONTACT
Ana Mandara Resort
Beachside Tran Phu Blvd
Nha Trang, Vietnam
T +84 58 829 829 ext 8130
F +84 58 829 629
E spaana@dng.vnn.vn
W www.sixsenses.com

Six Senses Spa at Evason Hideaway at Ana Mandara

NHA TRANG, VIETNAM

Majestic rock formations flank the white sandy beach. Within its waters lie colourful coral reefs where equally vibrant marine life play. Towering mountains hug the back of the property, rendering a wonderfully nurturing sense of being at one with nature. Such is the setting of the Evason Hideaway at Ana Mandara. Nestled on the dramatic Ninh Van Bay, the resort's architecture reflects the traditions of its host country, with classic Vietnamese structures that were painstakingly transported across waters and assembled on site.

Within these breathtaking premises hides the Six Senses Spa. Built into the tranquillity of the thick jungle, the spa was fashioned with equally natural materials—granite, bamboo, local hard woods and

thatched roofs, which conspire with the strains of a gentle waterfall to deliver an utterly serene spa experience. Here, holistic treatments have been carefully created to suit the different needs of every individual. Using the Six Senses Sodashi range of spa products—all made of 100 per cent natural plant essences and extracts—the spa constantly seeks to balance the senses of all who visit.

In any one of its beautifully designed treatment rooms or outdoor pavilions, guests can surrender to the spa's signature Vietnamese Massage. Incorporating a pressure point technique with invigorating movements, the massage warms and relaxes muscle tissues before small suction cups are placed on the back to aid muscle relaxation and to

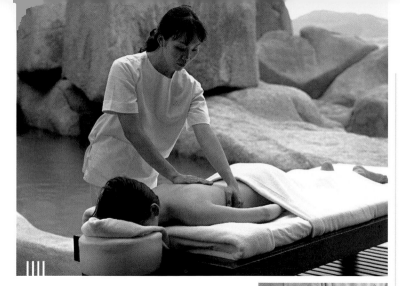

improve circulation. To pamper the skin, the Vietnamese Fruit Body Smoother is an exotic blend of tropical fruit such as papaya, pineapple and aloe vera, which helps to slough away dead skin cells and leave the skin tingling with freshness. To complete the experience, guest can opt for a Vietnamese Facial treatment, which encompasses basic skin cleansing, gentle exfoliation and a face mask made of all-natural ingredients that invigorates the complexion, leaving you glowing with well-being.

The spa boasts an extensive range of treatments, from baths and body scrubs to purifying back treatments and reflexology. Guests can make an event of Six Senses treatments, beginning or ending each day of their Hideaway holiday with an exquisite beauty or body ritual.

Post-treatment, guests can enjoy a meal or snack from the vast selection of Vietnamese culinary delights at the resort's restaurant, safe in the knowledge that each dish is perfectly healthy.

Those seeking a further extension of Six Senses Spa's calming offerings can participate in tai chi or yoga classes which are conducted at the summit of an impressive rock formation overlooking the magnificent sea below. It is a truly uplifting experience of a lifetime; holding poses invented by spiritual ancients while paying homage to nature at its most spectacular.

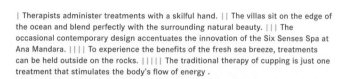

| Therapists administer treatments with a skilful hand. || The villas sit on the edge of the ocean and blend perfectly with the surrounding natural beauty. ||| The occasional contemporary design accentuates the innovation of the Six Senses Spa at Ana Mandara. |||| To experience the benefits of the fresh sea breeze, treatments can be held outside on the rocks. ||||| The traditional therapy of cupping is just one treatment that stimulates the body's flow of energy .

Spa Statistics

SPA AREA
3,500 sq m (37,675 sq ft)

FACILITIES
4 double indoor treatment villas, 2 double indoor treatment rooms; 1 consultation room; 1 meditation room, 1 relaxation room; 4 Jacuzzi baths; 2 saunas, 2 steam rooms; 1 hair salon station and 1 nail salon station; 2 outdoor yoga pavilions, 1 fully-equipped gymnasium; 1 outdoor swimming pool

SIGNATURE TREATMENT
Vietnamese Facial, Vietnamese Fruit Body Smoother, Vietnamese Green Tea Scrub, Vietnamese Massage

OTHER TREATMENTS AND THERAPIES
Baths, body scrubs, facial treatments, hair treatments, hand and foot treatments, holistic treatments, hot stone therapies, jet-lag treatments, manicures/pedicures, massages, purifying back treatments, reflexology, waxing

PROVISIONS FOR COUPLES
Available

SPA CUISINE
Available

ACTIVITIES
Biking, hiking, scuba diving, snorkelling, tai chi, tennis, yoga

SERVICES
Spa consultations, personal training

MEMBERSHIP/ADMISSION
Not required

CONTACT
Beachside Tran Phu Blvd
Nha Trang, Vietnam
T +84 58 728 222 ext 677
F +84 58 728 223
E sixsensesspa@evasonhideaways.com
W www.sixsensesspa.com

Angkor Spa at Sofitel Royal Angkor Golf & Spa Resort

CAMBODIA

With the magnificent Angkor Wat temple complex just a stone's throw away, the Sofitel Royal Angkor Golf & Spa Resort serves like a palace for visitors who come here to pay homage to the World Heritage Site. Located in tranquil landscaped gardens and representing the best of French and Khmer architecture, the resort is a luxurious oasis of pristine calm in this dusty ancient city.

Within the resort lies the glorious Angkor Spa. This world-class haven of health and beauty melds the best of Western spa experiences with the traditional healing practices of Khmer culture. And the result is a sanctuary of well-being, unlike any other, complemented by the use of all-natural spa products, pure essential oils, and fresh fruit and herbs from the region.

Within its exquisitely appointed suites, guests can rejuvenate mind and body with a selection of treatments performed by experienced therapists. For most, temple-hopping constitutes the main part of the holiday, and the spa offers quick reflexology sessions to soothe and refresh tired feet between excursions. For a more complete indulgence, Angkor Spa's signature treatments will not disappoint.

The Asian Blend is a delightful and unusual massage that combines two popular Asian techniques. It incorporates Thai massage techniques with an oil massage to deliver a splendid treatment for those who like their massage pressure firm. To address specific muscular concerns, a deep tissue massage can also be added to this repertoire.

Rice has long played an important part in Khmer Life, and in Angkor Spa's Rice Body Polish, ground rice is blended with a mix of herbs and pure honey to sweep away dry, rough skin and reveal a youthful, hydrated complexion.

In keeping with the centuries-old facial care practices of Khmer women, the Khmer Traditional Facial begins with a deep cleansing and exfoliation using gentle herbs. A massage using pure essential oils then softens and prepares the skin for a mask made of turmeric, tomatoes, clay and cucumber. This time-honoured mask brightens, purifies and tones the skin, restoring a youthful glow to your visage.

| The stunning backdrop of Angkor Wat is always in view at the Sofitel. || The free-form swimming pool is surrounded by sunbeds and massage salas where guests can relax after a day's sightseeing. ||| Khmer touches are dotted around the resort. |||| Treatments are available in one of the many indoor treatment rooms, massages draw on ancient Asian traditions. ||||| The expansive grounds provide peaceful spots to sit back and relax. |||||| The huge double treatment rooms, for couples who want to share their pampering.

Spa Statistics

SPA AREA
1,025 sq m (11,035 sq ft)

FACILITIES
8 single indoor treatment rooms that can be converted into 4 doubles, 1 double indoor treatment room; 1 relaxation room; 2 Jacuzzis; 2 indoor saunas, 2 outdoor saunas; 46 sun beds, 4 locker rooms; 1 manicure and pedicure station; 1 gymnasium, 1 outdoor swimming pool; 1 spa boutique

SIGNATURE TREATMENT
Asian Blend, Rice Body Polish, Khamin & Honey Body Wrap, Khmer Traditional Facial

OTHER TREATMENTS AND THERAPIES
Aromatherapy, baths, body scrubs, body wraps, facial treatments, foot treatments, jet-lag treatments, manicures/pedicures, men's facial treatments reflexology, scalp treatments, Thai therapies, waxing,

PROVISIONS FOR COUPLES
Villa Mira and Villa Soma

ACTIVITIES
Biking, table tennis

SERVICES
Babysitting

MEMBERSHIP/ADMISSION
Available but not required

CONTACT
Vithei Charles de Gaulle
Khum Svay Dang Kum
Siem Reap
Kingdom of Cambodia
T +855 63 96 46 00
F +855 63 96 46 10
E angkor.spa@sofitel-royal-angkor.com
W www.accorhotels.com/asia

Two special treatment rooms are available for couples, these come complete with a romantic outdoor sala and private courtyard garden, which provide the ambience for special occasions. The Mira and Soma suites are the ideal setting for the spa's packages, like the special two-hour Harihari treatment, which combines a Relaxation Massage (that pays special attention to the back, neck and shoulders) and an Aromatic Facial treatment that fills the room with the sweet scent of fresh flowers.

It's possible for guests to upgrade their room to the Mira and Soma Suites where they can enjoy complimentary use of the spa's private sauna, herbal steam room and the Jacuzzi, which is set amidst the suite's private courtyard garden.

For those inclined, the spa has recently introduced energizing Morning Yoga classes and Lunch Crunch sessions. Helpfully, instruction is given in both French and English.

Thankfully, the sight of Angkor Wat in the distance serves as a reminder of why most people come to Siem Reap. Because with so many luxurious pursuits within the Sofitel Royal Angkor Golf & Spa Resort, it's easy to want to stay in and never leave.

Anantara Spa at Anantara Resort and Spa Golden Triangle

CHIANG RAI, THAILAND

Perched on a hilltop ridge, overlooking the borders of Thailand, Myanmar and Laos, The Anantara Spa is a serene and unique retreat. Its three-storey volume reception area is simply stunning and a grand entrance for those who pass through here in search of relaxation and restoration.

Two massive muslin-draped swings accord guests the chance to kick back with a cup of warm ginger tea. From this vantage point, gaze beyond the lush canopy of the Thai and Burmese jungle, to the Mekong Valley and the misty green hills of Laos.

After choosing your treatment, stroll to one of the spa's five terrazzo and teakwood suites where the atmosphere and ambience can be adapted to suit your preferences. The volume of music played, as well as the air-conditioning, can be individually controlled so guests are optimally comfortable.

When the temperature dips, as it is wont to do in this northernmost tip of Thailand, eschew air-conditioning for the fresh mountain air by throwing open the balcony doors. Each suite balcony has an alfresco sunken soaking tub or a Thai massage platform. Both can accommodate two and can be shielded from the outside world with muslin drapes.

Using traditional beauty essences such as ylang ylang, sandalwood, patchouli, and mandarin, coupled with natural ingredients like volcanic pumice, Thai coffee beans and sweet woods, the Anantara Spa delivers indulgent treatments designed to deliver radiance, relaxation and a sense of well-being.

Its signature Papaya and Honey Body Wrap is a luscious treatment made from fresh papaya and honey. Rich in vitamins C and A, as well as alpha-hydroxy acids (AHA), this hour-long treatment leaves

skin silky smooth and with a velvety glow. Those with stiff or sore muscles can benefit from the Thai Herbal Hot Compress treatment that dates back to the Ayutthaya period. In those days, the treatment catered to war weary soldiers and has since been performed for over 200 years. Steamed herbal pouches containing five Thai herbs touted for their healing and rejuvenating properties are used to massage the body in light, soothing strokes. These help to rebalance and bring back a sense of serenity.

For unbridled luxury, opt for the five-and-a-half-hour Anantara Indulgence. This exquisite treatment comprises a steam bath, your choice of Anantara Body Scrub or Enzymatic Sea Mud Wrap, a floral bath, Nature's Healing Touch Massage, a spa cuisine meal, deep cleansing facial treatment, manicure or pedicure, and a cup of lemongrass tea. Then float out the door, refreshed, cleansed and utterly relaxed.

Spa meals are sensory affairs, taken at the salon balcony with the opulent jungle spread out before you. Some of Anantara's specially created dishes include Jungle Curry with Mixed Vegetables, Grilled Fillet or Sea Bass and Pan Fried Chicken Breast Topped with Spinach Sauce, Vegetables and Mashed Potatoes.

A special three-night spa package makes the Anantara Spa a destination to aim for. Designed for two, it includes three 60-minute treatments per person, airport transfers, room and breakfast.

| Sat on a hilltop ridge in Chiang Rai, the resort affords views of the stunning backdrop. || Each suite has a massage platform protected by muslin drapes that evoke a dreamy ambience. ||| Also, on the suite's balconies are the glorious sunken bath tubs that can be enjoyed in privacy behind the muslin drapes. |||| The Thai herbal hot compress treatment is a great tradition and is used to rejuvenate tired bodies.

Spa Statistics

SPA AREA
351 sq m (3,770 sq ft)

FACILITIES
5 treatment suites; 1 steam room; 3 hair salon stations; 3 nail salon stations; 1 gymnasium; 1 outdoor swimming pool; library; Thai cooking school; elephant mahout training camp

SIGNATURE TREATMENT
Anantara Cocoon, Ananatara Indulgence

OTHER TREATMENTS AND THERAPIES
Anti-cellulite treatments, anti-ageing treatments, aromatherapy, ayurveda, baths, body scrubs, body wraps, eye treatments, facial treatments, firming and slimming treatments, hand and foot treatments, holistic treatments, hot stone therapies, Indonesian therapies, jet-lag treatments, manicures/pedicures, massages, purifying back treatments, reflexology, salon services, scalp treatments, Thai therapies

PROVISIONS FOR COUPLES
Anantara Indulgence, Body Symphony, Spa Bliss, All Anantara Spa suites were designed for couples

SPA CUISINE
Available in spa

ACTIVITIES
Cooking classes, hiking, life enhancement classes, nail care classes

SERVICES
Personal training

MEMBERSHIP/ADMISSION
Not required

CONTACT
299 Moo 1, T Wiang Chiangsen
Chiang Rai 57150
Thailand
T +66 53 784 084
F +66 53 784 090
E ms_argt@minornet.com
W www.mspa-international.com

Banyan Tree Spa

PHUKET, THAILAND

Located on Bang Tao Bay, on the north-western coast of Phuket Island, is the multiple award-winning Banyan Tree Phuket. A cluster of 151 luxuriously appointed villas surrounded by tropical gardens and Asian water courts, the resort is a dreamy hideaway, where privacy is so valued that guests often feel like they are the only ones around.

Anchoring the resort is the Banyan Tree Spa, one of Asia's most exclusive Oriental spas and the proud pioneer of the tropical garden spa experience. As the first luxury resort spa in Asia, Banyan Tree Phuket has never been bettered, a testament to its undying quest for providing the best possible experience for all discerning spa goers.

The spa's philosophy is grounded on its 'high-touch, low-tech' approach that celebrates the human touch and the use of natural and indigenous ingredients. These ingredients are picked and prepared fresh every day from the resort's impressive herbal and floral garden. Designed to harness the healing powers of nature, the Banyan Tree Spa has developed its own signature treatments, recipes and techniques. Its therapists exude an aura of calm and confident expertise, each having received a total of 420 hours of theoretical and practical training at the highly acclaimed Banyan Tree Spa Academy.

The spa's extensive treatments draw on ancient traditions and natural remedies which focus on a holistic approach to healing and rejuvenation. The Royal Banyan, a signature therapy uses massage traditions that have been practised for centuries in the Royal Thai Palaces. It begins with an oil-free acupressure massage to improve blood circulation and alleviate muscle tension. Then Banyan Herbal Pouches filled with lemongrass, cloves and coriander are used to apply warm sesame oil to the body. The Royal Banyan culminates in a Banyan massage, which uses both eastern and western techniques to balance the mind, body and soul.

Each of the spa's 12 pavilions are recreations of royal Thai salas, with walls beautifully adorned with stone sculptures of dancing Thai maidens and meditating Buddhas. Six pavilions are equipped with jet-pools, while two have sauna rooms and 10 have steam rooms. The architecture blends seamlessly with the natural environment, turning the spa experience into a complete sensory encounter.

When your spa experience is complete, immerse yourself in the tranquillity of your private villa or steep in your own private lap pool, luxuriating amongst the sweet sounds of nature. You'll soon return home rested and rejuvenated from the Banyan Tree experience and ready to face the world again.

| The Spa Pool Villa is a sumptuous delight offering guests a truly beautiful sanctuary. || Looking out from the Spa Pool Villa. ||| Banyan Tree's outdoor sunken bath blends in with the stunning flora that surrounds it. |||| Banyan Herbal Pouches filled with skin nourishing and natural ingredients are used to apply warm oil to the body and is part of the Royal Banyan treatment.

Spa Statistics

SPA AREA
5,000 sq m (53,820 sq ft)

FACILITIES
5 double indoor treatment rooms, 12 outdoor treatment pavilions; 6 jet-pools; 2 saunas, 10 steam rooms; 2 hair salon stations, 4 nail salon stations; 1 gymnasium; 2 outdoor swimming pools; 1 golf course, 3 tennis courts; 1 spa boutique, Banyan Tree Gallery

SIGNATURE TREATMENT
Harmony Banyan, Royal Banyan, Thai Ginger Healer

OTHER TREATMENTS AND THERAPIES
Aromatherapy, baths, body scrubs, body wraps, facial treatments, hair treatments, hand and foot treatments, holistic treatments, Indonesian therapies, manicures/pedicures, massages, salon services, waxing

PROVISIONS FOR COUPLES
Time Honoured Traditions, Javanese Lulur, Hawaiian Lomi Lomi, Renewal, Rejuvenation, Thai Ginger Healer, Banyan Essentials, Banyan Back Reviver, Spa Pool Villas, all outdoor treatment areas have side-by-side massage beds, Special Spa Packages

SPA CUISINE
Available at Tamarind Restaurant or in-villa dining

ACTIVITIES
Aerobics, cooking classes, golf, massage lessons, meditation classes, sailing, tennis, yoga

SERVICES
Babysitting, corporate programmes, free transfer to nearby hotels in Laguna Phuket

MEMBERSHIP/ADMISSION
Available but not required

CONTACT
33 Moo 4 Srisoonthorn Road Cherngtalay
Amphur Talang
Phuket 83110
Thailand
T +66 76 324 374 ext 8950
F +66 76 271 463
E spa-phuket@banyantree.com
W www.banyantreespa.com

CHI The Spa at Shangri-La

BANGKOK, THAILAND

Lately, the spa crowd has been beating a path to this newly rejuvenated hotel. In 2004, Shangri-La Hotel, Bangkok held one of the biggest launches on the international spa scene to welcome its CHI Spa. And it would seem that CHI Spa has hit on a winning formula with its concept that is based on Chinese and Himalayan healing treatments and techniques.

Located on the banks of the Chao Phraya River, Shangri-La Hotel, Bangkok is set amidst beautiful tropical gardens and enjoys convenient access to the central business and shopping districts of the city. Consistently voted one of the best hotels in the world, Shangri-La Hotel, Bangkok boasts unrivalled hospitality and the CHI Spa is undoubtedly its gem.

The spa complex houses the most spacious treatment rooms in the city. Each suite is decorated in an exotic Himalayan style with distinctive artwork

and accessories, which reflect the wonders of Shangri-La. With an infinity bathtub, herbal steam facilities, private changing and vanity area, and relaxation bed in each suite, guests are given the luxury of personal space and time to indulge the senses, soothe the body and revitalize the spirit.

Each treatment begins with Tibetan singing bowls to help promote deep calm and relaxation. These ancient instruments are said to have a profound effect on the body's subtle energy or Chakra system, permeating to levels beyond the physical.

CHI's signature therapies are based on the Five Elements Theory, in which water, earth, fire, metal and wood are in balance to harmonize with the body's yin and yang energy. It also draws inspiration from the origin of the Shangri-La legend, which is said to have occurred on the mystical Himalayan

landscape. As such, ancient secrets from this magical world were revived and recreated, and then fused with traditional Chinese therapies to offer rituals and treatments that are unique to the spa.

One such treatment is the signature CHI Balance in which a blend of Asian techniques is personalized to suit the individual's yin and yang status. Focusing on the earth element (which builds chi), the wood element (which moves chi) and the fire element (for clarity and peace of mind), its techniques include acupressure, energizing massage for yang stimulation and a relaxing massage for yin calm. Pure Oriental element oils are used to harmonize chi flow. At the end of every treatment, cymbals are used to calm and centre guests.

The CHI concept carries through to the hotel's dining menus, with healthy spa cuisine options available at the riverside Pool Bar, in the NEXT2 Café and Terrace or through Room Service.

When restored and rejuvenated, guests can head back to their Shangri-La Bangkok room and be immersed in the bustle of Bangkok and its famed river without even breaking a sweat.

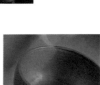

| The Himalayan healing stones play a central role at the CHI Spa. || Luxuriously appointed and spacious treatment rooms cater for both couples and those who are alone. The décor is an eclectic mix of modern Himalayan and Chinese style. ||| The inner sanctum of CHI spa where guests can sit back and relax and soak in the warmth of the spa's colour scheme. |||| A Tibetan singing bowl and ||||| signature incense, adds to the Himalayan ambience at CHI. ||||| The Himalayan stone therapy uses healing stones to warm the skin and rejuvenate.

Spa Statistics

SPA AREA
1,000 sq m (10,760 sq ft)

FACILITIES
5 single indoor treatment suites, 3 double indoor treatment suites, 1 outdoor treatment pavilion, 1 garden double suite; 6 Jacuzzis; 8 steam rooms; 1 gymnasium; 2 swimming pools, 2 tennis courts, 2 squash courts; 1 spa boutique

SIGNATURE TREATMENT
Chi Balance, Himalayan Healing Stone Massage, Mountain Tsampa Rub, Yin Yang Couples Massage

OTHER TREATMENTS AND THERAPIES
Anti-ageing treatments, baths, body scrubs, body wraps, eye lash tinting, facial treatments, hand and foot treatments, massages, reflexology, Thai therapies, waxing

PROVISIONS FOR COUPLES
Available

SPA CUISINE
Available at NEXT2 Café & Terrace, Pool Bar, Room Service

ACTIVITIES
Aerobics, ballroom dance classes, Thai cooking classes, yoga

SERVICES
Babysitting, city shuttle services, corporate programmes, five elements consultation, general health consultations, gift certificates, personal butler service in suite, private spa parties, skin care consultations

MEMBERSHIP/ADMISSION
Not required

CONTACT
89 Soi Wat Suan Plu
New Road, Bangrak
Bangkok 10500
Thailand
T +66 2 236 7777
F +66 2 236 8579
E chi.bangkok@shangri-la.com
W www.shangri-la.com/chispa

Chiva Som International Health Resort

HUA HIN, THAILAND

In Thailand and around the world, Chiva-Som is synonymous with wellness. This luxury health retreat located in the royal beach resort of Hua Hin is certainly unique—while most hotels add spas to their premises, Chiva-Som was designed first as a spa, with rooms added later.

In the heart of the Chiva-Som estate lies a cluster of guest pavilions that were inspired by traditional Thai architecture. These are surrounded by tropical gardens, lakes and waterfalls that are a sheer joy to stroll around. The grounds are massive, and guests can hop on golf buggies for transfers between their rooms—at the far end of the grounds— and Chiva-Som's 57 treatment suites.

Grounded in the belief that it is the combined health of the mind, body and spirit that leads to personal fulfilment, Chiva-Som takes a truly holistic approach. Each guest is considered not only in terms of their immediate mental, physical and spiritual needs, but also encouraged to be guided on a journey to a healthier, happier lifestyle.

People have come here for years to lose weight, quit smoking or kick a hard-partying lifestyle. Upon arrival, a private consultation identifies each guest's current state of health and determines the goals of their visit. Careful attention is then paid to creating personalized treatments and programmes accordingly. Guests can, of course, simply relax and

enjoy the peace and tranquillity of the resort. Manicured gardens, reflection pools, elegant Thai design and the gentle lapping of waves on Chiva-Som's quiet beach restore a sense of harmony with nature and calm the soul. Furthermore, Chiva-Som has a strict policy of no children, no mobile phones and no computers.

Chiva-Som's services include fitness, holistic health and medicine. There is an extensive menu of treatments or guests can leave themselves in the hands of Chiva-Som's Health and Wellness Advisors, all of whom are qualified natural health practitioners and who have attended to some of the biggest stars in the world. To achieve their goals, guests go on a unique journey that encompasses three phases of wellness: Foundation, Discovery and Transformation.

The Foundation phase is dedicated to restoring function, balance and harmony. From sunburn to

I The pristine grounds at Chiva-Som offer a tranquil sanctuary. II All part of the service, guests receive a massage every day during their stay. III Back to nature, a holistic approach is key to the journey of well-being. Meditation amongst the resort's grounds can make up just part of an extensive personalized programme. IIII Treatments range from traditional Thai to new international style and all ailments are cared for.

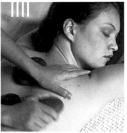

stress management, Chiva-Som offers an impressive array of facilities and treatments to relieve symptoms of stress and disease. The resort's wet and heat treatments detoxify the body, relax muscles, tone skin and clarify the mind. Fitness and mind-body development classes, such as tai chi, are also on offer, with a range of options for all ages and levels. To complement its health and fitness programmes, the resort offers its own gourmet spa cuisine, prepared by a team of master chefs, using fresh herbs, vegetables and fruit grown in Chiva-Som's own organic garden.

With the foundations of health firmly laid, the journey of Discovery begins. In this phase, guests undergo spa treatments that are designed to explore wellness through new cultures. One such example is a therapy from Kerala, India. It involves a warm aromatic oil massage followed by a sprinkling of fine herb powder on the skin. This prepares the body for a full exfoliation using liquorice, a key ingredient in ayurvedic and traditional Chinese medicine.

To expand the mind, explore body awareness and improve function and performance, there are specialized programmes such as pilates, personal training and Chiva-Som's proprietary Functional Integrated Training (FIT). An Intensive Yoga Retreat is available to both beginners and advanced yoga guests. Meanwhile, discovery of the spirit is explored through art, beauty and nature.

The Transformation phase confirms Chiva-Som's commitment to ensuring that the benefits of a stay here last a lifetime. For permanent, positive changes in its guests' lifestyles, there are education, empowerment and homecare programmes.

It is this dedication to results, coupled with its consistent level of unsurpassed service that has won Chiva-Som a star-studded list of clientele and awards over the years. In 2004, it was voted the Best Spa in Asia by readers of the US magazine *SpaFinder*, as well as the Best Overseas Destination Spa Retreat by *Condé Nast Traveller* (UK).

Chiva-Som's latest offering, a medi-spa, opened on July 25, 2005 and comes equipped with the latest technology in laser and radio frequency.

Another feather in its cap is that Chiva-Som is the only destination spa to have appeared in the top three in *Condé Nast* award listings over the last six years. With pedigree like this, it's no wonder some of the world's most discerning individuals hotfoot it over to be treated like kings.

Spa Statistics

SPA AREA
1,200 sq m (12,900 sq ft)

FACILITIES
32 single indoor treatment rooms, 3 double indoor treatment rooms, 3 outdoor treatment pavilions; 5 consultation rooms, 5 medical consultation rooms; meditation pavilion, 2 relaxation rooms; 2 flotation chambers, watsu pool, 3 Jacuzzis, 3 plunge pools; 3 saunas, 3 steam rooms; 7 hair salon stations, 3 nail salon stations; 1 aerobics studio, 1 gymnasium, pilates studio; 1 indoor swimming pool, 1 outdoor swimming pool; 1 spa boutique, library

SIGNATURE TREATMENT
Invigorating Massage, Iridology, Exclusively for Gentlemen Treatments

OTHER TREATMENTS AND THERAPIES
Anti-ageing treatments, anti-cellulite treatments, aqua therapy, aromatherapy, ayurveda, Bach flower remedies, baths, body bronzing, body scrubs, body wraps, Chinese therapies, colonic irrigation and enemas, facial treatments, firming and slimming treatments, flotation therapy, hair treatments, hand and foot treatments, hot stone therapies, homeopathy, hydrotherapy, iridology, jet-lag treatments, lymphatic drainage massage, make-up services, manicures/pedicures, massages, movement therapies, naturotherapy consultations, pre- and post-natal treatments, purifying back treatments, reflexology, salon services, scalp treatments, Thai therapies, thalassotherapy, waxing

PROVISIONS FOR COUPLES
Available

SPA CUISINE
Available in Taste of Siam and The Emerald Room

ACTIVITIES
Aerobics, aquaerobics, aqua exercise, biking, cooking classes, dance classes, horseback riding, kickboxing, life coach counselling, life enhancement classes, lifestyle management classes, make-up classes, massage classes, meditation classes, pilates, sports instruction, stretching classes, tai chi, talks by visiting consultants, water pilates, yoga

SERVICES
Body composition analysis, corporate programmes, free transfers to nearby towns and airport, general healthcare consultations, nutrition consultations, personal butler service, personal training, skincare consultations

MEMBERSHIP/ADMISSION
Available but not required

CONTACT
73/74 Petchkasem Road
Hua Hin, Prachuabkhirikhan 77110
Thailand
T +66 3 253 6536
F +66 3 251 1154
E reserv@chivasom.com
W www.chivasom.com

I Yoga, Tai Chi and stretching sessions are part of the Foundation of well-being and together restore balance and harmony. II The suites continue the elegant Thai style. III Healthy food is not necessarily uninspiring. The delicious spa cuisine makes it easy to commit to long-term lifestyle changes. IIII Watsu therapy is another innovative treatment available at Chiva-Som. IIIII All around the vast grounds, Thai-inspired architecture and Thai artefacts decorate the setting.

Dheva Spa
at Mandarin Oriental Dhara Dhevi

CHIANG MAI, THAILAND

Like a mirage in the secluded grounds of the incomparable Mandarin Oriental Dhara Dhevi in Chiang Mai, the Dheva Spa floats on carved wooden balusters. This magnificent teak palace stands regally in a grey granite courtyard, flanked by looming kapok trees. A spectacular recreation of the ancient royal palace of Mandalay, the 3,100-square-metre (33.370-square-foot) Dheva Spa features a seven-tier roof, symbolic of the seven steps to nirvana. Every inch of it is adorned with ornate mouldings and sculptures depicting animals or Buddhist motifs, based on the original Burmese template in Mandalay, Myanmar.

Dheva Spa's breathtaking exterior is matched by its beautiful interiors. Within these carefully sculpted walls, guests can enjoy a wonderful blend of oriental and international therapies that employ ancient secrets of herbal remedies and holistic techniques.

Some of these treatments have origins that date back over 4,000 years, and were part of the ancient Lanna Kingdom, of which Chiang Mai was the royal capital.

Indeed, amongst its white marble courtyards and dark wood pavilions, guests are transported back to a time when rituals and ceremonies were a part of daily life. In those days, spiritual awareness was considered key to physical and mental well-being. Thus, these same beliefs were brought to bear at Dheva Spa, where a tiny bell chimes to welcome guests as they are escorted through its grand reception.

An extensive spa menu offers treatments that are unique to Thailand, as well as relaxation rituals that are inherent to northern Lanna culture. In keeping with the spa's heritage, guests often opt for The Lanna Signature Ceremony, a treasure trove of Chiang Mai's secret beauty rituals. It begins with a herbal footbath infused with fresh miang. A luxurious

herbal bath then prepares the body for the Oriental Body Glow treatment. This is followed by an exquisite body wrap that uses fang, a Lanna ingredient used to awaken and refresh the skin. To top off this signature ceremony, a Lanna massage is administered.

Called the Tok Sen, this stimulating massage technique was once popular in Northern Thailand and is rarely practised outside of Dheva Spa today. In Tok Sen, warm herbal oil is applied to the entire body before tissues along the pressure points are gently massaged. A light gavel made from the bark of the tamarind tree is then tapped rhythmically along the muscles. This even, repetitive motion renders a hypnotic effect, which in turn eases muscle tension and promotes relaxation.

To complement its rituals and treatments, the spa offers a menu of wholesome delights, created by executive sous chef Fabrizio Aceti. Hailing from northern Italy, chef Aceti is no stranger to 'food that nourishes the soul' and has designed a selection of seasonal dishes that each contain between 100 and 380 calories. Each item carries details of its nutritional breakdown so guests are always aware of what—and how much of it—passes through their lips.

Naturally, one of the most memorable aspects of the Dheva Spa is its impeccable service. After all, it was modelled after an ancient Lanna palace. As such, staff observe gracious protocol, bowing their heads often and moving gently. With service like that, and in surroundings so grand, it's easy to feel like a member of royalty.

| The Dheva Spa sits in all its grandeur proudly displaying its palace-like exterior. || The ornate style is immaculate when lit up at night. ||| And the style continues into the lobby and throughout. |||| A traditional Thai massage is a welcome treat especially outside with views of the spectacular surroundings. ||||| One option is a session in the spa's rasul room.

Spa Statistics

SPA AREA
3,100 sq m (33,370 sq ft)

FACILITIES
2 single indoor treatment suites, 5 double indoor treatment suites; 1 consultation room, 1 medical consultation room; watsu pool, 7 whirlpools; 1 rasul chamber, 1 hammam chamber, 7 steam rooms; 2 hair salon station, 5 nail salon stations; 1 gymnasium, 1 yoga pavilion; 2 outdoor swimming pools, 2 tennis courts, 1 spa boutique

SIGNATURE TREATMENT
Lanna Ceremony, Lanna Massage, Mandalay Ceremony

OTHER TREATMENTS AND THERAPIES
Anti-cellulite treatments, anti-ageing treatments, aqua therapy, aromatherapy, ayurveda, baths, body scrubs, body wraps, Chinese therapies, facial treatments, hair treatments, hand and foot treatments, holistic therapies, hydrotherapy, jet-lag treatments, lymphatic drainage massage, manicures/pedicures, massages, pre- and post-natal treatments, purifying back treatments, reflexology, salon services, scalp treatments, Thai therapies, waxing

PROVISIONS FOR COUPLES
Available

SPA CUISINE
Available at Rice Terrace

ACTIVITIES
Biking, cooking classes, holistic health workshops, life enhancement classes, massage classes, meditation classes, nailcare classes, pilates, sports instruction, stretching classes, talks by visiting consultants, tennis, yoga

SERVICES
Babysitting, body composition analysis, corporate programmes, free shuttle service to city centre (three times a day), general healthcare consultations, nutrition consultations, personal training, skincare consultations

MEMBERSHIP/ADMISSION
Not required

CONTACT
51/4 Chiang Mai - Sankampaeng Road
T Tasala A Muang
Chiang Mai 50000
Thailand
T +66 53 888 888
F +64 53 888 978
E mocnx-dhevaspa@mohg.com
W www.mandarinoriental.com

Devarana Spa at Dusit Resort

HUA HIN, THAILAND

The charming Thai town of Hua Hin is home to a rustic mix of wooden beach houses, bustling night markets and backstreets that have remained largely unchanged for centuries. Located just 10 kilometres (six miles) north of the town centre is the idyllic Dusit Resort, Hua Hin. Set directly in front of the beach, the resort faces the sunrise side of the Gulf of Siam. Needless to say, the views from here are simply stunning and sunrises are almost too beautiful for words.

The Dusit Resort's magnificent swimming pools are flanked by a sparkling ornamental lake, a shimmering lily pond and opulent tropical gardens. A stone's throw away is a sprawling polo field where guests can enjoy a couple of hours' horseback riding. Alongside this patch of greenery sits the divine Devarana Spa.

Inspired by a literary garden in heaven, the spa's reception area is linked to its treatment rooms and villas by a large, serene pond. Textured copper and

steel makes for unconventional yet breathtaking spa design, accentuated by ebony teak and frescoed walls. Devarana's furnishings are decidedly contemporary—its sleek, clean lines are softened with plain silk upholstery that is endowed with a shot of vibrant colour. Careful lighting provides a dramatic contrast to its palette of white and grey, and an ever-changing interplay between light and shadow creates illusionary textures upon its pale floors.

The soothing strains of classical music greet guests as they enter this sanctum of tranquillity. Lemongrass tea, bale fruit tea or Roselle juice is served as skilled therapists listen attentively to the goals and needs of your visit. Devarana's treatments are all informed by age-old therapies and updated with modern knowledge designed to revitalize and heal. On its menu are a host of therapies that include body polishes, anti-stress massages, body wraps and beauty treatments. These are complemented by Algotherm products and herbal

preparations using the freshest natural ingredients. Many guests have emerged from Devarana's treatments refreshed and inspired to take home a piece of the exquisite experience. To that end, the Devarana Gallery offers the outstanding spa products, as well as the Devarana music collection and spa apparel.

Naturally, the spa's most popular treatments are its signature treatments—the Devarana Massage, Devarana Body Scrub and Devarana Bath. The Devarana Polish and Bath draw on the healing properties of rare Thai flowers that cleanse and awaken the skin, while the Devarana Massage combines various techniques such as Thai, aromatherapy and Shiatsu to knead away the stresses of modern day living. For the ultimate indulgence, the glorious Half-Day Pampering package is a four-hour treatment that includes a bath, body wrap and a 60-minute massage, together with a 60-minute facial treatment and an ayurvedic head massage. Couples may enjoy this treatment in the spa's luxurious villas or at the sumptuous Grand Villa at an hourly surcharge.

Once sated and relaxed, guests can head over to the beautiful beach and watch the sun go down behind the horizon. When night falls, there is no better way to celebrate such a heavenly spa experience than to slumber in the plush comforts of the luxury Dusit Resort Hua Hin.

| Treatments are drawn from various cultures. || The extremely stylish décor displayed in the spa evokes a truly calm and serene feel. ||| The treatment rooms are well equipped and decorated in soothing tones. |||| The resort offers space for relaxation and a swim, as well as stunning views of the sunset. ||||| Drawing on traditional Thai techniques, herbs play an important role in the spa treatments.

Spa Statistics

SPA AREA
730 sq m (7,850 sq ft)

FACILITIES
4 single indoor treatment rooms, 1 double indoor treatment room, 2 deluxe villas, 1 grand villa, manicure and pedicure treatment room; 6 steam rooms; 1 spa boutique

SIGNATURE TREATMENT
Devarana Bath, Devarana Body Scrub, Devarana Massage

OTHER TREATMENTS AND THERAPIES
Anti-ageing treatments, aromatherapy, ayurveda, baths, body scrubs, body wraps, facial treatments, firming and slimming treatments, hand and foot treatments, hydrotherapy, jet-lag treatments, lymphatic drainage massage, manicures/pedicures, massages, reflexology, Thai therapies, waxing

PROVISIONS FOR COUPLES
Half Day Harmony, Half Day Pampering, Grand Villa

SERVICES
Corporate programmes, general health care consultation, gift certificates, skincare analysis, skincare consultation

MEMBERSHIP/ADMISSION
Available but not required

CONTACT
Dusit Resort
1349 Petchkasem Road
Cha-Am
Petchburi 76120
Thailand
T +66 3 244 2494
F +66 3 244 2495
E huahin@devaranaspa.com
W www.devaranaspa.com

Devarana Spa at Dusit Resort

PATTAYA, THAILAND

On the secluded northern end of Thailand's Pattaya Bay sits the lavish Dusit Resort Pattaya. Within this playground of sun, sea and sand resides the tranquil pleasures of the Devarana Spa. Tucked away adjacent to the hotel lobby, Deverana beckons with the soft, soothing gush of a waterfall that draws frazzled souls through its serene doors.

The name Devarana (pronounced te-wa-run) derives from Thai Sanskrit and means 'garden in heaven'. In an ancient Thai work of literature titled 'Tribhumphraruang', its author describes a garden at heaven's gate, surrounded by verdant gardens and crystalline ponds, the air is redolent with a heavenly perfume and a soft melody plays, formed by a harp, flute and a bevy of traditional musical instruments. Filled with natural stones and gems, this Devarana also glimmers with the sparkle of gold and silver.

Inspired by the literary garden in heaven, the Devarana Spa in Pattaya entices the senses and makes each guest feel uniquely special. A menu of sumptuous pampering and healing treatments are offered in a peaceful ambience, matched by a level of service that is unsurpassed.

Its contemporary décor, centred around ochre wood and a warm colour scheme, evokes an otherworldly atmosphere. A beautiful pond set in front of Deverana's grand suite further reflects its garden-in-heaven approach.

Its nine indoor treatment rooms and suites are elegant and spacious, each like an inner sanctum of tranquillity with panels of handwritten traditional Thai poetry encrypted on its walls. The strains of Thai classical music, exclusively arranged and recorded for Devarana complete this rendition of heaven on earth.

| The décor's simple clean lines at the Devarana Spa calm the mind and prepare you for the treatments that lie ahead. || Treatment rooms are well equipped and give guests the space they need pre- and post-treament. ||| A Devarana bath treatment moisturizes the skin and soothes the senses. |||| The unique algotherm products are made from seaweed brought in from the coast of France. ||||| Post-treatment, the pool is a great place to unwind.

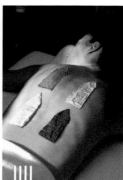

Spa Statistics

SPA AREA
920 sq m (9,900 sq ft)

FACILITIES
5 single treatment suites, 3 deluxe suites, 1 grand suite (all with outdoor areas); 7 steam rooms; 1 spa boutique

SIGNATURE TREATMENT
Devarana Bath, Devarana Body Scrub, Devarana Massage

OTHER TREATMENTS AND THERAPIES
Anti-ageing treatments, aromatherapy, ayurveda, baths, body scrubs, body wraps, facial treatments, firming and slimming treatments, hand and foot treatments, hydrotherapy, jet-lag treatments, lymphatic drainage massage, massages, reflexology, Thai therapies, waxing

PROVISIONS FOR COUPLES
3 deluxe suites, 1 grand suite, Half Day Harmony, Half Day Pampering

SERVICES
Corporate programmes, general healthcare consultations, gift certificates, skin analysis, skincare consultations

MEMBERSHIP/ADMISSION
Available but not required

CONTACT
Dusit Resort 240/2
Pattaya Beach
Cholburi 20150
Thailand
T +66 3 837 1044
F +66 3 837 1045
E pattaya@devaranaspa.com
W www.devaranaspa.com

Devarana's skilled therapists deliver treatments that rejuvenate, calm and restore its guests. And exclusive to the spa is the Devarana Massage that combines various techniques—Swedish, ayurvedic, aromatherapy, Shiatsu and Thai. The luxurious Devarana Bath lasts for 30 minutes and is filled with fresh, delicate lotus petals and the aroma of exquisite essential oils distilled from rare Thai flowers. Treasured for its delicate fragrance and healing properties given by the flowers, the bath not only refreshes, but moisturizes the skin, reduces stress and brings a serenity to the mind.

To further pamper the skin, the Devarana Body Scrub expertly combines the healing properties of rare Thai flowers with mineral sea salts to revitalize and induce calm. At the same time, the scrub promises skin that is velvety soft and faintly perfumed.

All of Devarana's therapies are complemented by natural Algotherm products. These are made of seaweed, which are harvested from the Brittany coast of France, and herbal preparations using fresh, natural ingredients. Its massage blends use only the finest quality cold-pressed oils combined with specially formulated pure essential oils to further elevate the exquisite experiences.

If guests need an extension of the Devarana experience, the Devarana Gallery carries its range of spa products for purchase. Besides massage and essential oils, guests can take home the Devarana music collection and its very own line of spa apparel.

Devarana Spa at The Dusit Thani

BANGKOK, THAILAND

Bustling markets, bumper-to-bumper traffic and throngs of people surround Bangkok's Dusit Thani hotel. Located in the heart of the business, shopping and entertainment district, the Dusit Thani offers comfort and style complemented by the finest Thai hospitality. Sequestered on its upper floor is an idyllic retreat that promises a feast for the senses. The award-winning Devarana Spa is inspired by the concept of a garden in heaven.

Suffused with soft lighting and classical Thai music arranged and recorded exclusively for the spa, Devarana represents warmth, peacefulness and calm to all who walk through its doors. As such, the Devarana Bangkok's guest list boasts a star-studded cast—Gwyneth Palthrow and husband Chris Martin, Sting, Enrique Iglesias, Sir Cliff Richard, Whitney Houston, and Juan Carlos Ferrero.

The centrepiece of the spa is a sparkling pond that runs almost the entire length of the room. Canopied couches line the room, covered by an undulating ceiling that renders a cloud-like effect. Shades of cream, silver and gold lend a rarefied ambience. And archetypal Thai shapes and textures abound, lifted with touches of contemporary style. On its walls are etched and encrypted traditional Thai handwritten poetry—a nod to its literary leanings. The name Devarana means 'garden in heaven' that was inspired by an ancient Thai literature text titled *Tribhumphraruang*. In it, its author describes a garden at heaven's gate, replete with glimmering ponds, precious stones, silver and gold.

Within its 14 well-appointed treatment rooms and suites, guests can experience a host of beauty and body rituals that were derived from age-old therapies. These were then updated with modern knowledge and technology to offer Devarana guests the best of both worlds. All its treatments are complemented by the use of highly-acclaimed Algotherm products, which are made from seaweed harvested in the Brittany coast, combined with fresh, and all-natural herbs.

Special packages for couples can be taken in Devarana's deluxe suites, which have their own steam shower, massage area and luxurious bathtub.

| Yoga is an integral part of well-being and is available at the spa. || The deluxe suites offer a luxurious bath before a massage treatment for couples. ||| A stay at the hotel is a calming experience where guests can enjoy the impeccable Thai style. |||| The spa offers a serene space in which to gather your senses and indulge in some luxury pampering. ||||| The pond that lines the whole of the spa is surrounded by the sumptuous relaxation area.

Spa Statistics

SPA AREA
1,200 sq m (12,900 sq ft)

FACILITIES
9 single indoor treatment rooms, 4 deluxe suites,
1 grand suite; 8 steam rooms; 1 spa boutique

SIGNATURE TREATMENT
Devarana Bath, Devarana Body Scrub, Devarana Massage

OTHER TREATMENTS AND THERAPIES
Anti-ageing treatments, aromatherapy, ayurveda, baths,
body scrubs, body wraps, facial treatments, firming and
slimming treatments, hand and foot treatments,
hydrotherapy, jet-lag treatments, lymphatic drainage
massage, massages, reflexology, Thai therapies, waxing

PROVISIONS FOR COUPLES
Half-Day Harmony, Half-Day Pampering, deluxe suites,
grand suite

SPA CUISINE
Available in spa relaxation area and hotel's restaurant

ACTIVITIES
Yoga

SERVICES
Corporate programmes, general healthcare consultations,
gift certificates, skin analysis, skincare consultations,

MEMBERSHIP/ADMISSION
Available but not required

CONTACT
Dusit Thani Hotel
946 Rama IV Road
Silom, Bangrak
Bangkok 10500
Thailand
T +66 2 636 3596
F +66 2 636 3597
E bangkok@devaranaspa.com
W www.devaranaspa.com

With a surcharge, they may opt to upgrade their
treatment premises for the Grand Suite.

There are two half-day packages available to
pamper, indulge and offer a touch of romance. The
Half-Day Harmony, which lasts four and a half hours
begins with an Aromatic Thai Herbal Steam before
continuing with a bath, body polish, Detoxifying
Spirulina Facial and massage of your choice. If you
can't decide, opt for Devarana's signature
treatments—its signature massage is a unique blend
of Swedish, ayurvedic, aromatherapy, shiatsu and
Thai techniques; the Devarana Bath is filled with fresh
lotus petals and essential oils distilled from rare Thai
flowers; and the Body Scrub combines mineral sea
salt with the healing properties of flowers to leave the
skin soft and perfumed.

To complete the day of unbridled pampering,
enjoy a meal from Devarana's spa cuisine menu.
Healthy, light, and very colourful, the meals use only
the freshest ingredients for the fullest flavour and
encompass plenty of fruit and vegetables. These can
be enjoyed in the spa relaxation area or in the hotel's
restaurant. If, however, you prefer a soothing
beverage as a sweet ending, the spa serves
lemongrass tea, bale fruit tea or Roselle juice.

The Earth Spa by Six Senses at Evason Hideaway at Hua Hin

THAILAND

Innovative style best describes the Evason Hideaway Hua Hin. Modern architecture mingles with traditional Thai accents, while generous space ensures an uncompromised standard of luxury. This boutique resort is tucked away in Pranburi, which lies approximately 23 kilometres (14 miles) south of the tranquil holiday town of Hua Hin. Adjacent to it is the Earth Spa by Six Senses, a haven for revitalizing and relaxing experiences.

Luxuriously appointed, The Earth Spa has set top standards in spa design with its uncontrived simplicity. More impressively, it is part of a pilot scheme for sustainable community development in rural areas, with particular application for a spa. Based on Six Senses' core values, which call for environmental awareness and back-to-nature living, the concept of 'green building' was implemented

here. Thus, the long abandoned local wisdom of construction based on human energy consumption was revived and reinforced by modern knowledge.

Relying on natural and tactile materials like wood and bamboo, the spa's ambience is one of complete serenity, warmth and care. Inside, four treatment rooms, steam rooms, and a stylish cave room provide the perfect setting for Six Senses' range of exquisite spa treatments.

The spa's therapists have been specially trained to take guests on exhilarating sensory journeys through myriad forms of holistic healing. These they deliver with serene professionalism, using products made from 100 per cent natural ingredients. There is a comprehensive selection of massages, baths, facial treatments and body wraps, all designed to direct energy towards the total harmony of the senses.

Those in need of rebalancing after extended hours of travel will find relief in The Earth Spa's Jet Lag Recovery treatment. Comprising a body and head massage with aromatherapy, this ritual revives circulation while awakening the senses so you can best enjoy your vacation hideaway.

After a day of soaking in the sun, guests can also benefit from the spa's Sunburn Soother. Cool lavender infused towels ease burnt skin, while soothing aloe vera moisturizes and encourages new cell growth. To add a touch of luxury to this treatment, a foot acupressure or scalp massage is added in.

Exclusive to The Earth Spa is the range of Skin Food treatments. The concept is based on the four elements of nature that are present and synergistically utilized throughout the spa. Together they provide a completely holistic journey. The four elements are Earth (mud), Water (which surrounds the mud caves), Air (the natural ventilation provides health and vitality) and Fire (which is present in heat-based treatments, for example hot stones or herbal compresses). A balance of all four is the aim of the treatments, which are based on ancient healing philosophies and make excellent use of this unique setting.

While the spa offers excellent treatment rooms and facilities, guests may still prefer to take treatments in the privacy of their own personal villas. The Hideaway's pool villas are the perfect setting for this personalized service, with indoor air-conditioned comforts or in the outdoor poolside salas. Wherever they choose, the experience will no doubt be a truly unforgettable one.

| Mud, also one of the defining elements of the spa, is used throughout. || Couples can enjoy privacy in this one-of-a-kind cave where therapists administer innovative treatments. ||| The Earth Spa's treatment rooms are surrounded by water, one of the four holistic elements. |||| Traditional buildings create an unusual landscape.

Spa Statistics

SPA AREA
1,386 sq m (14,920 sq ft)

FACILITIES
4 treatment rooms each with private outdoor Jacuzzi; 1 meditation cave; 1 relaxation area; 2 steam rooms; 1 yoga and tai chi area, 1 gymnasium (at the resort); 1 outdoor swimming pool (at the resort); 1 tennis court (at the resort); library and internet (at the resort)

SIGNATURE TREATMENT
The Sensory Spa Journey, Skin Food Treatments

OTHER TREATMENTS AND THERAPIES
Anti-cellulite treatments, aromatherapy, baths, body scrubs, body wraps, facial treatments, hair treatments, hand and foot treatments, holistic therapies, hot stone therapies, jet lag treatments, life coach counselling, lymphatic drainage massage, manicures/pedicures, massages, meditation, naturatherapy consultations, physiotherapy, purifying back treatments, reflexology, Reiki, scalp treatments, Thai therapies, waxing

PROVISIONS FOR COUPLES
Available

SPA CUISINE
Available at all dining outlets and in-villa dining

ACTIVITIES
Aromatherapy in daily life class, cooking classes, cosmetic kitchen classes, life enhancement classes, lifestyle management classes, massage classes, five types of meditation classes, personal training, pilates, stretching, tai chi, talks by visiting consultants, tennis, water exercises, water tai chi classes, five types of yoga

SERVICES
Body composition analysis, general healthcare consultations, gift certificates, naturopathic analysis, nutrition consultations, personal butler service, private spa parties, skincare consultations

MEMBERSHIP/ADMISSION
Not required

CONTACT
9/22 Moo 5 Paknampran, Pranburi
Prachuap Khiri Khan 77220
Thailand
T +66 32 618 200
F +66 32 618 201
E spahuahin@evasonhuahin.com
W www.sixsenses.com

Four Seasons Resort Chiang Mai

THAILAND

One of Northern Thailand's finest resorts is spread over eight hectares (20 acres) of landscaped grounds in the Mae Rim Valley, far away from the bustle of the city. Grace and calm preside over this prestigious resort that has left one celebrity guest enthusing, "...you delivered me with great tenderness back to myself".

The resort opened its doors in 1995, on the eve of the 700th anniversary of the foundation of the Lanna Kingdom, drawing a different breed of traveller to the mountains and its hill tribes. Its design pays tribute to Chiang Mai's artistic and cultural heritage, with clusters of Lanna-style pavilions that mirror the layout of a traditional northern Thai village. At its heart are the resort's lush rice paddies, where a family of resident water buffalos—perhaps the most pampered in the Thai kingdom—graze serenely.

Though style, beauty and tranquillity abound at every turn in the resort, its pièce de résistance is undoubtedly the exquisite Spa. Its standard of impeccable service and luxury is unrivalled in the region and it is no wonder the Spa is often referred to as the ultimate in indulgence.

Set in a palatial three-storey villa, the Spa is decked in rich shades of burgundy, gold leaf and black—this distinctive décor is based on the design of northern-Thai temples. Inside lies a cocoon of private herbal aromatherapy steam rooms, individual deep-soaking tubs on semi-enclosed sala terraces, and double tropical rainshower beds. A relaxation room, complete with its own fireplace and floor-to-ceiling windows afford enchanting views of the resort's grounds where waterfalls, roosters and cicadas create a background symphony of nature's harmony.

| The traditional Lanna style, shown here in the Pavilion Suite, features throughout the resort. || Situated in the Mae Rim Valley, a serene calm pervades the air. ||| Guests can make use of the yoga barn and the breathtaking views of the valley beyond. |||| Treatments draw on ancient Lanna techniques and are delivered in truly authentic surroundings. ||||| The plunge pool where guests can unwind before treatment.

All treatments are inspired by ancient Thai rituals and ingredients, and the Spa's signature Samunprai or Herbal Heat Energizer treatment is no different. This unforgettable traditional hot massage has remained unchanged since the Ayutthaya period, when a hot pack was administered to war weary soldiers with muscle aches and bruises. The balancing poultice opens the pores and draws deep medicinal heat to the muscles to release tension and revitalize the mind. For a gentler and more languid experience, try the Spa's four-hour Herbal Blend treatment. It comprises a traditional Thai herbal steam, Lanna herbal body polish, Thai herb wrap, Thai massage and herbal elixir.

Traditional Lanna therapies dominate the spa menu but ayurvedic remedies are also available. The Ancient Arts Awakener blends a gentle foot massage with a Reiki healing session and closes with a Shirodhara treatment—the perfect restorative.

There are treatment suites for both couples and individuals, each with its own private changing rooms and shower facilities. For unbridled privacy and luxury, guests can check into the palatial penthouse spa suite, Laan Chang, which features a terrazzo bathtub that overlooks the unending canopy of treetops and mountains.

Spa Statistics

SPA AREA
900 sq m (9,700 sq ft)

FACILITIES
1 single indoor treatment suite, 6 double indoor treatment suites; 4 rain shower beds, outdoor soaking tubs; 5 steam rooms; 3 hair salon stations, 3 nail salon stations; 1 cardio studio, 1 yoga barn; 2 outdoor swimming pools, 1 infinity-edged lap pool; 2 tennis courts, 1 spa boutique; 1 library.

SIGNATURE TREATMENT
Herbal Blend, Samunprai: Thai Herbal Heat Energizer, Ancient Art Awakener, Synchronized Massage

OTHER TREATMENTS AND THERAPIES
Anti-ageing treatments, aromatherapy, ayurveda, baths, body scrubs, body wraps, Chinese therapies, eye treatments, facial treatments, firming and slimming treatments, hair treatments, hand and foot treatments, holistic treatments, hot stone therapy, jet-lag treatments, manicures/pedicures, massages, reflexology, salon services, scalp treatments, Thai therapies, waxing

PROVISIONS FOR COUPLES
Romance package, Tropical Rain package, Laan Chaang Room, Chakra Lights Steam Room

SPA CUISINE
Available in Terraces Restaurant, private veranda in guest pavilion and in the spa by prior arrangement. Vegetarian, low carb, low fat and special medicinal diets can be accommodated with advance notice.

ACTIVITIES
Aerobics, biking, cooking, kickboxing, tai chi, tennis, yoga

SERVICES
Babysitting, childcare, free transfers to Chiang Mai, gift certificates, personal training, private spa parties with advance reservation

ADMISSION
For hotel guests, no membership needed.

CONTACT
Mae Rim-Samoeng Old Road
Mae Rim
Chiang Mai 50180
Thailand
T +66 53 298 181
F +66 53 298 189
E spa.chiangmai@fourseasons.com
W www.fourseasons.com/chiangmai

The Hideaway Spa
at Sila Evason Hideaway at Samui

THAILAND

Located on a headland on the northern tip of Samui Island, the Sila Evason Hideaway Samui is set amongst eight hectares (20 acres) of indigenous plants with stunning views of the ocean. Within this dreamy resort are villas hidden among natural vegetation offering utmost privacy while offering unsurpassed views. Private infinity edge swimming pools in these villas blend into the horizon, further enhancing the feeling of utter seclusion even though all the resort facilities are close at hand.

At the heart of the resort is the Hideaway Spa. Perched up on the cliffs with an ocean view that extends as far as the eye can see, the spa is almost a hideaway within a hideaway, with luxurious treatment villas that boast unbridled privacy.

Its décor is all about simple, elegant practicality. Shades of wood, beige, brown, sand, white and green bestow an earthy sophistication, enhancing the spaciousness of each treatment villa. Sunrise and sunsets are positively breathtaking from this vantage point and made even more exquisite when witnessed while being pampered under the dedicated hands of the spa's therapists.

A glass of cool lime water begins the treatment and guests can choose from a menu that focuses on bringing out the inner beauty by indulging the body's needs. Some of the spa's signature treatments include the Oriental Blend Massage and Four Hands Hot Stone Therapy. The former uses an ancient recipe of Asian exotic oils and involves a massage that boasts a mixture of Thai, shiatsu, Indonesian lulur and deep tissue strokes with a pressure point massage at the scalp. The latter is a deluxe body treatment that sees two therapists working in harmony to create an emotional and physical balance while promoting deep relaxation.

Guests at a crossroads in their lives may find the spa's Life Mapping Therapy beneficial. Using healing and relaxation techniques from Eastern and Western traditions, this creative coaching process helps guests tune into their passions, innate qualities and wisdom. Each session is personally tailored and is a powerful transformation experience that helps individuals make practical changes in their lives.

Another similar therapy available at the spa are the Transformational Life Sessions. In these sessions, guests are coached to shift consciousness and discover an awareness of their true being. This altered perspective creates within the individual a recognition of what is most valuable within their lives and an opportunity to release everything else that is not.

With the mind cleared, the consciousness lucid and the body soothed, indulge your appetite in the Hideaway's spa cuisine menu that focuses on the use of the freshest ingredients and marvellous tastes. When your belly is satiated, retire to your plush villa to soak in your new sensation of utter peace.

| Comfort and great service at every turn will ensure the ultimate relaxing break. || After treatment, guests can relax on their balcony and take a swim in their own inifinity-edged swimming pool. ||| Couples can undergo their treatments together in the privacy of their own balcony. |||| Facial treatments are a speciality at the Hideaway Spa. ||||| The benefits of fresh sea air accompany a soak in the tub and the view from this island paradise completes the experience.

Spa Statistics

SPA AREA
2,500 sq m (26,910 sq ft)

FACILITIES
5 double indoor treatment villas, 4 outdoor treatment pavilions; 1 consultation room; 1 meditation room, 2 relaxation rooms; 2 saunas, 2 steam rooms; 2 hair salons; 1 gymnasium; 1 outdoor swimming pool; 1 spa boutique

SIGNATURE TREATMENT
Dermalogica facial treatments, Four Hand Hot Stone Therapy, Hypnotherapy, Life Mapping, Life Readings with Numerology and Tarot Cards, Myotherapy, Integral Bodywork, Naturotherapy, Oriental Blend Massage, Transformational Life Sessions

OTHER TREATMENTS AND THERAPIES
Anti-ageing treatments, aromatherapy, Bach flower remedies, baths, body scrubs, body wraps, eye treatments, facial treatments, hair treatments, hand and foot treatments, holistic treatments, hot stone therapies, homeopathy, inhalation therapies, iridology, life coaching, massages, make-up services, manicures/pedicures, naturotherapy consultations, reflexology, salon services, scalp services, Thai therapies, waxing

PROVISIONS FOR COUPLES
Available

SPA CUISINE
Available at the spa

ACTIVITIES
Aerobics, cooking classes, golf, life enhancement classes, lifestyle management classes, meditation classes, pilates, sailing, scuba-diving, snorkelling, stretching classes, talks by visiting consultants, yoga

SERVICES
Babysitting, body composition analysis, free transfers to nearby towns and airport, general healthcare consultations, gift certificate nutrition consultations, skincare consultations,

MEMBERSHIP/ADMISSION
Not required

CONTACT
9/10 Moo 5, Baan Plai Laem
Bophut, Koh Samui
Suratthani 84320
Thailand
T +66 77 245 678
F +66 77 245 671
E silaspa@evasonhideaways.com
W www.sixsenses.com

Oriental Spa at The Oriental

BANGKOK, THAILAND

Since its debut in 1993, the Oriental Spa has been widely recognized as a pioneer in Thailand's spa industry. Throughout the years, it has maintained and set a high standard for luxury spa experiences in the country by consistently introducing new and innovative facilities and services. As a testament to its longstanding commitment and expertise, in October 2004 the Oriental Spa was voted the Number One spa in the "Top City Hotels Spas" worldwide category by readers of *Travel + Leisure* magazine.

After a recent $1.2-million refurbishment, the spa—set in a century-old teakwood house—boasts 14 exclusive treatment rooms appointed in understated antique style. To get there, hop on the complimentary shuttle-boat service from the Oriental Bangkok's private pier and sail across the Chao Phraya River.

The treatments at the Oriental Spa draw on traditional Thai healing techniques and herbal preparations that date back almost 2,000 years. These are fused with modern techniques and state-of-the-art equipment to ably soothe away the stresses of modern life and dissolve impurities that are invariably picked up from day to day.

A visit to the Oriental Spa could last an hour, a day or even a week, with treatments that promise to benefit the mind, body and soul. A typical day might begin with an Oriental Body Glow or a herbal wrap

treatment. Soothed and invigorated, a Thai massage follows, continuing with an energizing leg and foot massage. The end of the day heralds an exquisite Discovery Treatment before a delicious and hearty yet healthy Thai meal is served.

Natural ingredients are used in the Oriental Spa's treatments. Fragrant oils, aromatic herbs and the juices from fruit and vegetables all feature strongly in the spa's secret healing formulas. Rich massage oils, such as lemongrass, ginger and galangal, cleanse and stimulate the skin as well as the muscles, while honey, mint and lavender form the base of the Oriental Body Glow.

Fresh from its recent renovation, the spa now features improved in-suite facilities including temperature-controlled scrub tables and a vitality pool designed to stimulate all the senses with a full-body water jet massage.

New speciality treatments have been added to the menu, such as the Rasul Experience and Essence of Aqua. Both treatments make use of the newly installed rasul bath, a harmonized treatment that combines the basic elements of water, earth, heat and air to create a feeling of well-being. In addition, this temple of wellness features a new line of full- and half-day spa packages so you can spend as much or as little as you want in this oasis of calm in the bustling city of Bangkok.

| The Oriental Bangkok's stylish pool surrounded by palms, is an oasis amongst the bustle of Thailand's captial. || A lotus pond sits at the base of the traditional Thai pavilion in The Oriental's lobby. ||| All new spa suites come complete with bath and its own Thai massage bed. |||| The Oriental Spa's lobby decked in its original teakwood décor. ||||| In its recent renovation the spa was given new temperature-controlled scrub tables, which can be enjoyed in the wet spa with a full body water jet massage.

Spa Statistics

SPA AREA
1,958 sq m (21,000 sq ft)

FACILITIES
3 single indoor treatment rooms, 11 double indoor treatment rooms (including 3 deluxe suites and 1 Oriental suite); meditation room; rasul chamber, 4 Jacuzzis, 4 heated marble scrub tables; 14 steam rooms; 3 nail salon stations; 1 spa boutique

SIGNATURE TREATMENT
Essence of Aqua, Rasul Experience, Vitality Experience

OTHER TREATMENTS AND THERAPIES
Aromatherapy, ayurveda, body scrubs, body wraps, facial treatments, hand and foot treatments, jet-lag treatments, lymphatic drainage massage, massages, manicures/pedicures, reflexology, scalp services, Thai therapies, waxing

PROVISIONS FOR COUPLES
Available

SPA CUISINE
Available at the spa and Sala Rim Naam

ACTIVITIES
Aerobics, cooking classes, meditation classes, pilates, tai chi, sports instruction, stretching classes, squash, tennis, yoga

MEMBERSHIP/ADMISSION
Not required

CONTACT
597 Charoennakorn Road
Khlongsan
Bangkok 10600
Thailand
T +66 2 439 7613/4
F +66 2 439 7885
E orbkk-spa@mohg.com
W www.mandarinoriental.com

Pimalai Resort & Spa

KOH LANTA, THAILAND

The first deluxe property to open on the Southern Thai island of Koh Lanta, the Pimalai Resort & Spa is deserving of its reputation as a haven of beauty and relaxation. Recipient of the 2004 Thailand Tourism Award and a member of Small Luxury Hotels of the World, the property spreads across 40 hectares (100 acres) of verdurous hilly land, and opens up to a 900-metre (2,950-foot) stretch of pristine sandy beach with waters so blue it almost hurts your eyes.

Tucked away behind the resort is Pimalai Spa. Its architect Khun Chakorn Niyomsuk has cleverly designed this village-style spa to look as if it was grown into the surrounding jungle. Surrounded by lush foliage, the Pimalai Spa comprises seven thatch-roof salas with double and single beds.

The spa's primary aim is to bring all its guests back to the glory of nature. In keeping with this philosophy, the salas were fashioned out of the most natural materials such as stone, native wood, bamboo, iron ropes and ceramics. Throughout the spa, Japanese fancy carp glide languidly through an emerald pool of water that gurgles softly beneath its wooden walkways and platforms. A soft breeze tinged with the saltiness of the sea constantly wafts through the spa as its therapists soothe, awaken and ease with their experienced hands.

| The lush surroundings at the Pimalai Spa offer a tropical paradise in which to relax. || The double treatment room opens out onto the surrounding jungle providing the ultimate backdrop to the spa experience. ||| Traditional Thai herbs offer a healing therapy. |||| Plunge pools can be enjoyed in the privacy of your own salas. ||||| The resort's swimming pool sits above Koh Lanta's stunning beach.

After a steaming hot cup of chrysanthemum or ginger tea, lie back and experience one of Pimalai Spa's many acclaimed treatments. To fully soak up the spa experience, opt for the Royal Koo Rak package that was designed as the ultimate indulgence for couples. The treatment begins with a herbal steam bath, which allows the healing vapours to penetrate the body through the lungs and the skin's open pores. This boosts vitality, promotes relaxation and clears the head.

A body scrub then exfoliates and polishes the skin while preparing the body for the main event. Guests can choose from one of three hour-long massages—the Asian Aroma Massage induces deep relaxation through long, slow movements and strokes; The Royal Siam Massage dates back to the time of Buddha and rejuvenates the body and spirit by applying firm thumb and palm pressure on the body's energy lines and pressure points. The more active will benefit from the Pimalai Sports Massage that uses both soft and firm movements to relax and soothe while preparing the body for more activity.

When these are done, a relaxing facial treatment—employing a wonderful blend of natural plants, fruit and Thai herbs—completes the ritual, leaving you restored and ready to face the world.

Spa Statistics

SPA AREA
810 sq m (8,720 sq ft)

FACILITIES
4 indoor treatment salas, 3 double indoor treatment salas, 1 outdoor treatment pavilion; 1 Jacuzzi; 2 steam rooms; beauty salon; 1 gymnasium; 1 swimming pool; 1 spa boutique, library

SIGNATURE TREATMENT
Royal Koo Rak Couple Package

OTHER TREATMENTS AND THERAPIES
Aromatherapy, baths, body scrubs, body wraps, facial treatments, manicures/pedicures, massages, reflexology, salon services, waxing

PROVISIONS FOR COUPLES
Royal Koo Rak Couple Package; Pramaisuree room with private steam room and flower bath

SPA CUISINE
Provisions for special dietary requirements available on request

ACTIVITIES
Biking, cooking classes, sailing, scuba diving, snorkelling

SERVICES
Babysitting

MEMBERSHIP/ADMISSION
Not required

CONTACT
99 Moo 5, Kan Tiang Beach
Koh Lanta
Krabi 81150
Thailand
T +66-(0) 7560 7999 ext 1999
F +66-(0) 7560 7998
E spa@pimalai.com
W www.pimalai.com

Six Senses Spa at Evason Hua Hin Resort

THAILAND

In the tranquil town of Pranburi, 230 kilometres (143 miles) away from the bustle of Bangkok, hides the Evason Hua Hin Resort & Spa. Set amongst eight hectares (20 acres) of gorgeously landscaped tropical gardens, the resort boasts a sleek and contemporary design along with the well-known five-star Evason service that embodies its philosophy of re-defining experiences for its guests.

Set on the beachfront overlooking the Gulf of Siam, the resort appears as a serene gem in the heart of Thailand's oldest holiday destination of Hua Hin. On these grounds, so close to the pristine beach, is the luxurious Six Senses Spa.

Here a truly relaxing and revitalizing experience awaits, with a long menu of therapeutic treatments that promise to rejuvenate the senses. Inside the spa, there are three treatment rooms for couples which make the perfect spots for the spa's special rituals such as the Romantic Spa Package. This exquisite treatment begins with an Exotic Flower Bath for two before a holistic full body massage and face and scalp massage sends guests into a state of complete relaxation.

Those indulging in solitary pleasures will find the ultimate treat in the signature Sensory Spa Journey. This 90-minute treatment sees two

therapists working in complete harmony to take guests on a voyage of the five senses and beyond. Warm scented towels, a luxurious footbath and skin renewing indulgences are only the beginning. These are followed by a body aroma massage applied in long, smooth strokes while a cleansing facial treatment and stress relieving scalp massage is performed simultaneously. It isn't long before the mind and body releases every last hint of stress to recess into a deep and wonderful calm. Indeed, it is a complete mind and body encounter that continues long after guests leave the spa. To remind guests of this exquisite experience, a special gift is presented at the end of the treatment, which has been packaged lovingly by individuals who work for the Mae Fah Luang Foundation (an organization that's dedicated to promoting traditional handicrafts of the hill tribes).

For those more actively inclined, the resort boasts a host of recreational activities, from tennis lessons to windsurfing and archery. Top quality golf courses nearby make for a superb day out on the fareway, whilst excursions to the nearby hiking and mountain bike trails provide an opportunity for a spot of soft adventure.

Naturally, the spa is a perfect place to return to. Guests can soothe away any aches and strains with a signature massage or relieve the skin from the sun's rays with a gentle facial treatment. All products used at Six Senses Spas are made from 100 per cent natural ingredients, and all aspects of the spa are kind to the environment. Indeed total harmony (of mind, body and nature) takes on a new meaning at this Six Senses Spa.

| The warm glow of the resort entrance. || The spa lobby, situated away from it all and surrounded by calming water. ||| Style is paramount and the sleek design of the rooms create a relaxing sanctuary. |||| The numerous spa packages mean couples can enjoy the spa experience together. ||||| A Thai massage; just one of the expert massages on offer.

Spa Statistics

SPA AREA
900 sq m (9,700 sq ft)

FACILITIES
5 outdoor treatment pavilions, 5 double indoor treatment rooms, 1 single indoor treatment room; 3 relaxation areas; 2 Jacuzzis; 2 saunas, 2 steam rooms; 1 gymnasium (at the resort); 1 outdoor swimming pool (at the resort); 1 tennis court (at the resort); 1 spa boutique, library and art gallery (at the resort)

SIGNATURE TREATMENT
The Sensory Spa Journey

OTHER TREATMENTS AND THERAPIES
Anti-cellulite treatments, aromatherapy, baths, body scrubs, body wraps, facial treatments, hand and foot treatments, holistic therapies, hot stone therapies, jet-lag treatments, life coach counselling, manicures/pedicures, massages, purifying back treatments, reflexology, reiki, waxing

PROVISIONS FOR COUPLES
Available

SPA CUISINE
Available in all restaurants at the resort and in guest villas

ACTIVITIES
Aromatherapy in daily life class, cooking classes, cosmetic kitchen class, life enhancement classes, lifestyle management classes, massage classes, meditation classes, talks by visiting consultants, tai chi, yoga

MEMBERSHIP/ADMISSION
Body composition analysis, general healthcare consultation, gift certificates, naturopathic analysis, nutrition consultation, personal butler service, skincare consultation

CONTACT
9 Moo 3 Paknampran, Pranburi
Prachuap Khiri Khan 77220
Thailand
T +66 32 632111
F +66 32 632112
E spahuahin@evasonhauhin.com
W www.sixsenses.com

Six Senses Spa
at Evason Phuket Resort

THAILAND

On Rawai Beach, on the south-eastern side of Thailand's Phuket Island, lies the gorgeous Evason Phuket Resort & Six Senses Spa. Set amongst 26 hectares (64 acres) of beautifully landscaped gardens facing the Andaman Sea, the resort successfully embodies the Evason philosophy of redefining experiences.

As ever, at an Evason resort, the atmosphere here is welcoming and friendly, and the famed Evason service standards ensure great attention to detail that never leaves guests wanting. This level of excellence is also evident in the resort's stylish design, which takes a fresh approach to traditional materials, finishes and colour. Choose to stay in one of 260 elegantly appointed rooms, suites and pool villas, all of which are nestled gracefully in a tropical garden setting. Activities abound, from swimming in the resort's three dazzling pools, playing volleyball on its two courts or diving the nearby waters with help from the resort's fully equipped dive shop.

For a more sublime experience, however, guests should head to the Six Senses Spa. Spread over three floors, this luxe spa has set new standards in spa design with its treatment rooms located in salas overlooking the cerulean ocean. Surrounded by beautiful lotus ponds, they are a tranquil escape from the rest of the world and where professional and highly experienced therapists dedicate their craft to balancing the senses.

Plushly appointed, the spa uses Six Senses' signature Sodashi products in all their treatments, ensuring that all elements are 100 per cent natural and never tested on animals. Opt for the spa's signature Sensory Spa Journey and experience a unique variation of the four-hand massage by two highly skilled therapists. Long, smooth strokes on the body are matched by a synchronized cleansing facial and stress relieving scalp massage. The effect is divine and induces a deliciously deep state of calm.

For more exotic selections, the spa also offers a range of Specialist Bodyworks. These include hot stone therapy using basalt stones, authentic Indian head massages traditionally known as Champi, and ear candling, an ancient natural therapy used by Shaman healers to cleanse and harmonize the different energy fields of the body. Aromatherapy takes on its truest meaning here as special oils are custom blended to suit each individual's needs. The oil is then used for a light pressure massage to promote self-healing.

Staying in is also a wonderful experience with the spa's fabulous bath menu. Luxurious options such as a Cleopatra Milk Bath, Exotic Flower Bath or a Jacuzzi bath for two complete with sparkling wine can be set up in the resort's Jacuzzi baths or in the privacy of your own room. When you are cleansed, refreshed and revitalized, follow with an exquisite meal indoors, or head out to the sea to bask in the afterglow of exquisite well-being.

| Therapists use only the most natural ingredients at the Evason Phuket. || The stunning pool and its surroundings set a great stage for impressive views of the Andaman Sea. ||| Couples can luxuriate in their treatments together and share the experience either indoors or out. |||| The spa's extensive bath menu includes an Exotic Flower Bath.

Spa Statistics

SPA AREA
1,500 sq m (16,145 sq ft)

FACILITIES
3 double indoor treatment villas, 1 single indoor treatment room, 4 outdoor treatment pavilions, 5 double indoor treatment rooms; 1 meditation room; 3 Jacuzzis; 2 saunas, 2 steam rooms; 8 sun beds; 1 cardio studio, 1 aerobics studio, 1 gymnasium; 3 outdoor swimming pools; 2 tennis courts, 2 volleyball courts; 2 spa boutiques, library

SIGNATURE TREATMENT
The Sensory Spa Journey

OTHER TREATMENTS AND THERAPIES
Anti-cellulite treatments, baths, body scrubs, body wraps, facial treatments, hair treatments, hand and foot treatments, holistic treatments, hot stone therapies, hydrotherapy, jet-lag treatments, manicures/pedicures, massages, purifying back treatments, reflexology, scalp treatments, Thai therapies, waxing

PROVISIONS FOR COUPLES
Romance package, couple treatment rooms

SPA CUISINE
Available in-villa and at all resort restaurants

ACTIVITIES
Aerobics, biking, cooking classes, elephant trekking, fishing trips, golf, kickboxing, meditation classes, sailing, scuba diving, snorkelling, spinning, stretching classes, sunset and moonlight cruises, tai chi, tennis, yoga

SERVICES
Babysitting, childcare, corporate programmes, personal training

MEMBERSHIP/ADMISSION
Not required

CONTACT
100 Vised Road
Tambon Rawai
Muang District
Phuket 83100
T +66 76 381 010/7
F +66 76 381 018
E spa@evasonphuket.com
W www.sixsenses.com

The Spa at Four Seasons Hotel

BANGKOK, THAILAND

Tucked away on the second floor of the Four Seasons Hotel Bangkok, The Spa managed by MSpa International boasts a rare design, blending Lanna-style architecture with accents of Moroccan flair.

The corridors are lined with an interplay of Lanna images, with curved door architraves surrounded by natural earthy colours. The spa's Lanna roots are further embedded in the selection of natural materials and fabrics—engraved stone pieces which give heft to the surroundings and sumptuous Thai silks that are accentuated throughout. This visual impact takes guests back to ancient Northern Thailand, where grand ceremonies were a part of daily life.

The mellow waft of lemongrass greets guests at the entrance of The Spa and a bell tinkles as guests enter; a nod to the Asian belief that the voice of a bell carries messages of prosperity, protection, control and positive energy. Indeed, these elements are well in place at The Spa, whose treatments are influenced by myriad cultures and traditions.

From Bali to India and, of course, Thailand, ancient health and beauty rituals were cultivated to suit the luxury of the spa and the expectations of its discerning guests. A sense of ritual and devotion is nurtured within this sanctuary of well-being to reflect the grace and refinement of the ancient times from which the treatments evolved.

To reflect the hotel in which it is situated, The Spa has four signature treatments to symbolize the mood of the different seasons. The Fall Mood Balancer, Spring Inspiration, Winter Body Glow and Summer Spirit are all indulgent rituals that encompass

an exquisite bath and massage. All treatments are preceded by a floral footbath and end with a soothing refreshment to ease and awaken the body.

With nine treatment rooms in total, the largest of the couple's suites is an opulent affair. Decked in Moroccan style, it features a rattan-style bed flanked by a generous bathtub and two treatment beds. Here, couples can enjoy a five-and-a-half-hour Ultimate Indulgence, comprising a Steam Bath, Aromatic Floral Bath, a choice of body scrub or wrap, an Aromatherapy Massage, a spa meal, an Aromatic Facial and a spa manicure or pedicure.

There are other packages that range from four to four-and-a-half hours for languorous indulgences. To complement its treatments, The Spa uses the award-winning Elemis range of products, all of which are on sale at its well-stocked spa boutique.

| The Lanna style is evident throughout the whole property and all suites come complete with luxurious bath tubs. || The dramatic and modern style of the spa lobby blends with the more traditional interior. ||| Spa products include the Elemis range which can be bought at the spa boutique. |||| The double treatment rooms offer an array of indulgences for couples to enjoy together.

Spa Statistics

SPA AREA
400 sq m (4,305 sq ft)

FACILITIES
2 double indoor luxury suites, 4 single indoor treatment rooms, 1 double indoor treatment room; 2 facial treatment rooms, 4 nail salon stations; 1 gymnasium, 1 aerobics studio; 1 outdoor swimming pool; 1 spa boutique

SIGNATURE TREATMENT
Fall Mood Enhancer, Spring Inspiration, Summer Spirit, Winter Body Glow

OTHER TREATMENTS AND THERAPIES
Anti-ageing treatments, anti-cellulite treatments, aromatherapy, baths, body scrubs, body wraps, eye treatments, facial treatments, firming and slimming treatments, hand and foot treatments, hot stone therapies, Indonesian therapies, jet-lag treatments, lymphatic drainage, massages, manicures/pedicures, reflexology, scalp treatments, Thai therapies

PROVISIONS FOR COUPLES
Ultimate Indulgence, Total Relaxation, Romantic Getaway, 2 suites, 1 double room

SPA CUISINE
Available in spa suite or by the poolside

SERVICES
Babysitting, personal butler service, personal training

MEMBERSHIP/ADMISSION
Not required

CONTACT
Four Seasons Hotel
155 Rajadamri Road
Bangkok 10330
Thailand
T +66 2 652 9311
F +66 2 651 9314
E ms_fsbk@minornet.com
W www.mspa-international.com

Angsana Spa

KUALA LUMPUR, MALAYSIA

Smack in the heart of Malaysia's capital city, the
Angsana Spa Kuala Lumpur sits quietly over a
1,000-square-metre (10,765-square-foot) space on
the fifth floor of the Crowne Plaza Mutiara. Within
walking distance are KL's main shopping and
entertainment areas, with sky-high buildings and the
bustle of traffic signalling the pulse of the city.

Yet within the Angsana Spa's trademark lime
green and tangerine walls lies a luxurious haven of
tranquillity and relaxation. This 22-room spa boasts
12 indoor single treatment rooms, two indoor
twin-bedded rooms, four indoor single facial
treatment rooms, and two outdoor spa pavilions; of
particular note are the two Rainmist rooms—a recent
innovation by Angsana Spa and the very first of its
kind in Malaysia. These rooms offer their own spa
packages that use the steam and wet treatment
facilities, which include rain showers and overhead
jets that send water gently trickling over the body.
Clad in Angsana's vibrant signature colours and
complemented by bamboo blinds, a fluid combination
of contemporary architecture is interspersed with
charming Asian artwork.

A soothing selection of time-honoured
massages inspired by techniques from all over the
world is available on the extensive spa menu. Also,
wraps, scrubs and facial treatments serve to nourish
the body from head to toe, while the ancient art of
aromatherapy is brought to bear in order to help
elevate the senses. Specially developed oils are
mixed and adapted by the spa's therapists so that all
individual needs are met whilst complementing
Angsana's signature treatments that offer the
seasoned spa-goer something different every time.

| One of the double indoor treatment rooms in the stylish and
calming Angsana décor. || The outdoor pavilion comes complete
with private shower. ||| The bath is used to complete many of the
spa's treatments. |||| The sesame body polish treatment, part of
the Essence of Angsana, is used to soften the skin.

As its name suggests, Angsana Spa's signature Rainmist package encompasses all the wonders of hydrotherapy. This complete body treatment begins with a 10-minute steam session to prepare your body for a deep cleansing and conditioning therapy. Next, an exfoliating body polish smoothens the skin before another steam session complements the moisturizing attributes of a special skin enhancer.

To experience the Essence of Angsana, guests are led to the spa's beautiful outdoor pavilion where the ultimate indulgence begins with a skin-softening body polish of your choice. Surrender to the experienced therapists as you feel your tension and stress melting away with one of the specially developed massages on the menu. Then luxuriate in a revitalizing facial treatment, followed by a relaxing bath to end the session.

Completely unique to the spa is the wonderfully relaxing Angsana Massage. By using long palm strokes and thumb pressure, the highly skilled therapists work on your body's key pressure points to alleviate stress and strengthen your inner chi. This 90-minute massage uses Euphoria oil to further enhance the experience.

All of Angsana Spa's therapists were trained at the acclaimed Banyan Tree Spa Academy in Phuket, which will ensure that every one of them is highly skilled and able to provide safe, effective treatments. The spa's 'high-touch, low-tech' approach celebrates the power of the human touch and the use of fresh botanicals and as such offers some of the best spa treatments in the world.

Spa Statistics

SPA AREA
1,000 sq m (10,765 sq ft)

FACILITIES
12 single indoor treatment rooms, 2 double indoor treatment rooms, 2 outdoor pavilions, 2 Rainmist rooms, 4 indoor facial rooms; separate male and female changing areas with private showers, 1 relaxation area; 1 spa bath; 4 nail salon stations; Angsana Gallery spa boutique

SIGNATURE TREATMENT
Angsana Massage, Essence of Angsana-Bliss, Rainmist

OTHER TREATMENTS AND THERAPIES
Aromatherapy, baths, body scrubs, body wraps, facial treatments, hand and foot treatments, holistic treatments, hydrotherapy, Indonesian therapies, manicures/pedicures, massages, Thai therapies

PROVISIONS FOR COUPLES
Couples packages and double treatment rooms

SERVICES
Gift certificates

MEMBERSHIP/ADMISSION
Available but not required

CONTACT
Level 5 Crowne Plaza Mutiara, Kuala Lumpur
Jalan Sultan Ismail
50250 Kuala Lumpur
Malaysia
T +60 3 2141 4321
F +60 3 2141 1321
E spa-kualalumpur@angsana.com
W www.angsanaspa.com

Four Seasons Resort Langkawi

MALAYSIA

Echoing an intimate Malaysian kampong (or village), the luxurious Four Seasons Resort Langkawi is a study in traditional Malay architecture. But look a little closer and you'll see touches of Arabian and Indian accents reflecting the various cultures that make up Malaysia's multi-heritage.

At the heart of this exquisite resort is the breathtaking spa with its six thatched roof pavilions perched beneath a dramatic limestone cliff. Here, the focus is on reconnecting with your self, refreshing the body and relaxing the mind.

Each pavilion is surrounded by tranquil reflecting ponds and lush gardens that render the illusion of a floating sanctuary. They all boast their own outdoor rain showers and soaking tubs and are spacious enough to accommodate a private yoga lesson and an indulgent spa treatment for two.

To match these idyllic surroundings, a selection of treatments inspired by Malaysia's rich diversity is on offer—from Malaysian and Thai massages, to ayurvedic therapies and ancient Chinese rituals. Mirroring this mix of cultures are the spa's staff who hail from all over Asia, bringing with them the expertise of their homeland's healing treatments.

Many of Four Seasons Spa's treatments were custom designed to fuse the best of each culture's rituals. An example is its signature Shanti Shanti Shanti, a special combination of sacred practices that begins with an hour-long private session with the resort's Indian guru. During this session, he teaches techniques in breathing, stretching and meditation.

Armed with a renewed calm, guests then receive an Indian herbal oil massage and Shirodhara, where a steady stream of warm herbal oil is poured onto the

forehead. Taking it one step further, the treatment then incorporates elements of reiki to eliminate every last trace of stress and encourage utter relaxation. Finally, bask in this afterglow of well-being with a gentle steam and an invigorating shower.

Equally special is the Malaysian Mist. This treatment echoes the dewy mist that cloaks the magnificent forested limestone hills of Langkawi. To do this, guests are treated to a hot steam bath and cooled with a shower before enjoying a traditional Malay massage. An organic lemongrass and coconut scrub follows, and is rinsed off under a tropical cascade from three oversized rain shower-heads. Guests then immerse themselves in a special outdoor bath infused with special oils and fresh flowers. When they emerge, the body is hydrated with a soothing tropical lotion as they sip on a cup of hibiscus herbal tea.

Adjacent to the main pool area is a series of interconnecting private spaces. Here, several Jacuzzis are set within alcoves, which lead to larger asymmetrical pools. These are the perfect spots to luxuriate in post-treatment perhaps—if it suits you— with a cool cocktail in hand.

Famed for its cuisine worldwide, this Four Seasons Resort does not disappoint. While it may not boast a specific menu of spa cuisine, it does welcome special requests. That means whatever your palate fancies, your palate will probably get. And isn't that the true definition of luxury?

| Distinctive Langkawi landscape dramatically frames the resort. || The brilliantly designed spa pool affords nooks and crannies where guests can escape and unwind. ||| A Turkish hammam-inspired bath. |||| The luxurious Beach Villa overlooking stunning sunsets over the Andaman Sea. ||||| The simple yet stylish Beach Villa bathroom.

Spa Statistics

SPA AREA
1,496 sq m (16,100 sq ft)

FACILITIES
6 double indoor treatment villas each with their own indoor soaking tubs, 20 beach villas with their own double spa room; 2 consultation bales; 1 meditation pavilion; 3 relaxation bales; 8 steam rooms; 3 hair salon stations, 2 nail salon stations; 1 gymnasium; 2 outdoor swimming pools; 1 tennis court; 1 spa boutique, 1 spa bar

SIGNATURE TREATMENT
Earthlight Ritual, Malaysian Mist, Shanti Shanti Shanti

OTHER TREATMENTS AND THERAPIES
Anti-cellulite treatments, aromatherapy, ayurveda, baths, body scrubs, body wraps, facial treatments, firming and slimming treatments, hair treatments, hand and foot treatments, holistic treatments, manicures/pedicures, massages, reflexology, Thai therapies, waxing

PROVISIONS FOR COUPLES
Available

SPA CUISINE
Available

ACTIVITIES
Biking, golfing, hiking, sailing, scuba diving, snorkelling, tennis, yoga

SERVICES
Babysitting, childcare, corporate programmes, gift certificates, private spa parties

MEMBERSHIP/ADMISSION
Not required

CONTACT
Jalan Tanjung Rhu
07000 Langkawi
Kedah Darul Aman
Malaysia
T +60 4 950 8888
F +60 4 950 8899
E spa.langkawi@fourseasons.com
W www.fourseasons.com/langkawi

Mandara Spa
at Prince Hotel & Residence

KUALA LUMPUR, MALAYSIA

The assaults of city living can certainly drain the good energies of even the most well balanced of people. And sometimes, the ability to escape into a sanctuary of calm in the thick of it all is nothing short of necessary. The Mandara Spa at the Prince Hotel & Residence Kuala Lumpur provides exactly that sort of escape, situated 10 floors up in the heart of the restless capital city.

Step into its doors and time immediately slows to an unhurried pace. Close off the outside world for several hours and surrender yourself to the expert hands of Mandara's professional staff. Here, luxuriously appointed treatment rooms and villas are the perfect place to get away from it all.

Mandara's exotic treatment range combines the wisdom of the world's ancient rejuvenation and beauty traditions with the sophistication of modern spa techniques. Its treatments draw influences from all over the world—from Bali and Thailand to Europe and Hawaii—to offer a global fusion of massage, body and face treatments designed to relax and renew the body, mind and spirit. One of Mandara's most notable treatments is the ayurvedic shirodhara.

This ancient therapy, which hails from India, restores calm to the mind, balances the emotions, releases toxins and encourages deep relaxation of the nervous system. A ritual footbath begins this treatment, followed by an ayurvedic pressure massage. For the next 20 minutes, a gentle flow of aromatic oil is streamed down onto the third eye area of the forehead, known to many as the window to the soul. A gentle head, neck and shoulder massage brings this calming and uplifting therapy to an end, and the result will no doubt be a rejuvenated being, ready to face the rigours of the modern world once again.

If you need a little more, the Mandara Massage, performed by two therapists working in tandem, should do the trick. This unique blend fuses five different massage styles—Japanese shiatsu, Thai,

Hawaiian lomi lomi, Swedish and Balinese—rendering a sublime massage experience that is simply too exquisite for words.

Meanwhile, couples can luxuriate in the Ultimate Indulgence, a package that encompasses an aromatherapy floral footbath, lavender body wash, traditional body scrub, herbal steam and tea ceremony. And that's just the beginning—the treatment continues with a four-hand Mandara Massage and a facial treatment and ends with a fabulous foot massage—it's not called Ultimate Indulgence for nothing.

Last but not least, an exclusive facial treatment designed by French skincare specialist Decléor is available for both men and women. This can be combined with a detoxifying and refining body treatment from the spa menu for optimum results. Indeed, when the blissful nurturing of body, mind and soul is complete, head back down to the city with a new vitality and spirit for life.

| The lobby combines simple elegance with stylish tropical touches. || The bustle of the city continues below whilst guests luxuriate in the treatment rooms. ||| Hot stone therapies are just one of the options on the menu. |||| The colour scheme and style of the spa induce an overall feeling of calm. ||||| In the relaxation room, guests can slowly rebalance and bring their senses back to reality.

Spa Statistics

SPA AREA
400 sq m (4,305 sq ft)

FACILITIES
2 double indoor treatment villas, 4 single indoor treatment villas, 2 double grand suites; 2 relaxation rooms; 4 steam rooms (inside double suites), 2 steam rooms (in male and female changing areas); 1 spa boutique

SIGNATURE TREATMENT
Ayurvedic Shirodhara, Mandara Massage

OTHER TREATMENTS AND THERAPIES
Aromatherapy, baths, body scrubs, facial treatments, hot stone therapies, Indonesian therapies, massages

PROVISIONS FOR COUPLES
Ultimate Indulgence, double treatment villas and grand suites

MEMBERSHIP/ADMISSION
Not required

CONTACT
Prince Hotel & Residence
Level 10, Jalan Conlay
50450 Kuala Lumpur
T +60 3 2170 8777
F +60 3 2170 8776
E infoasia@mandaraspa.com
W www.mandaraspa.com/www.princehotels.co.jp

Spa Village at Pangkor Laut Resort

MALAYSIA

A 'retreat within a retreat' best describes the amazing Spa Village at Malaysia's highly acclaimed Pangkor Laut Resort. Bringing together the myriad healing cultures from across the region, the Spa Village comprises eight treatment pavilions spread over one and a half hectares (four acres) on a quiet bay between the sea and the age-old rainforest. Designed to soothe the senses, its pavilions face the ocean and are interspersed with open courtyards, lotus ponds, a herb garden and a reflexology path.

All Spa Village treatment programmes are based on one of four umbrella concepts: Rejuvenation and Longevity, Relaxation and Stress Reduction, Detoxification, and Romance.

Treatments begin with the Spa Village's unique Bath House Ritual, symbolic of the various bathing traditions around Asia. This ritual commences with a footbath and an invigorating Chinese Foot Pounding, once solely the privilege of concubines in feudal China. Guests are then escorted to the Bath Houses to experience the traditional Malay 'circulating' bath, a throwback to when villagers bathed in streams and rivers. The next stop: Japanese-style cleansing with a 'goshi-gohsi' cloth before a stimulating soak in the exquisitely heated rotten-buro, or outdoor bath.

As your body buzzes from the warmth of the rotten-buro's steaming waters, a spa assistant leads you to the Spa Village's private scrub house, where she invigorates the senses with an energizing Shanghai Scrub. To still your piqued senses, a cup of calming tea is served as you luxuriate in these tranquil surroundings.

The à la carte menu of body treatments features the signature Campur-Campur. Its name connotes the blending of varieties in Malay, and thus, the Campur Campur combines the best techniques of Malay and Thai massage, using touch, tone and aromatherapy. Throughout the treatment the sweet and mellow scent of lemongrass and pandan leaves permeates the air as steam pouches of herbs are pressed soothingly along the body.

Those in a deeper search of the region's health rituals are advised to meet the Spa Village's Malay, Chinese or ayurvedic health specialists for a

complimentary consultation. Each speciality boasts its own Hut, where the different 'diagnosis' are made and treatments prescribed.

As a tropical spa, much attention is naturally devoted to soothing and nourishing the spirit as well as the skin. All the Spa Village's treatment pavilions have been designed to provide the best in aesthetics, temperature, lighting, sound and smell, establishing the optimum environment so guests can be completely relaxed. Each pavilion comes with an oversized sunken tub and outdoor shower, as well as a private deck to chill out on post-treatment.

For true exclusivity, ask for the Ultimate Spa Experience at the Belian Spa Pavilion, where couples may indulge in an entire day of custom-designed treatments. Hidden away in a private compound, the Belian Spa Pavilion is like your very own exclusive retreat, boasting an outdoor whirlpool, yoga pavilion, nap gazebo, steam room and private treatment area.

Such luxury is easy to get used to, which could explain why guests often stay for as long as two weeks, sampling the various healing treatments and experiencing life at its most blissful.

| The Malay bath, the first stage of the spa's unique Bath House Ritual which begins all treatments. || The overlapping infinity-edged lap pools overlook the beach. ||| A spa hut by the beach, right by the spa villas where people can stay and receive treatments throughout their holiday. |||| Dotted around the gardens, nap gazebos provide a perfect hideaway. ||||| The Malay bath leads you on to the Japanese bath.

Spa Statistics

SPA AREA
16,187 sq m (174,240 sq ft)

FACILITIES
8 twin pavilions, 1 deluxe pavilion, 3 spa huts, 3 nap gazebos; 1 ayurvedic consultation hut, 1 Malay consultation hut; 1 Chinese consultation hut; 3 steam rooms (attached to pavilions), 2 bath houses; 1 yoga pavilion; 1 outdoor swimming pool; spa boutique, herb garden, reflexology path

SIGNATURE TREATMENT
Bukit Gantang Warrior (for men), Campur-Campur, Royal Secrets of Puteri Lindungan Bulan (for women)

OTHER TREATMENTS AND THERAPIES
Ayurveda, baths, body scrubs, body wraps, Chinese therapies, facial treatments, hair treatments, manicures/pedicures, massages, waxing

PROVISIONS FOR COUPLES
Couple's Spa Experience, Ultimate Spa Experience

SPA CUISINE
Available in the spa at the Jamu Bar or at the Belian Spa Pavilion

ACTIVITIES
Aquaerobics, cooking classes, golf, jungle trekking, sailing, snorkelling, sports instruction, squash, tai chi, tennis, windsurfing, yoga

SERVICES
Babysitting and childcare, body consultation analysis, general healthcare consultations, gift certificates, nutrition consultations, skincare consultations

MEMBERSHIP/ADMISSION
Only for resort guests

CONTACT
Pangkor Laut Island
32200 Lumut, Perak
Malaysia
T +60 5 699 1100
F +60 5 699 1025
E spavillageplr@ytlhotels.com.my
W www.pangkorlautresort.com

Spa Village at The Residences at The Ritz-Carlton, Kuala Lumpur

MALAYSIA

The Spa Village Kuala Lumpur may well be the poshest village you will ever come across. Spread over 1,115 square metres (12,000 square feet) on the fourth storey of The Residences at The Ritz-Carlton, Kuala Lumpur, it has been designed as a tropical paradise with outdoor cabanas, landscaped gardens and gorgeous water features.

Within this heavenly space are eight luxurious treatment suites, outdoor showers and sunken baths embraced by lush, verdant greenery. Hidden around its gardens are a lap pool, a hot spa and cool plunge pool, turning the Spa Village into an entirely different world from the bustling city just outside.

The Spa Village offers the best spa therapies from around the world, and pays tribute to the cultural diversity and rich healing heritage of the Nusantara region—the archipelago that encompasses the mainland from Myanmar to Peninsular Malaysia and the islands of Indonesia and the Philippines.

The Spa Village's ultimate signature treatment is the hour-long Sensory Exploration. This unique treatment is performed in the Sensory Room—the first of its kind in the region. Step in and be surrounded by sounds, sights, smells, tastes and touch that heighten your connection to the world and to your inner self. Guests are guided through aromatherapy, tasting, vibration, ancient and natural sounds, and sensory relaxation, all of which culminate in a scalp and foot massage.

For a more languorous experience, try the three-hour Chinese Peranakan Treatment. A tribute to the unique culture derived from the marriage of Malay and Chinese heritage, the treatment begins with a Milk Nectar Meditation to calm the nerves. When you are soothed and relaxed, a pearl and rice facial follows, which also includes a mulberry leaf eye treatment. Next, a moxa naval activation improves metabolism and eases digestion and jet

lag. Afterwards, a rattan tapping massage preps the body for a Chinese Tui-Na An-Mo massage, which places an emphasis on the acupressure points and the directional flow of the body's subtle channels.

The Nusantara Treatments refer to the historic uses of herbs and plants unique to this region to enhance beauty and sensuality. Gentlemen are prescribed the Gandapura which begins with a rejuvenating hair treatment and papaya body masque to exfoliate the skin. Relaxing in the steam room allows the oils to be better absorbed into the hair and body before it is washed away in a luxurious bath. A full body massage then tops the treatment.

Ladies get the Rose Therapy, which begins with a rose and lavender hair treatment and follows with a rose petal body masque. This masque is left as you relax in the steam room before it is washed away by a milk bath infused with roses. To end, ladies get a full-body massage that leaves them utterly relaxed and rejuvenated. The Spa Village's main aim is to embody the true meaning of joie de vivre and with its all-encompassing approach to looking and feeling good, the spa ably meets this goal.

| Treatments at the Spa Village KL are quite unique, egg endulation face treatments draw upon a Peranakan therapy. || Outdoor cabanas are perfect for Thai massages. ||| Senses are soothed and gently awakened in the spa's unique Sensory Room. |||| Outside, the pool provides a welcome sanctuary from the bustling city below. ||||| A milk nectar treatment calms the nerves.

Spa Statistics

SPA AREA
1,115 sq m (12,000 sq ft)

FACILITIES
2 single indoor treatment suites, 6 double indoor treatment suites, 3 outdoor cabanas for Thai massage, 1 Sensory Room, 1 relaxation lounge; 1 plunge pool, 1 whirlpool; 4 steam rooms; 2 hair salon stations, 2 nail stations; 1 outdoor swimming pool; spa retail outlet

SIGNATURE TREATMENT
Chinese Peranakan Treatment, Gandapura Treatment, Hang Tuah, Rose Therapy, Tun Teja, Sensory Exploration

OTHER TREATMENTS AND THERAPIES
Anti-ageing treatments, aromatherapy, baths, body scrubs, Chinese therapies, facial treatments, hot stone therapies, manicures/pedicures, massages, salon services, waxing

PROVISIONS FOR COUPLES
Couple's Spa Experience in Couple's treatment suites

ACTIVITIES
Meditation (in Sensory Room), yoga

SERVICES
Chinese consultations, gift certificates, private spa parties skincare consultations

MEMBERSHIP/ADMISSION
Not required

CONTACT
4th floor, The Residences at
The Ritz-Carlton, Kuala Lumpur
168 Jalan Imbi
55100 Kuala Lumpur
Malaysia
T +60 3 2782 9090
F +60 3 2782 9099
E spavillagekl@ytlhotels.com.my
W www.ytlhotels.com

The Oriental Spa
at The Mandarin Oriental

SINGAPORE

Like the prestigious hotel it is located in, The Oriental Spa reflects its exotic roots through interior design that focuses on Asian culture. Deep walnut timber flooring, Asian motif panels and traditional Chinese furniture imbue a sense of the old Orient in these tranquil surroundings. The 'journey of the senses' begins the moment guests enter into the spa. To begin each treatment, a soothing foot ritual is performed as experienced spa therapists assess each guest's individual needs.

The innovative and restorative treatments from The Oriental Spa fuse both modern and ancient techniques and philosophies. Using pure essential oils and herbs, the spa's goal is to take each guest on a personalized journey to wellness. Guests can enjoy The Oriental Spa's exquisite treatments in one of four luxurious treatment rooms or in the Couples' Suite. There is also a private relaxation lounge for guests to relax before and after each treatment.

An extensive range of facial and body treatments, massages and packages leaves guests spoiled for choice. Recommended is the signature Oriental Massage, where techniques from all over Asia are combined to create a sublime 85-minute experience. The special shiatsu and Thai massage room provides enough space for couples to enjoy the traditional treatments together. For a more indulgent affair, opt for one of the day packages that includes a light spa lunch and use of the outdoor pool.

The Oriental Reviver Day begins with a Renewal Body Peel. This fruity concoction contains jojoba spheres and uses a gentle peeling action to deeply

exfoliate and hydrate the skin. Soft and luminous, the skin is then slathered in a Monticelli Mud Wrap. In this treatment, rich and creamy algae mud is spiked with pure essential oils and plant extracts. This mixture is blended with thermal spring waters from Monticelli Terme in Northern Italy and applied warm to the body to soothe sore muscles and swollen joints. It also detoxifies the body and restores energy levels. Next, a heavenly 25-minute deep tension Stress Relieving Back Massage is performed before you pick from your choice of two facial treatments—Rebalance or Hydrate. Whichever you choose, you are promised a glowing complexion with even skin tone.

Special Couples Suite Packages are also available such as the Oriental Romance Ritual. These can be taken side by side in the Couples' Suite or separately in private rooms. The Oriental Romance Ritual comprises a Renewal Body Peel, Tranquillity Bath and Hot Stone Massage, while the Best of Friends package features a Renewal Body Peel, Aroma Soul Massage and Illuminate Facial.

A special Spa Cuisine set menu is available at the hotel's Mediterranean restaurant, Dolce Vita. Situated by the spa and outdoor pool, the restaurant must be pre-booked to avoid disappointment. The luxury spa product line—including bath, skincare, apparel and spa gifts—means guests can now take home a piece of the Oriental Spa as a reminder of the exquisite experience that is unrivalled anywhere.

Spa Statistics

SPA AREA
400 sq m (4,300 sq ft)

FACILITIES
4 single indoor treatment rooms, 1 double indoor treatment room; 1 relaxation room, 1 shiatsu/Thai massage room; 1 steam room (must be pre-booked as it is part of the Couples' Suite); 1 yoga room, 1 gymnasium; 1 outdoor swimming pool

SIGNATURE TREATMENT
The Oriental Massage

OTHER TREATMENTS AND THERAPIES
Anti-cellulite treatments, anti-ageing treatments, aromatherapy, baths, body scrubs, body wraps, Chinese therapies, eye treatments, facial treatments, firming and slimming treatments, holistic treatments, hot stone therapies, hydrotherapy, jet-lag treatments, lymphatic drainage massage, massages, pre- and post-natal treatments, scalp treatments, Thai therapies

PROVISIONS FOR COUPLES
Couples Suite

SPA CUISINE
Available at Dolce Vita. Must be pre-booked. Special dietary requirements must be made clear at the time of booking.

ACTIVITIES
Yoga, fitness centre

SERVICES
Gift certificates, personal training, private spa parties

MEMBERSHIP/ADMISSION
Available but not required

CONTACT
Level 5, The Oriental Singapore
5 Raffles Avenue, Marina Square
Singapore 039797
T +65 6885 3533
F +65 6885 3542
E orsin-spa@mohg.com
W www.mandarinoriental.com

| The Dolce Vita restaurant is situated next to the spa and the outdoor swimming pool. The spa cuisine menu makes it a popular choice with spa-goers. || The spacious double treatment room comes complete with two bath tubs and a private relaxation area. ||| Couples can enjoy their spa experience together in the double treatment room. |||| The signature treatment—the Oriental Massage—blends techniques from all over Asia to create a truly sublime experience.

RafflesAmrita Spa
at Raffles The Plaza

SINGAPORE

Spread over 4,650 square metres (50,000 square feet), the RafflesAmrita Spa at Raffles the Plaza is one of Asia's largest luxury spas. Set in the heart of Singapore's commercial district, it exists like an urban oasis tucked away from the bustle of modern city life. Here, members and guests can take advantage of RafflesAmrita's cutting-edge fitness facilities, its signature spa cuisine and its private label of aromatherapy products. However, it goes without saying that those who come here come in search of more exquisite pursuits—namely the immense range of body and beauty treatments.

The name Amrita, meaning 'Elixir of Youth', is derived from the ancient Sanskrit legend. The story goes that Hindu deities have searched for Amrita, or eternal youth, since the beginning of time. The legend inspires many of the treatments here and although the legendary elixir remains elusive the therapies on offer come pretty close.

As a tribute to its namesake, the spa's signature treatment is aptly called the RafflesAmrita Elixir of Youth. This two-hour ritual begins with a speciality herbal foot bath. Once warmed and relaxed, guests are cocooned in an anti-ageing Spirulina algae body masque, which is renowned for its anti-oxidant properties. A therapeutic soak in holistic herbal waters follows to capture its lightly tranquilizing effects. The treatment concludes with a soothing massage using a blend of calming lavender, intoxicating ylang ylang and entrancing Melissa.

Also on the menu is the Anti-Ageing Caviar Facial. Rich with nutrients, the key ingredient in this facial is the protein-laden caviar, long recognized as a powerful skin regenerator. The caviar works with bupleurum falcatum extract—a medicinal tonic plant common to the Chinese and known as Chai Hu—and caffeine, famed for its toning properties. This decadent facial treatment firms, tones and deeply

| RafflesAmrita's very own aromatherapy products prove very popular in the spa's boutique. || The wet spa where much of the water therapy is carried out. ||| Guests can relax and unwind before or readjust after treatment in the sumptuous relaxation lounge. |||| From the extensive menu, guests can select the one-and-a-half-hour Ayurvedic Pancha Karma package and experience a truly ancient therapy. |||||The VIP suites offer space and a romantic setting for couples to enjoy some of RafflesAmrita's unique treatments.

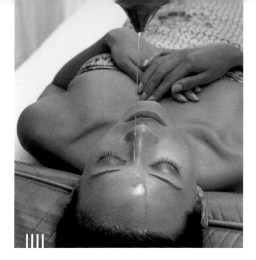

hydrates the skin, endowing it with nutrients that can smooth fine lines and improve skin texture. It also stimulates and activates cell regeneration promising a renewed and youthful complexion.

Male and female treatment areas are segregated for exclusive privacy, but couples looking to share the RafflesAmrita experience can opt for the spa's VIP suites. These double suites are fitted with their own Jacuzzi, aromatherapy steam room and private showers for that special aura of romance.

As befits its stature as one of the largest luxury spas in Asia, RafflesAmrita's menu of services is amazingly extensive. Everything from massages, body wraps, ayurveda, water therapy, facial skincare, manicures, pedicures and salon services are available within its peaceful complex.

Afterwards, guests may venture outside to luxuriate further in the spa's fabulous pool or Jacuzzi amidst lush, green foliage perched above the city. Yoga, pilates or tai chi sessions are also available at its very own state-of-the-art gym.

Perhaps the best way to enjoy the RafflesAmrita Spa at Raffles the Plaza and to further indulge, is to check into one of the hotel's gorgeous rooms and make a full holiday out of it. After all, some of the best shopping, dining and local sights of Singapore are within walking distance of the spa and hotel.

Spa Statistics

SPA AREA
4,650 sq m (50,000 sq ft)

FACILITIES
35 treatment rooms (2 double RafflesAmrita Pavilions, 3 double VIP suites, 26 individual treatment suites), 2 Dermalife rooms, 2 Hydrotone rooms; 2 meditation alcoves, 2 relaxation lounges; 2 Jacuzzis, 2 whirlpools, 2 cool plunge pools; 2 saunas, 2 steam rooms; 1 state-of-the-art cardio studio, 1 gymnasium; 2 swimming pools, 6 tennis courts; 1 lifestyle boutique

SIGNATURE TREATMENT
RafflesAmrita Elixir of Youth, Ayurveda Pancha Karma Treatment, Caviar Facial, Hot Stone Therapy

OTHER TREATMENTS AND THERAPIES
Anti-ageing treatments, anti-cellulite treatments, aqua therapy, aromatherapy, ayurveda, baths, body bronzing, body scrubs, body wraps, eye treatments, facial treatments, hair treatments, hand and foot treatments, holistic treatments, hot stone therapies, hydrotherapy, jet-lag treatments, lymphatic drainage massage, manicures/pedicures, massages, pre- and post-natal treatments, purifying back treatments, Thai therapies, thalassotherapy, waxing

PROVISIONS FOR COUPLES
VIP Suites

SPA CUISINE
Available in VIP suites and Alligator Pear Poolside Restaurant and Bar

ACTIVITIES
Kick-boxing, pilates, tennis, yoga, yoga-lates

SERVICES
Corporate programmes, gift certificates, personal training, skincare and nutrition cosultations

MEMBERSHIP/ADMISSION
Available

CONTACT
Level 6, 80 Bras Basah Road
Singapore 189560
T +65 6336 4477
F +65 6336 1161
E enquiries@amritaspas.com
W www.amritaspas.com

Spa Botanica at The Sentosa Resort and Spa

SINGAPORE

Just 10 minutes away from Singapore's Central Business District, The Sentosa Resort and Spa is one of Asia's best-kept secrets. Tucked away on Singapore's Sentosa Island, this stylish sanctuary is spread over 11 hectares (27 acres) of lush tropical greenery, with age-old trees conserved and included as part of the resort's opulent landscape.

Within The Sentosa's magnificent grounds is Singapore's first garden destination spa—Spa Botanica which boasts Asia's first labyrinths from which guests can quieten their minds through meditative walks. Check into the Spa Botanica Suite and you'll be greeted with your own private outdoor deck, spacious treatment areas and a hydro-bath. More decadent is the Royal Suite, with its King's Bath, a 450-kilogram (990 pound) hand-tooled tub fashioned from cast bronze so that it retains the

warmth of a sensuous milk, floral or herbal bath. All of Spa Botanica's treatments were thoughtfully designed to incorporate the beneficial properties of plants, flowers and herbs unique to this region. Its signature Galaxy Steam Shower is no different. Drawn from practices dating back to the Roman Empire, this unique yet classic treatment combines a special mud pack with a herbal steam bath.

Guests are shown into their 'chamber', a room walled with ornate Moorish tiles and roofed with a starry night sky, replicating that of the Northern Hemisphere. After a short shower, special medicinal earths are applied to the entire body before the room is slowly heated with various steam infusions. The warmth of the room helps dry the mud on the skin as the aroma of herbs being steamed on the stove lends a heavenly therapeutic scent. Later, the

| The treatment pavilions sit behind the spa's lush gardens. | | The Japanese-style outdoor bath is a welcome and relaxing treat. | | | A main feature of the superb gardens is the waterfall. | | | | The swimming pool, next to a stunning water lily pond, leads to the beach. | | | | | The labyrinths offer a calming and meditative spot.

room's humidity increases and triggers perspiration, causing the medicinal earth to liquefy and draw toxins out of the body. To remove dead skin cells, the loosened earth is gently rubbed on the skin, simultaneously stimulating blood circulation. As this cleansing ceremony draws to a close, a warm rain falls inside the steam room, washing the earth from the skin. Out of the steam room, guests then apply nourishing oils according to their needs and moods.

For a more contemplative experience, guests may walk one of two Spa Botanica labyrinths—one for women only and the other open to both sexes. It is a popular belief that walking a labyrinth with the right mental approach provides a means of meditation, opening up a 'space' to listen to ourselves. After all, the labyrinth is shaped like our inner landscape-the swirl of a thumbprint, the coiling surface of the brain, and the undulating patterns of the inner ear. A person who journeys her way out of a labyrinth is said to discover a rebirth as one prepares to re-enter the outside world with a renewed purpose.

Should you emerge from the labyrinth and find yourself hungry, head to the resort's all-day restaurant, The Terrace, for a healthy and light meal accompanied by a selection of fragrant herbal teas. Then spend quiet time exploring the lush grounds upon which the resort is built and luxuriate in this quiet haven just minutes from the city, yet a peaceful other-world unto itself.

Spa Statistics

SPA AREA
6,000 sq m (64,580 sq ft)

FACILITIES
9 single indoor treatment rooms, 3 double indoor treatment rooms, 3 suites, 6 outdoor treatment pavilions, 2 labyrinths; 2 Galaxy Steambaths, 1 indoor Vichy shower, 1 outdoor Vichy shower, 2 cold plunge pools, 2 whirlpools, 2 mud pools, 2 flotation pools; Botanica Hair Spa, 1 nail salon station; 1 pilates studio, 1 gymnasium; 1 outdoor swimming pool, 2 tennis courts; 1 spa boutique, 1 Japanese tea house

SIGNATURE TREATMENT
Galaxy Steam Shower

OTHER TREATMENTS AND THERAPIES
Anti-ageing treatments, anti-cellulite treatments, aqua therapy, aromatherapy, baths, body scrubs, body wraps, eye treatments, facial treatments, firming and slimming treatments, flotation, hair treatments, hand and foot treatments, holistic treatments, hot stone therapies, hydrotherapy, Indonesian therapies, jet-lag treatments, manicures/pedicures, massages, movement therapies, pre and post-natal treatments, scalp treatments, Thai therapies

PROVISIONS FOR COUPLES
Indoor and outdoor couple treatment rooms with bath features, indoor and outdoor shower facilities

SPA CUISINE
Available at The Terrace
Provision for dietary requirements available upon request

ACTIVITIES
Biking, cooking classes, nature trail walk, pilates, stretching classes, talks by visiting consultants, tai chi, team building

SERVICES
Babysitting, body composition analysis, corporate programmes, free transfers to nearby shopping areas, general healthcare consultations, gift certificates, nutrition consultations, personal training, private spa parties, skincare consultations

MEMBERSHIP/ADMISSION
Not required

CONTACT
2 Bukit Manis Road
Sentosa
Singapore 099891
T +65 6275 0331
F +65 6275 0228
E thesentosa@beaufort.com.sg
W www.spabotanica.com, www.thesentosa.com

Javana Spa

JAKARTA, INDONESIA

Spread over 23 hectares (57 acres) in the pristine rainforest on the slopes of Mount Salak, the Javana Spa sits in a centuries-old area which is renowned for its therapeutic and healing properties. Just 54 kilometres (33½ miles) south of Jakarta, Javana Spa is a unique and exclusive haven of good health and offers some of the most specialized spa treatments and traditional therapies in Indonesia.

The spa's facilities are extensive, and include private rooms for massages, facial treatments, mud treatments, herbal wraps and hair and nail care. A lean but specific treatment menu of eight therapies includes an Indonesian massage, a strawberry mint skin scrub and a herbal and floral body wrap. Unique to the spa is the Volcanic Mud Body Masque that draws from the healing powers of nature by using forest plant elements, mud and volcanic ash to tone and tighten skin, while nourishing and detoxifying at the same time. Complement this treatment with a Javana Aromatic Massage that uses essential oils for calming, toning, and invigorating the body.

While it's tempting to stay indoors and sample every treatment on the menu, it's hard to ignore the grandeur of nature outside. The crisp, fresh air offers the perfect excuse to indulge in a spot of soft adventure from rock climbing to white water rafting, both of which can be arranged by the spa.

Those with less adventurous leanings may prefer to take advantage of the spa's two swimming pools, tennis courts, gym or jogging track. And Javana

Spa's manicured gardens and the Onsen-An Japanese sulfur bath, whose waters come directly from the source, will keep you in the great outdoors.

Unique to the Javana Spa are the personalized programmes that its staff can put together to meet the individual needs of each guest. Depending on your goals and preferences, this could encompass a morning yoga session, a hike to one of the seven magnificent waterfalls nearby, a meditation session in the evening and a massage to end the day.

Javana Spa's accommodations are elegantly simple, with large bungalows and well-appointed rooms that surround the steaming waters of the Onsen bath. Dining here is also a healthy and hearty experience. The spa's chefs have created a mouth-watering array of dishes that make use of the organic vegetables grown in their gardens, as well as the freshest meats and fish.

Whether it is a day trip to the spa, or a week or weekend stay, guests are assured one thing: By the end of the trip, they'll be rejuvenated, refreshed and ready to face the world again with newfound vigour.

| Nestled on the slopes of Mount Salak, the outstanding views at sunrise start off the day perfectly. || The Japanese Onsen is filled with natural spring waters straight from the source. ||| The great outdoors is a major feature during any stay. |||| Programmes are drawn up for each individual guest and yoga is just one of the activities available. ||||| Mount Salak gives a dramatic backdrop to the spa and views can be enjoyed from the manicured gardens.

SPA AREA
1,200 sq m (12,900 sq ft)

FACILITIES
6 single indoor treatment rooms, reflexology station; 1 Jacuzzi, 1 whirlpool, 1 Japanese-style onsen; 1 sauna, 1 steam room; hair salon, nail salon; 1 aerobics studio, 1 gymnasium; 2 outdoor swimming pools, 1 tennis court

SIGNATURE TREATMENT
Aromatherapy Facial, Body Herbal and Floral Wrap, Body-Skincare Relaxation Treatment, Hot Stone Massage, Javana Aromatic Massage, Strawberry Body Exfoliation, Traditional Indonesian Massage, Volcanic Mud Body Masques,

OTHER TREATMENTS AND THERAPIES
Aromatherapy, body scrubs, body wraps, facial treatments, hair treatments, hand and foot treatments, hot stone therapies, hydrotherapy, manicures/pedicures, massages, reflexology, salon services, scalp treatments

SPA CUISINE
Available

ACTIVITIES
Aerobics, aquaerobics, biking, hiking, meditation classes, rock climbing, white water rafting, yoga

SERVICES
Free transfers to nearby towns and airport, gift certificates, personal training, private spa parties

MEMBERSHIP/ADMISSION
Not required

CONTACT
Plaza Bisnis Kemang II
Jalan Kemang Raya No 2
Jakarta 12730
Indonesia
T +62 21 719 8327/28
F +62 21 719 5555
E javana@javanaspa.co.id
W www.javanaspa.co.id

Mandara Spa at Alila Ubud

BALI, INDONESIA

The calm road that leads to the Alila Ubud offers a glimpse of what lies ahead at one of Ubud's most sought after resorts. Past a traditional Balinese temple and through emerald sculpted rice paddies, Alila Ubud rises in the distance. It is a serene hillside retreat and home to one of Bali's most celebrated and established spas.

First opened in 1996, The Mandara Spa was given a facelift in 2002, bestowing upon it a delicate sophistication that simply exudes the treasures of peace and quiet. As soon as you step into its breezy central foyer and feel the pebble-deck flooring underfoot softly massaging your bare feet, you begin to prepare for the sensorial journey that lies ahead. The 840-square-metre (9,040 square-foot) spa comprises one double spa pavilion, a double spa suite, another suite dedicated to Thai massages, and two single spa suites for those who prefer to bask in the pleasures of the spa alone. Its design features traditional Indonesian touches such as alang alang roofs, local stonework and a variety of Indonesian timbers, alongside silk fabrics that line the walls and cover the soft furnishings.

On the spa menu is a wide range of health and beauty treatments, instilled with the allure of ancient traditions paired with the sophistication of modern spa techniques and products including the exclusive Elemis range. Various Asian cultures have inspired the treatments offered, with everything from ayurveda and traditional Balinese massages, to hot stone

| Meditation opportunities abound in this exotic setting. It's the perfect environment to switch off from the rest of the world. || The stunning pool is perched high above the Ayung River Valley below. ||| The villas at Alila Ubud afford a view of the treetops and the surrounding jungle. |||| Treatments at the Mandara Spa take place in one of the many spa suites. ||||| Spa products are available in the boutique. |||||| Out in the jungle on a hillside, Alila Ubud is a remote sanctuary.

therapy, Thai massages and foot reflexology. If you find yourself spoiled for choice, then make the Mandara Massage—the spa's signature treatment—your first option. A sublime experience to say the least, the Mandara Massage brings together a unique blend of five different massage styles—Japanese shiatsu, Thai, Hawaiian lomi lomi, Swedish and Balinese. What makes this treatment particularly exquisite is the careful synchronization of two therapists working together on your body.

To clear the mind and encourage deep relaxation, the ayurvedic shirodhara is a definite must. This oil flow treatment begins with an ayurvedic pressure massage before a gentle flow of aromatic oil is poured onto the third eye area of the forehead. Guests emerge refreshed and uplifted from the 50-minute experience, ready to face the modern world again with newfound vigour.

Each Mandara Spa experience is gently fused with the daily rituals of Balinese life. These small touches may not be immediately evident to the guests, but it manifests itself in the soft calm of the therapists, in the serenity of the surroundings, the intoxicating aromas and the overall air of tranquillity that welcomes and soothes every visitor that comes to Alila Ubud. And should guests want to take home a piece of this sublime world, the boutique stocks the spa's signature products that are all made from high quality natural ingredients.

Spa Statistics

SPA AREA
840 sq m (9,040 sq ft)

FACILITIES
2 double indoor treatment villas, 2 single indoor treatment rooms, 1 double indoor treatment room; 1 manicure and pedicure pavilion; 1 outdoor swimming pool; 1 spa boutique

SIGNATURE TREATMENT
Ayurvedic Shirodhara, Mandara Massage, Royal Thai Massage

OTHER TREATMENTS AND THERAPIES
Aromatherapy, ayurveda, baths, body scrubs, Chinese therapies, facial treatments, hot stone therapies, Indonesian therapies, manicures/pedicures, massages, movement therapies, reflexology, Thai therapies

PROVISIONS FOR COUPLES
2 treatment villas

ACTIVITIES
Meditation classes, tai chi, yoga

MEMBERSHIP/ADMISSION
Not required

CONTACT
Desa Melinggih Kelod Payagan
Gianyar 80572
Bali, Indonesia
T +62 0 361 975 963
F +62 0 361 975 968
E infoasia@mandaraspa.com
W www.mandaraspa.com/www.alilahotels.com

Maya Ubud Resort and Spa

BALI, INDONESIA

A lush secluded river valley situated in the physical and spiritual heart of Bali, offers an astoundingly beautiful setting in which to create a spa. The award winning Spa at Maya houses a cluster of enchanting, double and single, thatched treatment pavilions that are dramatically suspended on a steep cliff side, seemingly defying gravity. Fringed by verdant jungle foliage, the canopied bathtub in each pavilion literally overhangs the swirling waters of the Petanu River as it carves its way through the narrow valley below.

After descending into this serene haven by the considerate means of an outdoor elevator, guests have the opportunity to enjoy a rebalancing and enriching experience that will ease fatigue, stimulate the senses and awaken the spirit. Removed from the world and totally encompassed by raw nature; local materials and natural colours have been blended to harmonize with the peaceful environment.

The spa menu offers a broad range of soothing and energizing treatments in secluded privacy. Massage and aromatherapy are combined with a choice of the finest 100 per cent essential oils; the exotic signature blend being an intoxicating combination of lavender, tangerine and cananga. Massage therapies include the 90-minute Harmony Duo, a four hand massage with two therapists working in tandem and employing special techniques to revitalize tired muscles and improve blood circulation. Skin remedies showcase traditional body scrubs utilizing herbal exfoliates, and the Maya Facial is a recipe of fresh and natural ingredients including orange, avocado, cucumber, yogurt, egg, honey, mint leaf, apple cider vinegar and ground corn.

The three-hour Riverside Special is a luxurious traditional package featuring the Maya Massage followed by a choice of body scrub. Options include

the warm and exotic Cinnamon and Tangerine Scrub, or the Pandan Leaf Body Scrub which is an all natural exfoliant ground from the pure, fragrant leaves of the Balinese Pandan plant, rich in natural vitamins and amino acid. This pampering package finishes with a sweet-scented flower bath and a rejuvenating facial, leaving guests with a feeling of total renewal. Treatments for men include the 'Refined Man', an excellent package recommended after a day of intense physical activity that starts with a treat for the feet followed by a full body massage and an invigorating herbal bath.

Three exceptional restaurants offer culinary specialities from around the world; and the delightful accommodation includes individual Balinese-style villas, many of which boast their own private pools. The Maya Ubud Resort and Spa is located just a few minutes' drive from the famous artistic and cultural town of Ubud. Spread throughout hillside gardens, between the steep river gorge and the gently swaying fields of rice, it is a masterpiece of contemporary wonder and ethnic chic.

| The exquisite traditional décor welcomes you at the very beginning of your Maya Ubud experience. || Balinese treatments are a speciality here and the flower bath completes many spa packages. ||| Facial treatments at the spa use the most natural ingredients. |||| Balinese touches decorate the spa throughout. ||||| One of the two outdoor swimming pools at Maya Ubud, both are brilliantly carved into its surroundings.

Spa Statistics

SPA AREA
1,000 sq m (10,765 sq ft)

FACILITIES
3 single indoor treatment villas, 2 double indoor treatment villas complete with semi-outdoor bathtubs; 2 outdoor swimming pools, spa pool; mini golf course, 1 tennis court; spa boutique, library

SIGNATURE TREATMENT
Harmony Duo, The Refined Man, Riverside Special

OTHER TREATMENTS AND THERAPIES
Baths, body scrubs, facial treatments, hand and foot treatments, herbal treatments, Indonesian therapies, manicures/pedicures, massages, reflexology

PROVISIONS FOR COUPLES
Petanu Interlude, Riverside Special, double spa pavilions

SPA CUISINE
Available at River Cafe

ACTIVITIES
Aquaerobics, biking, cooking classes, free to do today programme, mini-golf, pilates, tennis, yoga

SERVICES
Babysitting, gift certificates

MEMBERSHIP/ADMISSION
Not required

CONTACT
Jalan Gunung Sari
Peliatan PO Box 1001
Ubud 80571,
Bali, Indonesia
T +62 361 977 888
F +62 361 977 555
E spa@mayaubud.com
W www.mayaubud.com

Parwathi Spa at Matahari Beach Resort and Spa

BALI, INDONESIA

Perched on the Java Sea next to Bali Barat National Park, Matahari Beach Resort and Spa is the island's only luxury hideaway off the beaten track. To get here, guests are driven through dramatic mountain ranges, past sacred temples and charming tropical villages. The journey itself is resplendent with the magic of Bali and arriving at the resort is akin to reaching an enchanted locale.

Meaning 'eye of the day', Matahari is nestled on a black sand beach and is everything that discerning travellers could ask for. A cool blend of East and West, it comprises handcrafted Balinese structures, from ornate and luxurious bungalows to its Parwathi Spa, a uniquely Indonesian refuge for mind and body that honours the Hindu gods Shiva and Parwathi.

Wander through its gardens and experience a dreamy oasis lush with bougainvillea, hibiscus, fragrant lilies, jasmine and frangipani. If the gods could have an official headquarters on the island of Bali, Matahari Beach Resort and Spa would be it.

At the Parwathi Spa, water fountains gurgle and the scent of lotus flowers and frangipani linger in the air. Resembling an ancient royal palace, it is a virtual botanical paradise steeped in the calming influence of Balinese art. The spa's Sthira massage is a revitalizing treatment designed to relieve stress and mental fatigue by releasing blocked energy from the muscles and connective tissue. This energy flow is then redirected throughout the body to rebalance and re-energize, while calming the mind. The Sukha massage eases tension with long, rhythmic movements, it also opens, balances and calms the body's subtle energy centres. At the same time, it serves to comfort and still the mind.

For a more romantic and decadent experience, opt for the Royal Parwathi package. Step back in time and be treated like members of the Brahmana cast preparing for their wedding with exquisite body treatments and rituals. The package begins with a Sthira or Sukha massage, all while sipping on an ice-cold bottle of champagne. Like true Balinese royals, guests are then served a 10-course gala dinner, serenaded by the sound of splashing water in the pavilion. As the sky darkens into night, sink into the Bali Sari, a king-sized bed, as the balmy night breeze caresses you into a sweet, easy slumber.

In addition to traditional Balinese preparations, all Parwathi Spa treatments use products from the world-famous Ligne St Barth range. The all-natural ingredients are extracted from the plants, fruit and flowers of the Caribbean. PABA-free, not tested on animals and approved by dermatologists, the Ligne St Barth range boasts a natural affinity with the complexion, leaving it radiant and soothed. With such attention to detail and services that care attentively for each guest, even the gods would approve.

| The resort is a tranquil Balinese paradise where lotus ponds dot the landscape. || At the spa, couples can be treated together to the four-handed Sthira or Sukha massage. ||| The Parwathi Spa stands grandly around its pond and garden courtyard. |||| Traditional houses make unique accommodation and celebrate Bali's rich cultural heritage. ||||| The villas offer complete privacy and luxury, somewhere to unwind before more pampering at the spa.

Spa Statistics

SPA AREA
1,200 sq m (12,915 sq ft)

FACILITIES
1 single indoor treatment room, 2 double indoor treatment rooms, outdoor treatment pavilion; 1 consultation room, 1 medical consultation room; 1 meditation room; 1 relaxation room; flotation chamber, 3 Jacuzzis; 1 steam room; solarium; bale sari, hair salon station, nail salon station; 1 gymnasium; 1 outdoor swimming pool, 1 tennis court; spa boutique, library

SIGNATURE TREATMENT
2-, 4- or 6-hand massage, Sthira Massage, Sukha Massage

OTHER TREATMENTS AND THERAPIES
Body scrubs, body wraps, facial treatments, hair treatments, hand and foot treatments, hydrotherapy, Indonesian therapies, jet-lag treatments, make-up services, manicures/pedicures, massages, salon services, foot baths, sun repair

PROVISIONS FOR COUPLES
Available

SPA CUISINE
Available in the spa, rooms and romantic pavilions

ACTIVITIES
Badminton, beach volleyball, biking, canang (palm leaf course), cooking classes, dance classes, fruit carving course, golf, horseback riding, massage classes, painting course, scuba-diving, snorkelling, table tennis, tai chi, tennis, tours and trekking, yoga

SERVICES
Babysitting and childcare, body composition analysis, day room usage, general healthcare consultation, nutrition consultation, personal training, skincare consultation

CONTACT
PO Box 194 Pemuteran
Singaraja
Bali, Indonesia
T +62 362 92312
F +62 361 92313
E mbr-bali@indo.net.id
W www.matahari-beach-resort.com

Pita Maha & Tjampuhan Resort & Spa

BALI, INDONESIA

Since 1934, the historical Tjampuhan area of Ubud, Bali has been the heart of its famed artistic community. It was here that the Prince of Ubud joined forces with celebrated Western artists Walter Spies and Rudolf Bonner to create an artists' association called Pita Maha. What began as a private guesthouse for artists soon became the undisputed centre for Balinese art.

As befits such a large source of inspiration for the artistic enclave, Pita Maha Resort and Spa overlooks the picturesque River Oos. From its lobby and restaurant, the foothills of Ubud are spread out as far as the eye can see. Designed by a descendent of the founding Prince, Pita Maha Resort and Spa is set out like an authentic Balinese Village with 24 villas set in a traditionally styled walled compound. Its workmanship is worthy of a Balinese palace, with wood and stone fixtures and furnishings each complementing the carefully tended gardens lush with tropical greenery.

This restful resort is anchored by its exquisite spa, which has played host to celebrities such as Cindy Crawford. Its tranquil Private Spa Villa is the ideal buffer against the assaults of urban life with healing treatments, tranquil surroundings and experienced therapists to offer the best options in holistic spa care. Relax in this haven of privacy and choose from a vast array of traditional treatments. A particular favourite of Pita Maha guests is the

Balinese massage. Lay back for a blissful hour as a therapist kneads the stress out of your system with a choice of aromatic perfume oils like ylang ylang, lotus or sandalwood.

Meanwhile, its signature Lulur treatment is one that cannot be missed. This ancient herbal skin scrub promises to rejuvenate the skin with ingredients that hark back to centuries past. The scrub is followed by a refreshing yoghurt massage and finished with a tropical flower bath in the Spa Villa's exclusive spring water pool that overlooks the sacred river valley.

The Pita Maha Kopi Scrub makes use of the traditional exfoliant, coffee. Starting with a 20-minute back massage, the scrub is gently for 40 minutes to remove dead skin cells and soften the skin. Afterwards, a carrot mixture is applied to replenish any lost moisture ensuring that the skin is left in optimum condition.

Couples can order up a special spa experience with the Harmony Package that encompasses two idyllic hours in a private villa. Spend the first hour under the healing hands of a therapist's Balinese massage before soaking in the energetic properties of the sauna, steam room and hot and cold Jacuzzis. To get the blood circulation going again, a steaming cup of ginger tea is served before a short stroll to the resort's Terrace Restaurant takes you to a specially prepared Balinese meal. What better way to end a heavenly spa experience than with a spread consisting sumptuous offerings like Bergedel Kepiting (deep fried crab cakes with mango and coriander sauce), Spicy Balinese Duck Consomme and Tenggiri Bakar (char-grilled mackerel fillet).

Spa Statistics

SPA AREA
400 sq m (4,305 sq ft)

FACILITIES
1 double indoor treatment villa, 1 outdoor treatment pavilion; 1 Jacuzzi, 1 plunge pool, 1 whirlpool; 1 sauna, 1 steam room; 1 outdoor swimming pool; spa boutique, library

SIGNATURE TREATMENT
Traditional Lulur

OTHER TREATMENTS AND THERAPIES
Baths, body scrubs, body wraps, facial treatments, hand and foot treatments, manicures/pedicures, massages, reflexology

PROVISIONS FOR COUPLES
2-hour Private Villa Spa

SERVICES
Babysitting, free transfers to Ubud area

MEMBERSHIP/ADMISSION
Not required

CONTACT
Jalan Sanggingan PO Box 198
Ubud 80571
Bali, Indonesia
T +62 361 974330
F +62 361 974329
E pitamaha@indosat.net.id
W www.pitamaha-bali.com

| The pool provides the opportunity to take in the fresh Balinese air. | | The flower bath follows the spa's signature Lulur treatment. Guests staying in the private villa spa can enjoy the exclusive spring water pool that overlooks the sacred river valley below. | | | The spa is perfectly nestled in the surrounding jungle. | | | | The resort's luxurious suites provide for a truly satifying holiday. | | | | | A calm tranquillity pervades the air.

Prana Spa at The Villas

BALI, INDONESIA

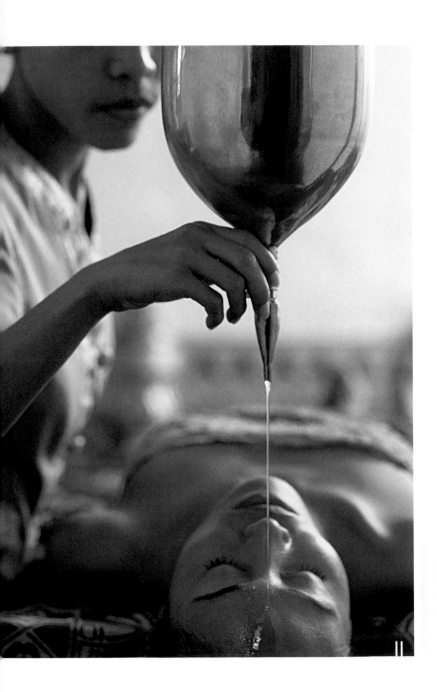

To enter Prana Spa At The Villas is to enter an entirely different dimension. Inspired by the legendary Moguls of Rajasthan, Prana Spa is one of life's sumptuous pleasures. Forget understated decorations that have come to be expected of spas around the world. Here lies a universe of sensorial delights, lavishly appointed in rich colour, gilded accents and voluptuous architecture.

A wonderfully heady, lingering fragrance permeates the air, evoking the first whispers of deep relaxation. As you walk through the lofty courtyard and past the exotic arched doorway, a sense of calm pervades, inspiring you to shrug off the strains of the modern world. Beneath this castle-like structure of restrained opulence, the ancient wisdom of Hindu ayurveda healing and relaxation arts are practised by skilled Balinese therapists who thoughtfully and carefully accompany guests through a medley of massages and treatments. Using exquisite blends of rare herbs, precious spices, fragrant oils and unctuous creams, these dedicated therapists knead, stroke and soothe every filament of stress away from your bodies as if your well-being were their lives' calling.

The mind and body must be rebalanced before it is rejuvenated. Hence, the signature Prana Rebalance treatment is the ideal start to the Prana Spa experience. This all-over detoxifier, originating from India, promises to deliver you into a perfectly grounded state of wellness. It begins with a Pizichill, a synchronicity massage where two therapists simultaneously knead warm medicated oils into your body. Next, healing powders and herbs specially imported from India—and unique to Prana—are

applied to stimulate circulation and recondition the body. This is followed by the Mavarakizhi, a traditional technique that uses poultice bags filled with curative herbs and powders to help alleviate fatigue, improve digestion and undo any stiffness of the body. Finally the Pina Sweda sees steaming towels infused with herbs draped over the body to cleanse and detoxify.

In order to take full advantage of the spa's facilities, three-, five- and seven-day packages can provide the ultimate rejuvenating break. Each programme is carefully drawn up and include all meals and daily treatments for the whole duration.

While wellness can be administered through spa treatments, Prana Spa believes that an integral part of good health is in developing flexibility and strength in the body to balance and calm the mind. To that end, the Prana Yoga room offers daily stretch classes. If guests prefer to stretch in the privacy of their own villas, personalized in-villa classes can also be arranged.

Meanwhile, as part of its holistic approach to wellness, a section of the Spa's food menu has been devoted entirely to 'Live Food'. Organically grown vegetables and salads are part of the health menu, while herbal ingredients and cleansing drinks have been infused into the daily fare.

With such a complete range of services and treatments dedicated to restoring the harmony of mind, body and soul, it is certainly difficult to leave this oasis of pleasure and healing. Luckily, guests can take home a piece of Prana through its gift shop which stocks a collection of jewellery, textiles and fine artworks from around Asia.

| The castle-like exterior makes Prana Spa a unique setting. || The ancient Shirodhara treatment is part of the spa's extensive ayurvedic menu. ||| Sumptuous body treatments include the clay body mask. |||| The unique style of the spa continues into the luxurious steam room.

Spa Statistics

SPA AREA
1,300 sq m (13,995 sq ft)

FACILITIES
19 single indoor treatment rooms, 4 double indoor treatment rooms; 1 meditation room; 1 hot plunge pool, 2 cold plunge pools; 2 saunas, 3 steam rooms; 8 nail salon stations; yoga room; Prana gift shop

SIGNATURE TREATMENT
Ayurvedic Simple Bliss, Prana Rebalance

OTHER TREATMENTS AND THERAPIES
Baths, beauty treatments, body scrubs, body wraps, massages, manicures/pedicures, facial treatments, reflexology, Shiatsu

PROVISIONS FOR COUPLES
4 couple treatment rooms

SPA CUISINE
Available at The Restaurant At Prana

ACTIVITIES
Yoga

CONTACT
Jalan Kunti 118X
Seminyak
Bali, Indonesia
T +62 361 730 840
F +62 361 734 758
E spa@thevillas.net
W www.thevillas.net

The Ritz-Carlton, Bali Thalasso Resort & Spa

BALI, INDONESIA

Everything about The Ritz-Carlton, Bali Thalasso & Spa makes it the perfect spot to offer the best of Thalasso therapy. For a start, its atmospheric pressure at sea level is ideal as it increases oxygenation of the body. Secondly, the winds that blow in from the sea are pure and dust-free. Yet it is charged with miniscule droplets of seawater, producing a powerful natural aerosol that relieves congestion. Add to that Bali's tropical climate and you get a year-round seaside spa escape that is unrivalled anywhere on this dazzling island.

This award-winning spa is home to one of the world's largest Aquatonic seawater pools, where guests can improve their fitness and circulation while toning and firming the body in its liquid comforts. In these pools, water from the Indian Ocean is warmed to optimum temperatures to rebalance mineral deficiencies and provide the body with its curative and preventative properties.

In the same vein, the spa's treatments incorporate long established European seawater therapies, focusing on relaxation and healing, while taking advantage of the resort's idyllic seafront location. Fittingly, six state-of-the-art thalasso therapy rooms, six private spa villas, two Spa on the

Rocks Villas, not to mention the 20 treatment rooms and suite, were specially built to provide guests with ultimate havens of relaxation, where these treatments can be enjoyed in unbridled luxury and privacy.

Some of the spa's signature Thalasso treatments include Jet Baths and Underwater Massages, seaweed body wraps, scrubs and beauty treatments. Besides their physical benefits, these treatments also bestow a sense of peace, rebirth and rediscovery, while forming a base for effectively improving lifestyles.

Of course, being situated in a land rich with a history of therapeutic body treatments, The Ritz Carlton, Bali Thalasso & Spa also offers traditional Indonesian beauty rituals. For centuries, Indonesian woman have used natural herbal concoctions, creams and oils to enhance their natural beauty and maintain their health. Today, the spa's selection of top-to-toe treatments draws from this centuries-old well of knowledge to renew, revive and restore.

All of the spa's 57 therapists and beauticians have been thoroughly trained to provide their guests with knowledgeable and flawless spa experiences. Unique and traditional spa facilities, including a Jacuzzi Grotto, separate men's and women's whirlpool baths, plunge pools and various outdoor meditation pavilions elevate The Ritz Carlton, Bali Thalasso & Spa experience from an exquisite to a sublime one.

Post-treatment, treat yourself to a healthy spa meal at the resort's Spa Café, which serves low-calorie cuisine that is both tasty and satisfying. And if you want to take home a memento of your stay, head to the spa boutique, which carries beautiful gift items and products from the Thermes Marin, Guinot and Aroma Therapy Associates ranges.

| Out in the fresh air, guests receive more than just a massage. The gentle breeze brings all the goodness from the surrounding ocean. || Luxury is key in the indoor treatment rooms where opulence intermingles with traditional style. ||| Relaxing is easy at The Ritz-Carlton Bali. This plunge pool situated at one of the Cliff Villas, offers spectacular views of the sea. |||| The Spa on the Rocks, a spectacular experience which takes full advantage of the setting.

Spa Statistics

SPA AREA
22,000 sq m (236,800 sq ft)

FACILITIES
6 spa villas, 1 spa suite, 6 thalasso therapy rooms, 20 indoor treatment rooms with en-suite shower and bath, 2 Spa On The Rocks Villas; 1 consultation gazebo; 3 Jacuzzis; 2 saunas, 2 steam rooms; 5 hair salon stations; 3 nail salon stations; 1 aquatic pool; 1 gymnasium; 18-hole golf course, 3 tennis courts; spa boutique

SIGNATURE TREATMENT
Arjuna, Balinese Thalasso Experience, Cinta Abadi–'Eternal Love', Drupadi, Frangipani Package, Marine Beauty, Marine Slimming, Marine Wave, Marine Wave Deluxe, Rama & Shita, The Thalasso Experience

OTHER TREATMENTS AND THERAPIES
Anti-ageing treatments, anti-cellulite treatments, aqua therapy, aromatherapy, baths, body scrubs, body wraps, bust treatments, facial treatments, firming and slimming, hair treatments, hand and foot treatments, holistic treatments, hot sand therapies, hydrotherapy, Indonesian therapies, make-up services, manicures/pedicures, massages, purifying back treatments, reflexology, salon services, scalp treatments, thalassotherapy

PROVISIONS FOR COUPLES
Eternal Love–'Cinta Abadi' package, Rama Shita, spa villas and spa suite

SPA CUISINE
Available at the Spa Cafe

ACTIVITIES
Aerobics, aquaerobics, biking, golf putting, nature walks, tennis, yoga

SERVICES
Free transfers to nearby towns and airport, gift certificates, personal training

MEMBERSHIP/ADMISSION
Not required
Available but not required for Aquatonic pool

CONTACT
Jalan Karang Mas Sehahtera
Jimbaran 80364
Bali, Indonesia
T +62 361 702 222
F +62 361 701 555
E spa.reservation@ritzcarlton-bali.com
W www.ritzcarlton.com

The Spa at Four Seasons Resort Bali at Jimbaran Bay

BALI, INDONESIA

The Four Seasons Resort Bali at Jimbaran Bay is a multiple award-winning resort designed around paved streets and laid out like a traditional Balinese village. This exclusive and exotic retreat, immersed in the mystique of Bali's unique and spiritual surroundings, boasts a fantastic beach, lavish facilities, beautiful gardens, and a private plunge pool in every villa. An example of flawless and impeccable service, the resort's staff are constantly on hand to ensure that every comfort is provided for and guests are never left wanting.

Within its tranquil premises is the Jimbaran Spa, which was voted the Best International Hotel Spa by *Travel + Leisure*'s 2005 World's Best Awards Readers Survey. Perched on a terrace surrounded by towering tropical greenery, the spa is spread over 1,000 square metres (10,760 square feet) and houses nine treatment rooms, including three large couples' spa suites and indoor and outdoor facilities. The Royal Spa Suite is its most popular offering, with double massage beds, Swiss shower, and a garden courtyard that is anchored by a large soaking tub and a cascading rinse shower.

| Each thatched-roof villa, with its own landscaped courtyard, comes complete with plunge pool and outdoor shower. || The tropical gardens flow all the way down to the sea providing a beautiful view of Jimbaran Bay. ||| and |||| The Royal Spa Suite can be enjoyed by couples where a gentle Rain Shower follows a Tropical Scrub. ||||| The ladies' Jacuzzi provides a perfect sanctuary. ||||||PJ's restaurant serves up delicious seafood from the day's catch.

Choose from a spa menu that draws inspiration from the ocean and local healing elements, featuring traditional and exotic rituals that celebrate the restorative heritage of Indonesia. Ancient recipes that incorporate healing flowers, plants, herbs and spices are fused with modern-day beauty regimes to deliver treatments that signify the very height of luxury.

Exclusive to the spa are body elixirs that promise to cleanse, detoxify and renew with its garden fresh ingredients. The most popular of these is the Ocean Ritual, which begins with a Blue Ocean Sea Salt Scrub, followed by a luxurious Sea Body Wrap and is completed with a relaxing scented Sea Salt Bath.

Not to be missed is the spa's signature Lulur Jimbaran treatment that begins with a relaxing Balinese massage, followed by an invigorating exfoliation. Using a traditional Javanese blend of turmeric, sandalwood, sweet woods, rice powder, ginger and spices, this magical mixture polishes and refreshes the skin before it is soaked off in an oversized bath, which has been infused with plants and flowers from the spa garden. A nourishing flower body lotion is then rubbed into your skin as you enjoy a piping hot jamu herbal beverage that serves to awaken all your senses.

A Mediterranean counter serves light spa cuisine and an extensive boutique features essential oils and spa products that allow guests to take home a piece of the unforgettable Jimbaran Spa experience.

Spa Statistics

SPA AREA
1,000 sq m (10,760 sq ft)

FACILITIES
3 single rooms, 3 double rooms, 2 facial treatment rooms; 2 plunge pools, 2 whirlpools; 1 sauna, 1 steam room, 1 aroma steam room; 2 hair salon stations, 2 nail salon stations; 1 gymnasium, aerobics studio; 2 outdoor swimming pools; 2 tennis courts; 1 spa boutique, library

SIGNATURE TREATMENTS
Lulur Jimbaran, Ocean Ritual

OTHER TREATMENTS AND THERAPIES
Aromatic massages, Balinese massage, body elixirs, body masks, body wraps, facial treatments, hair masks and treatments, healing waters and baths, foot treatments, manicures/pedicures, skin scrubs, waxing

PROVISIONS FOR COUPLES
2 Spa Suites and 1 Royal Spa Suite

SPA CUISINE
Nutritionally balanced cuisine and a vegetarian menu are available at the Resort's outlets

ACTIVITIES
Cooking, jamu herbal drinks course, junior tennis lessons, Kids For All Seasons activities, water sports

SERVICES
Babysitting, free transfers from hotel to shopping areas of Kuta and Nusa Dua, free transfers between Four Seasons Jimbaran Bay and Sayan, rental of sightseeing car and driver, rental of self-drive cars

CONTACT
Jimbaran 80361
Bali, Indonesia
T +62-361 701 010
F +62-361 701 020
E fsrb.jimbaran@fourseasons.com
W www.fourseasons.com/jimbaranbay

The Spa at Four Seasons Resort Bali at Sayan

BALI, INDONESIA

Since its inception in 1988, the Four Seasons Resort Bali at Sayan has served as a sanctuary for those seeking peace and quietude in the tranquil depths of Bali. Amid verdant rice terraces, ancient shrines, age-old banyan trees and lush jungle, the resort seems to emerge from the mountain mists like an ethereal kingdom. The entrance lies across a long bridge that leads to a pond and it is along this stretch where the pulse instinctively slows and the resort's ultra modern surroundings signal the beginnings of a spiritual getaway.

Nestled in Bali's central highlands, the spa at Sayan offers the calming influence of the sacred Ayung River and the beauty of lush, terraced rice fields rising in the distance. Here, the earth's elements play an integral part in restoring inner balance. Unique rituals and beauty therapies abound, all using a blend of ayurvedic traditions, natural clays, exotic spices and locally grown herbs and flowers. Through a celebration of the healing powers of nature, the spa's treatments soothe, rejuvenate and refresh frazzled city-dwelling souls.

| Drawing from its calming influence, The Spa at Sayan sits by the sacred Ayung River. || The two-tiered swimming pool allows guests to exercise or just lay back and relax whilst overlooking the resplendent valley. ||| At the top of the main building is the bridge guests need to cross in order to arrive at the resort's entrance. |||| Guests can enjoy a warm bath with specially blended essences in their own suite or villa. A scalp-neck-shoulder-back-arm massage is administered whilst the bath is being prepared. ||||| The spa bath is used during treatment to relax the body and soothe the skin.

A nod to this philosophy is its signature Suci Dhara treatment. Referring to the awakening and balancing of the body, heart and soul, the Suci Dhara treatment begins with a scalp massage to improve circulation and relax muscle and nerve fibres. Warm herbal oils are then rhythmically dripped onto the forehead for mental relaxation and clarity. To nourish the nervous system and aid detoxification, a warm herbal oil massage is administered before a steam bath completes the ritual and a comforting mug of herbal dosha tea is served. Indeed, the Suci Dhara works wonders for both the body and mind.

The spa's interiors combine the textures and native warmth from local stone facings, teakwood cabinets and floorings and glass windows shielded discreetly with Japanese rice paper blinds. Customized terrazzo massage tables and freestanding soak tubs provide a modern contrast to traditional layered alang alang thatched roofs. Spa villas for couples are connected to outdoor bathing facilities that offer steam showers and large bathtubs. The largest of these is the Cendana Villa, measuring 93 square metres (1,000 square feet) and designed for full- and half-day visitors.

Outside, in the centre of a lotus pond, a private swimming pool and lounge area is the ideal place to enjoy a light meal prepared by Four Season's acclaimed chefs. From this vantage point, the panoramic view of emerald rice terraces is an affirmation that life is good indeed.

Spa Statistics

SPA AREA
800 sq m (8,610 sq ft)

FACILITIES
2 single treatment rooms, 1 double treatment room, 3 spa villas; 1 Jacuzzi, 2 plunge pools; 1 hair salon station; 1 gymnasium; 1 outdoor swimming pool; 1 spa boutique, library

SIGNATURE TREATMENT
Lulur Sayan, Suci Dhara

OTHER TREATMENTS AND THERAPIES
Ayurveda, body scrubs, body wax, facial treatments, hair treatments, manicures/pedicures, massages, reflexology

PROVISIONS FOR COUPLES
3 spa villas, 1 double treatment room in the main building

SPA CUISINE
Nutritionally balanced cuisine and a vegetarian menu are available at the Resort's outlets.

ACTIVITIES
Biking, cooking, trekking, yoga

SERVICES
Free transfers to nearby towns, free transfers between Four Seasons Sayan and Jimbaran Bay

CONTACT
Sayan, Ubud,
Gianyar 80571
Bali, Indonesia
T +62-361 977 577
F +62-361 977 588
E fsrb.sayan@fourseasons.com
W www.fourseasons.com/sayan

CHI Spa Village at Shangri-La's Mactan Island Resort and Spa

CEBU, PHILIPPINES

Symbolism is everywhere at the CHI Spa Village, where the experience begins the moment guests reach its entrance. Here, an arresting fountain and water cascade structure represents the five elements while heightening your sense of arrival. Step across a CHI signature mandala, which symbolizes the Himalayan cosmic universe, and stroll across a wooden walkway stretched above a lotus pond that leads to The Sanctum.

This three-tiered open-air sanctuary houses the spa's reception, boutique and lounge. An intricate glass sculpture is suspended as if floating from the ceiling, evoking a sense of ethereal serenity. From here, guests can enjoy the CHI Water Garden Pavilion, which features an infinity-edged vitality pool and body scrub salas—preludes to a relaxing and revitalizing spa treatment.

As befits the Philippine's first and largest spa resort, the CHI treatment menu boasts over 30 face and body treatments, water therapies and special spa packages developed by a team of experts in traditional Chinese medicine and Himalayan healing traditions. All of CHI's signature therapies are based on the theory of the five elements while drawing inspiration from the healing customs of Sout-East Asia. To honour its location, a select number of treatments are based on the traditional folk practices of the Philippines. These use indigenous ingredients like banana leaf, coconut milk, papaya, mango and ginger to offer guests a unique taste of the tropics.

CHI's design takes its cues from a myriad of exotic sources, from the ethereal gardens of China's highlands to the hallowed halls of Kathmandu's Patan Museum. The spa itself draws inspiration from the Shangri-La legend, which is set amid the Himalayan landscape. Fittingly, local artisans in the Himalayas were employed to incorporate traditional elements throughout the spa's design. Wander through the building and you'll see bronze lotus flower inlays on the pathways that were made in Nepal using the traditional 'lost wax' process. Look skywards and witness wooden frames highlighting Himalayan

artefacts hanging from the ceilings on impressive interlocking hand-wrought metal straps.

Naturally, the spa boasts its own private label range of massage oils, mists and body and bath products. Like the treatments on offer, this exclusive CHI range of products was created based on the Chinese philosophy of the five elements.

On your visit here, don't miss out on CHI's signature therapies such as the CHI Balance, Himalayan Healing Stone Massage and the Mountain Tsampa Rub. And when in the Philippines, do as the Filipinas do with the traditional Hilot, a time-honoured healing massage that includes the divine Barako Coffee Bean Scrub and the Tropical Linen and Leaf Wrap.

Make a vacation of it by checking into the 547-room Shangri-La Mactan Island Resort & Spa and enjoy the unsurpassable, holistic experience of fine spa treatments, excellent food and flawless service. It is a sublime experience you won't soon forget.

| Herbal pouch containing 15 herbs. || Relaxation beds. ||| The spa's therapists administer treatments with a knowing and experienced hand. |||| Chi Spa is set in traditional cabanas and overlooks the stunning pool. ||||| The spa sits proudly amongst its surroundings.

Spa Statistics

SPA AREA
10,000 sq m (107,640 sq ft)

FACILITIES
8 single indoor treatment villas, 6 double indoor treatment villas, 3 outdoor treatment pavilions, body scrub salas; 1 meditation room; 1 Vitality Hydro pool, 1 watsu pool, 1 Jacuzzi, whirlpool; sauna, steam rooms; sun bed; hair salon, nail salon; 1 gymnasium, 1 cardio studio; 2 outdoor swimming pools, 1 golf course, 3 tennis courts; spa boutique

SIGNATURE TREATMENT
Barako Coffee Bean Scrub, Chi'atsu, Herbal Harmony, Himalayan Healing Stone Massage, Mountain Tsampa Rub, Philippine Touch Therapy (Hilot), Tropical Linen and Leaf Wrap

OTHER TREATMENTS AND THERAPIES
Aqua therapy, aromatherapy, baths, body scrubs, facial treatments, flotation, hair treatments, hand and foot treatments, hot stone therapies, jet-lag treatments, make-up services, manicures/pedicures, massages, reflexology, salon services, Thai therapies, waxing

PROVISIONS FOR COUPLES
Special treatment rooms for couples

SPA CUISINE
Available in the Tea Pavilion or in the treatment villas (if included in spa package), Provisions for vegetarian diet available, Provisions for special dietary requirements available on request

ACTIVITIES
(For resort guests only) Aquaerobics, golf (pitch and putt and putting green), sailing, scuba diving, snorkelling, stretching classes, tennis, yoga

SERVICES
Babysitting and childcare, corporate programmes, free transfers to nearby malls, personal training

MEMBERSHIP/ADMISSION
Available but not required

CONTACT
Punta Engano Road
PO Box 86, Lapu Lapu City 6015
Cebu, Philippines
T +63 32 231 0288
F +63 32 495 1259
E mac@shangri-la.com
W www.shangri-la.com/spa

The Farm at San Benito

BATANGAS, PHILIPPINES

Far away from it all, 90 kilometres (56 miles) south of Manila, The Farm at San Benito is a favourite hideaway for Filipino celebrities and international stars like Woody Harrelson. This sprawling complex is set in the verdant jungle and is entirely dedicated to the enjoyment, relaxation and wellness of its guests. In fact, well-being is taken very seriously here, and besides offering a range of pampering treatments like massages, scrubs and facials, it also offers medical vacations that focus on detoxification.

In these detox programmes, guests consume mostly vegetable salads and life-giving juices, and undergo colon hydrotherapy sessions. Programmes are supervised by doctors and medical professionals, ensuring that guests are in very safe hands.

Those seeking more indulgent experiences can opt for The Farm's 'Pampering Packages', which include gentle body scrubs to invigorate and exfoliate, as well as Therapeutic, Thai, Filipino or Balinese massages to soothe tense muscles.

A particular favourite at the Farm is its signature Hilot Haplos with Coco Cacao Body Scrub. Treatment begins with a refreshing scrub made of coconut cream and powdered cocoa. Once the body is slathered and scrubbed in the mix, it is washed off in a luscious bath of warm, fresh coconut milk. A sensational hilot, a traditional Filipino massage, follows, as therapists knead the strain out of the muscles before a mug of hot chocolate, made from the finest Batangas chocolate, is served. Another popular treatment is the Moxa Ventoza. Influenced by the Chinese therapy of moxibustion, this tradtional Filipino treatment is practiced by healers who use heat resistance cups to encourage blood flow.

Meals at The Farm are wonderfully healthy. The restaurant's menu is strictly vegetarian, with nary a fish, dairy product or egg in sight. Its chef, Felix Daniel Schoener, says that delicious meals can be made entirely out of vegetables, especially raw ones. Delicious rice and pasta meals can still be

found at the Farm, but Chef Schoener insists that his 'live food' system—essentially dishes made of organic vegetables, herbs, spices, seeds, and nuts that are raw, slightly marinated or gently heated—can be just as delicious as any gourmet meal.

When not luxuriating under the hands of the skilled therapists or supping on its excellent cuisine, guests can relax and unwind amongst its lush surroundings. Paths into the jungle lead to restful meditation spots, a library and a serene lake. There are several natural spring water swimming pools, one in the jungle under a waterfall. Fountains and exotic flowers abound, and beautiful songbirds fill the air. Around the large pond set between the reception and restaurant, ducks, peacocks and a black swan wander.

These make up The Farm's ambience and its entertainment—there are no televisions or radios, no smoking or alcohol. If you do find yourself desperate for some urban enjoyment, there are DVDs at the reception which can be enjoyed in the spa's library.

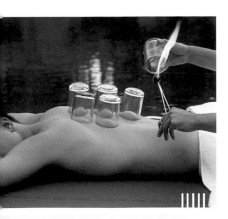

| After treatment, guests can relax in the well-appointed and luxurious villas.
|| Situated in the verdant jungle, the Farm's setting offers numerous peaceful spots where guests can meditate or practice yoga. ||| Treatments are not restricted to treatment rooms. Reflexology and Thai massage is administered by the pool against the awesome backdrop of the jungle. |||| Bringing the outside in, the spa's shower area takes full advantage of the setting. ||||| Moxa Ventoza is just one of the treatments on offer. This ancient practice uses cupping to improve blood circulation.

Spa Statistics

SPA AREA
1,225 sq m (13,200 sq ft)

FACILITIES
1 single indoor treatment room, 4 double indoor treatment rooms, 4 outdoor treatment pavilions; 3 consultation rooms, 2 colema rooms, 2 colonics rooms; 5 meditation rooms, meditation pavilions; 10 sun beds; gymnasium; 4 outdoor swimming pools; boutique, library, function rooms, amphitheatre

SIGNATURE TREATMENT
Hilot Haplos with Coco Cacao Body Scrub

OTHER TREATMENTS AND THERAPIES
Spa Menu: Body scrubs, facial treatments, foot scrubs, hot stone therapies, manicures/pedicures, massages, moxa ventosa, reflexology, reiki
Medical Menu: Art therapy, blood chemistry studies, body salt bath, colon hydrotherapy and enemas, creative visualization, curative arts, de-repression, iridology, kidney cleanse, live blood analysis, liver cleanse, neuro-linguistic programming, positive energy infusion, psycho-emotional counselling, subtle body nourishment
Facial Enhancement Procedures: Aptos/minimally invasive facelift, eye surgery, facial injections, mesotherapy in combination with the Wellness and Detoxification programmes

PROVISIONS FOR COUPLES
Available

SPA CUISINE
'Living Food' gourmet menu

ACTIVITIES
Breathing and walking exercises, golf, guided meditation, Living Food preparation classes, rotational meridian, lessons on sprouting greens and growing wheatgrass, life enhancement classes, personal training, stretching classes, talks by visiting consultants, Tibetan exercise, trail walking, weight training, yoga
Various programmes and workshops: Beauty and nutrition workshops, natural therapies, stress management workshops, weight loss workshops

MEMBERSHIP/ADMISSION
Not required

CONTACT
119 Barangay Tipakan, Lipa City
Batangas, Philippines
PO Box 39676
T +632 751 3498/+632 696 3795
F +632 751 3497/+632 696 3175
E info@thefarm.com.ph
W www.thefarm.com.ph

Mandala Spa

BORACAY ISLAND, PHILIPPINES

Named Best Spa by the Philippine *Tatler* in 2004, Mandala Spa oozes sun-kissed charm and unbridled serenity. Set on the idyllic Boracay Island, this 2.5-hectare (6-acre) spa estate nestles on a lush tropical hilltop overlooking Boracay's famous White Beach, often referred to as one of the most beautiful beaches in the world. Here 12 exquisitely crafted villas offer complete privacy, each are tastefully clad in bamboo, stone riprap and cogon roofing—all are natural materials which enable them to blend seamlessly with their tropical surroundings. Inside, glass walls and wooden finishes evoke a sense of the outdoors, while Italian designer bathroom fittings lend a surprisingly welcome modern edge.

A stone's throw away is the beautifully landscaped wellness sanctuary, where people from all walks of life come to experience Mandala's highly acclaimed spa treatments. The most talked about of these treatments is the Watsu therapy (water shiatsu), a deep relaxation therapy that is performed in a special pool of warm water. Through gentle movement and acupressure, the body is stretched, glided and gracefully turned and floated by Mandala's experienced practitioners. The deeply relaxing effects of the warm water and nurturing support combine with the Watsu movements to unleash a range of therapeutic benefits and potential healing on many levels.

In the same way, couples can indulge in Watsu For Two, which could help deepen their connection as they learn to safely cradle and nurture each other in the soft comforts of the water.

Mandala Spa's myriad other offerings include the Ayurvedic Shodhana Karma cleansing ritual, Swedana de-stress massage and sauna combination, Thalasso scrub and seaweed bath, lymph drainage and pre-natal massages. Luxurious facial treatments such as the Royal Liquorice and Green Tea facial treatment by Pevonia also cater to the visage of guests and leave them feeling refreshed, invigorated

and wonderfully healed. Evidently, the vast menu draws on spa traditions from around the world as well as new and more cosmopolitan therapies.

To offer guests better value, various award-winning deluxe spa holidays were specially designed. These holiday packages include daily breakfast and dinner, daily yoga classes, and of course, wonderful spa treatments. Those seeking to rid themselves of accumulated toxins while losing weight can opt for the Cleansing and Detoxification Holiday package. Meanwhile, Mandala's Yoga Holidays allow guests to learn the intricacies of yoga practice in privacy and under the experienced guidance of certified instructors. Mandala's Wellness Holidays are the ideal environment for inner and outer renewal while the Rejuvenation Holiday lets guests revel in holistic beauty treatments freshly prepared specifically for each individual. Suffice to say, Mandala Spa's Holidays are crafted with attention to detail and care for everyone's unique needs.

To complement this holistic approach to well-being, Mandala Spa nourishes the appetites of guests by reinventing vegetarian cuisine. Its delectable menu was developed exclusively by its top chefs and boasts a symphony of flavours drawn from Mediterranean and Asian culinary traditions, they are a sheer pleasure to the taste buds. Indeed, time spent at Mandala Spa at Boracay is time indulged in the mind, body and soul.

| Mandala Spa sits elegantly on one of the most beautiful beaches in the world, Boracay's White Beach. || The suites ensure your stay is of the utmost comfort. ||| The balcony looks over the serene tropical hillside. |||| The treatment rooms are housed in traditional Filipino villas which are crafted from all natural materials. ||||| Watsu is a popular treatment at the Mandala Spa.

Spa Statistics

SPA AREA
2.5 hectares (6 acres)

FACILITIES
4 single or double indoor treatment villas, 2 shared indoor treatment pavilions; 1 meditation and yoga room; watsu pool and pavilion; 2 saunas, 1 spa boutique/library

SIGNATURE TREATMENT
Lymph Drainage Massage, Mandala Signature Massage, Pre-natal Massage, Shodhana Karma, Stone Magic Therapy, Thalasso Suite, Water Journey, Watsu for Two

OTHER TREATMENTS AND THERAPIES
Anti-ageing treatments, anti-cellulite treatments, aromatherapy, ayurveda, baths, body scrubs, body wraps, colonic irrigation and enemas, facial treatments, firming and slimming treatments, holistic treatments, hot and cold stone therapies, life coaching, lymphatic drainage massage, massages, pre- and post-natal treatments, reiki, thalassotherapy

PROVISIONS FOR COUPLES
Available

SPA CUISINE
Available at Prana Restaurant

ACTIVITIES
Life enhancement, lifestyle management, massage classes, meditation classes, talks by visiting consultants, yoga and monthly yoga retreats

SERVICES
Corporate programmes, day use rooms, free transfers to nearby towns and airport (during peak season months), gift certificates, nutrition consultations, personal training, private spa parties

MEMBERSHIP/ADMISSION
Not required

CONTACT
Boracay Island
Malay Aklan 5608
Philippines
T +63 36 288 5858
F +63 36 288 3531
E info@mandalaspa.com
W www.mandalaspa.com

The Angsana Spa Double Bay

SYDNEY, AUSTRALIA

The Angsana Spa takes its name from the statuesque Angsana Tree found in the tropical rainforests of Asia. Best known for its towering magnificence and crown of golden flowers, the Angsana embodies the maxim of living life and savouring time as it passes by inexorably. To that end, the Angsana Spa Double Bay exists like a wizened old tree in Sydney's urban jungle. Set in a 19th-century Victorian house, it exudes calm and the power of revitalisation through its treatments and careful décor.

Within the spa, Victorian architecture mingles with traditional Asian accents and contemporary interior design. This spirited juxtaposition of modern chic with old world grandeur has been successfully achieved through the use of authentic Asian artefacts that stand out against the signature Angsana Spa colours of lime and tangerine. When it opened in January 2003, the spa was the first to

introduce traditional Asian nourishing remedies in such a contemporary setting. The combination works; it was ranked among the top 10 'Overseas Urban Day Spas' in the prestigious *Cond Nast Traveller* Readers' Spa Awards 2004.

Managed and created by the award-winning Banyan Tree Spa, Angsana's treatments reflect its roots with holistic massages, beauty wraps and tropical scrubs using fresh botanicals and the ancient art of aromatherapy. Its therapeutic sense of touch and a fusion of techniques from both east and west refresh and invigorate the mind, body and spirit.

To get a taste of what's on Angsana's exquisite treatment menu, opt for its signature therapies that embody its renowned 'high-touch, low-tech' philosophy. One such example is the Empress Veil, a 60-minute facial treatment that uses ginseng to coax the glow out of dull, tired skin. In Java Jive, the

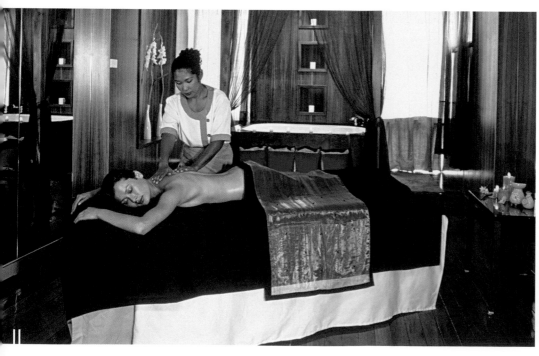

Javanese Lulur—Indonesia's best kept beauty secret and once the privilege of royalty—helps to buff away dead skin cells on the body to reveal fresh, new skin.

Created exclusively for the Angsana Spa, the deeply relaxing Angsana Massage combines slow, graceful palm strokes and thumb pressure at strategic pressure points to relieve tension and aid blood circulation. Specially blended Euphoria Oil that combines the extracts of ylang ylang and sweet basil is used to enhance the experience.

The wide range of beauty treatments is equally (and deliciously) irresistible. Using a fruity blend of papaya, tangerine and bananas, these treatments nourish and moisturize, unveiling beautifully calm skin and a radiant visage. Suffice it to say, all-natural ingredients are used extensively in each beauty and body treatment. Think cooling cucumber, honey, almond, yoghurt, milk, soybeans, aloe vera, ginger and sesame seed.

All of Angsana's 40 massages, body polishes, skin enhancers, facial treatments and fusion baths are performed by a team of dedicated therapists who have undergone more than 400 hours of training at the acclaimed Banyan Tree Spa Academy. You can take the experience away with you. Step into the charming Angsana Gallery where the spa's range of massage oils, floral-based essential oils and everything from fashion apparel to home furnishings, are on sale. Indeed, within the Gallery is a myriad of mementos of your time at the spa, that will help you sense the 'Angsana moment' even at home.

| The day spa is located in a Victorian house and the mix of old and new make a day at Angsana Double Bay a unique experience. || The Deluxe Double Therapy Room provides a perfect haven in which guests can luxuriate in treatments. ||| Hot compresses are used in massages to soothe warm oil over the body. |||| The décor in the treatment rooms is welcoming and warm with the signature tangerine tones of Angsana Spa. ||||| As part of the Essence of Angsana, guests can relax in a fusion bath, with nourishing ginseng, aromatic oatmeal or soothing jasmine tea leaves.

Spa Statistics

SPA AREA
150 sq m (1,615 sq ft)

FACILITIES
3 single indoor treatment rooms, 4 double indoor treatment room; foot reflexology area; relaxation lounge; spa bath, shower facilities, steam facilities; Angsana Spa Gallery

SIGNATURE TREATMENT
Angsana Massage, Empress Veil, Java Jive, Papaya Refresher

OTHER TREATMENTS AND THERAPIES
Aromatherapy, baths, body scrubs, body wraps, facial treatments, hand and foot treatments, Indonesian therapies, massages, Thai therapies, reflexology, pouch treatments

PROVISIONS FOR COUPLES
Java Jive, Serenity, Spirit, Deluxe Double Therapy Suite

SERVICES
Gift certificates

MEMBERSHIP/ADMISSION
Available but not required

CONTACT
15 Bay Street
Double Bay
Sydney
NSW 2028
Australia
T +612 9328 5501
F +612 9328 5517
E spa-doublebaysydney@angsana.com
W www.angsanaspa.com

Chuan Spa at Langham Hotel

MELBOURNE, AUSTRALIA

Set on the south bank of the Yarra River, the Langham Hotel, Melbourne sits in the heart of the city's cultural precinct. Within the Langham Hotel, Melbourne lies the Chuan Spa, a haven for contemplation, relaxation and renewal. The spa occupies two levels of the hotel and offers guests more than 40 speciality spa treatments inspired by the principles of traditional Chinese medicine.

Combining the finest traditions of the East and West, the spa's design was drawn from the idea of a Chinese garden, where men and women retreat from their everyday world into a place of calm. Accordingly its walls are lined with floral embossed panels of silk and intricate bamboo panels and its colour palette is soothingly warm. Meanwhile, clean lines, uncluttered furnishings and soft lighting evoke an ambience of calm.

In keeping with its Oriental roots, a feng shui master was consulted at the spa's conception. Thus, water features, smooth pebbles and curved hallways capture the elements of a natural landscape all in accordance with the ancient art of achieving harmony between humans and their surroundings.

Within its eight treatment rooms, guests can enjoy a myriad of services, from detox and deep relaxation treatments to jet-lag remedies and facial therapies. All the treatments on the menu are a nod to the pillars of traditional Chinese medicine—Wu Xing (the Five Elements), Yin and Yang, and Jing Luo (the Meridian System).

Chuan's holistic approach to well-being is best witnessed in its signature treatment called the Serenity Shen. This three-hour exclusive ritual transports guests to a dreamy state of relaxation with a nourishing stone therapy massage. The state of calm continues with a long soak in your private geisha tub before an indulgent facial mask of revitalizing cool marine algae is applied.

With the mind and body stilled and centred, an exquisite light meal is served. Comprising six delicate dishes—four savouries and two sweets—the meal is a taste sensation and the perfect end to the treatment.

Steam rooms, saunas, therapeutic snail showers, a conservatory covered pool and jacuzzi and an outdoor deck provide places for awakening after treatments, where mind and body can be restored and rebalanced. Furthermore, the Australian-made Chuan Spa private label products are available for sale as retail and gift items. This popular range of spa products was created in close consultation with a Chinese healthcare expert and comprise healing oils and body care products that smell as good as they feel.

Within Chuan Spa, the fitness centre offers 24 pieces of fitness equipment. Guests can enjoy a comprehensive full body workout with features such as a cardio theatre, eight televisions or simply taking in the Melbourne City skyline. The fitness floor located on level 10, offers passive classes including yoga, pilates, tai chi, and fitball.

| Asian touches dot the setting at Chuan, and a feng shui master has ensured that harmony abounds. || The stunning indoor pool affords fantastic views across the city which can be enjoyed during a relaxing swim. ||| The modern eclectic style is demonstrated in the spa's relaxation room. |||| Guests can take home signature Chuan products. ||||| The spa's sumptuous double treatment rooms are fully equipped and with impeccable style.

Spa Statistics

SPA AREA
1,060 sq m (11,410 sq ft) spa and health club

FACILITIES
1 double indoor treatment suite, 4 single indoor treatment rooms, 3 double indoor treatment rooms; 2 relaxation rooms; 2 snail showers, 1 Jacuzzi; 2 saunas, 2 steam rooms; 1 pedicure room, 1 manicure/make-up room; 1 gymnasium, 1 cardio theatre, 1 pilates studio; 1 indoor swimming pool, outdoor sun-deck

SIGNATURE TREATMENT
Serenity Shen

OTHER TREATMENTS AND THERAPIES
Anti-cellulite treatments, anti-ageing treatments, aromatherapy, baths, body scrubs, body wraps, Chinese therapies, facial treatments, firming and slimming treatments, hair treatments, hand and foot treatments, holistic treatments, hot stone therapies, hydrotherapy, jet-lag treatments, manicures/pedicures, massages, purifying back treatments, reflexology, salon services, scalp treatments, waxing

PROVISIONS FOR COUPLES
4 couple treatment rooms

SPA CUISINE
Available in spa, hotel restaurant and room service

ACTIVITIES
Aquaerobics, lifestyle management classes, martial arts, pilates, sports instruction, stretching classes, tai chi, talks by visiting consultants, yoga

SERVICES
Body composition analysis, corporate programmes, gift certificates, nutrition consultation, personal training, skincare consultation

MEMBERSHIP/ADMISSION
Available but not required

CONTACT
Langham Hotel, Melbourne
One Southgate Avenue
Southbank Victoria 3006
Australia
T +61 3 8696 8111
F +61 3 9690 6581
E mel.info@chuanspa.com
W www.chuanspa.com

Daintree Spa
at Daintree Eco Lodge & Spa

QUEENSLAND, AUSTRALIA

Set in the world's oldest living rainforest, in tropical North Queensland, the Daintree Eco Lodge & Spa pampers the environment as lavishly as it indulges its guests. This one-of-a-kind treehouse-style spa has won numerous worldwide accolades for its fantastic efforts to ensure that while giving its guests an unforgettable experience, it also cares for the impact it might have on its precious environment and the Indigenous people who live around it.

Cond Nast Traveller (UK) recently named it one of the Top 10 Spa Retreats of the World 2005. In 2004 it was awarded Best Spa Retreat in Australia and the South Pacific, and in 2003, it won two much coveted Australian Tourism Awards for Deluxe Accommodation and for Ecotourism.

Tucked away in a lush valley in the Daintree Rainforest, the Lodge and Spa sits adjacent to the majestic Daintree River, just 40 kilometres (25 miles) from Port Douglas, considered the gateway to the Great Barrier Reef. Here, 15 gorgeous 'hideaway' rainforest villas provide one of the world's most unique experiences of living within the lush beauty of nature's oldest gem.

The Lodge works closely with the Aboriginal Kuku Yalanji rainforest people to create experiences that acquaint guests with the intricacies, legends and traditions of their culture. This is carried through to the Daintree Spa's treatments which are best enjoyed at the spa's newly created waterfall pavilion. Simply called Gunya (the Yalanji word for shelter), the pavilion is nestled deep in the rainforest, in an area that is said to hold mystical healing powers. This spiritual area has been visited as a special place by the Kuku Yalanji women for thousands of years and today offers its essence to the spa treatments provided at Daintree Eco Lodge & Spa.

Daintree Spa's signature treatment, Walbul Walbul (which means 'butterfly') connects guests with the vibration of this ancient land by way of a warm oil and desert salt scrub. This is followed by a head treatment aptly called Milkanga Kaday (return to the mind), before the healing waters of a rain shower and a soothing massage unites the body with the sky. The treatment is likened to the brilliant transition of a caterpillar to a butterfly, which spreads its wings and soars when opened to nature.

Alongside the various spa treatments, the Kuku Yalanji guides offer insights on how their ancestors lived in harmony with nature. Dreamtime storytelling is perhaps the most unique method. Set in a clearing in the rainforest, and conducted in the early evening around a campfire, guests can listen to a telling of selected Dreamtime stories—always with the permission and approval of the Kuku Yalanji elders. The oldest folklore on earth, guests are connected to this special land in a truly unique way. As well, art workshops and cultural classes provide a glimpse into this ancient Aboriginal culture in a relaxed, interactive and non-contrived way.

A celebration of the rainforest, of its Indigenous people and the concept of well-being all mix to create a truly enriching experience. At the Daintree Eco Lodge & Spa, the unpolluted air is replete with oxygen; bands of pure sunlight filter through the thick canopy of trees; and the sounds and smells of clear running water are a constant reminder of how far back to nature you've come. The realization itself is intoxicating. As Brooke Shields succinctly put it: "To wake up in this rainforest is heaven on earth."

| The spa's ochre back treatment. || The 15 treehouse villas and restaurant have been built to complement their surroundings. ||| The waterfall where the Gunya spa (meaning shelter) is situated. It is the most spiritual area at the Lodge. |||| The superbly equipped spa offers all kinds of therapies. The rain shower is just one of them. ||||| Guests can enjoy a soak in their own private Jacuzzi amongst the treetops.

Spa Statistics

SPA AREA
200 sq m (2,150 sq ft)

FACILITIES
3 single indoor treatments rooms, 1 double indoor treatment room, 1 outdoor treatment pavilion, 1 waterfall treatment pavilion; 1 consultation room; 1 meditation room, 2 relaxation rooms; 1 Jacuzzi; 2 sun beds; pilates area; 1 swimming pool under cover; 1 spa boutique, library

SIGNATURE TREATMENT
Walbul Walbul

OTHER TREATMENTS AND THERAPIES
Anti-cellulite treatment, aromatherapy, Bach flower remedies, baths, body scrubs, body wraps, facial treatments, hair treatments, hand and foot treatments, holistic treatments, homeopathy, hydrotherapy, iridology, jet-lag treatments, lymphatic drainage massage, make-up services, manicures/pedicures, massages, naturotherapy consultations, purifying back treatments, reflexology, scalp treatments (salon services and some other treatments must be booked in advance)

PROVISIONS FOR COUPLES
Available

SPA CUISINE
Available

ACTIVITIES
Aboriginal art and culture classes, Aboriginal fishing and hunting tours, aquaerobics, cooking demonstrations, dreamtime storytelling, four-wheel safari drives, hiking, horseback riding, interpretive Aboriginal rainforest walk, jungle surfing, life coach counselling, life enhancement classes, lifestyle management classes, meditation classes, pilates, scuba diving, snorkelling, stretching classes, talks by visiting consultants. (Please contact the Lodge prior to arrival to arrange.)

SERVICES
Babysitting, body composition analysis consultations, childcare, corporate programmes, day use rooms, free transfers to nearby village, general healthcare consultations, gift certificates, nutrition consultation, personal training, private spa parties, skincare consultation. (Please contact the Lodge prior to arrival to arrange.)

MEMBERSHIP/ADMISSION
Not required

CONTACT
20 Daintree Road, Daintree
Queensland 4873
Australia
T +617 4098 6100
F +617 4098 6200
E info@daintree-ecolodge.com.au
W www.daintree-ecolodge.com.au/spastyleasia

Hush Spa

QUEENSTOWN, NEW ZEALAND

Queenstown, New Zealand has often been described as one of the most beautiful places on earth. It is rich with nature, magnificent with looming mountains and blessed with invigoratingly fresh air all year round. Aptly, Queenstown is now home to one of New Zealand's new premier day spas, which opened in November 2003.

Hush Spa, a boutique day spa facility, is situated on the mid-level of a three-storey building adjacent to Home Creek. Majestic snow-capped mountains surround the area, and through Hush's windows, guests can glimpse trout and native birds that call this rustic area home.

Step through its doors and Hush's soothing lighting signals a respite from the rigours of daily life. The soft hues of warming beige set the ambience for a pure haven of relaxation and well-being. As well, the strains of soft music, especially chosen for its healing sounds, calm the senses, helping guests to unwind almost as soon as they enter.

Once centred, guests are welcome to sip on a glass of fresh nectarine juice or a cup of soothing herbal tea, and choose from the vast array of spa treatments that include body and beauty therapies, massages, and facial treatments.

Hush Spa is owned by a local mother-and-daughter team Jan Butson and Amy Green, and their spa was created after five years of intensive research. The duo welcomed internationally qualified therapist Jenny Hodgson to the team and together they created a place that takes its lead "from some of the most exclusive spas in the world".

Hush's facial treatments are proving extremely popular. Each treatment begins with a skincare consultation so that the therapy can be customized to suit each individual's skin's needs. Best examples include the signature facial which aims to relax and rest the mind and The Hydradermie Lift Deluxe, which uses gentle microcurrent massages and targets unwanted wrinkles.

Not to be left out, the spa also specializes in a range of treatments for men. These include deep cleansing facials, aroma stone therapy and grooming services, such as male-centric manicures and sports pedicures, as well as waxing.

One treatment that appeals to both men and women alike is Hush's Seaweed Infusion Body Wrap. Excellent for treating aches and pains picked up on the nearby ski slopes, the treatment entails being slathered in a mixture of dried seaweed extract and essential oils. Guests are then cocooned in a special foil wrap and covered with blankets to allow the heat to draw those nasty toxins from the body. While you steep, a soothing mask is placed over the eyes and a blissful scalp and foot massage administered.

Also available at Hush is the comprehensive make-up service. Sessions include the Personalized Make-Up Application and the Professional Make-Up Lesson. And for that special day, brides are catered for with make-up trials and on the day services. Hush is a truly one-stop spa for beauty and well-being.

Should guests get hungry, a menu of freshly prepared salads, meats, deli meals and condiments, fresh fruit and vegetables are available, and can be taken in the comfort of Hush's relaxation rooms or at the nearby Mediterranean Market café. Hush also boasts its own boutique so guests can take home some of their favourite products from the spa.

| The spa welcomes you with its soft and welcoming tones and offers five-star pampering in an exclusive yet homely environment. || A soak in the vast and deep bath is a welcome completion to any massage. ||| Massages at Hush vary from Swedish style to a deep tissue, from chakra balancing to Aroma Stone therapy. |||| The spa is well equipped for well-being and beauty treatments; pedicures are a speciality. ||||| Manicures are available for both men and women. |||||| Stylish details decorate the spa and attention has been given to every detail.

Spa Statistics

SPA AREA
182 sq m (1,960 sq ft)

FACILITIES
4 single indoor treatment rooms, 1 double indoor treatment room, 1 wet treatment room; 2 relaxation rooms; 1 Kohler "Sok" Overflowing Bath; 1 steam room; 1 vertical tanner; 4 hair salon stations, 2 manicure stations, 3 pedicure stations; spa boutique

SIGNATURE TREATMENT
Hush Pure Relaxation Facial

OTHER TREATMENTS AND THERAPIES
Anti-ageing treatments, anti-cellulite treatments, body bronzing, body scrubs, body wraps, bust treatments, eye treatments, facial treatments, slimming treatments, jet-lag treatments, make-up services, manicures/pedicures, massages, pre- and post-natal treatments, purifying back treatments, reflexology, salon services and waxing.

PROVISIONS FOR COUPLES
Available

SPA CUISINE
Available in spa relaxation rooms or at Mediterranean Market café

SERVICES
Gift certificates, private spa parties

MEMBERSHIP/ADMISSION
Not required

CONTACT
Level Two - The Junction
Corner Gorge & Robins Road
Queenstown 9197
New Zealand
T +64 3 409 0901
F +64 3 409 0902
E relax@hushspa.co.nz
W www.hushspa.co.nz

Spa du Vin

POKENO, NEW ZEALAND

Just 45 minutes away from Auckland, this ultra romantic hideaway is set on a sprawling vineyard, surrounded by lush native bush alongside a gorgeous green valley. Its spa, arguably New Zealand's most unique wellness centre, is a clever fusion of East and West, and where Balinese-style interiors and treatments meet western technology and cuisine.

Only recently opened in 2004, Spa du Vin was created to cater to every individual need, with brand new technologies never before available in New Zealand, such as the NeoQi Cocoon. Using the natural healing properties of water and minerals, this unique hydrotherapy treatment offers customized body therapy programmes that are administered using the unique equipment that creates a snug and safe cocoon-like environment.

And to keep up with the growing trend of male spa enthusiasts, Spa du Vin offers a menu of services designed specifically for men. The Male Fitness treatment encompasses a deep tissue body massage using a special oil to warm the muscles and relieve built up tension. This is followed by a maintenance facial designed to relieve sensitivity and prevent ingrown hairs caused by shaving.

Pregnant mothers also get special treatment here. A gentle and nurturing ritual called Pregnancy Perfect assists in restoring the emotional and physical well-being with a softening body polish and conditioning full body mask. This safe and effective treatment also helps prevent and treat scar tissue and stretch marks.

The spa is completely flexible and guests are free to choose their own massage combination. Swedish, sports, aromatherapy and lymphatic massages can be combined with any Sodashi oil. The choice of which includes: balancing, energizing, serenity, fitness or a vitamin rich massage oil. With such choice all needs are certainly catered for.

Within easy reach of Auckland, the Spa offers stopover options that encompass one- or two-night stays and a VIP Prescription. That means spa treatments and meals that have been tailor-made for each individual need. Guests can enjoy the Relaxation Break. This one-day package is a journey of exquisite spa therapies that are prescribed to

| The spa, at Hotel du Vin, is surrounded by glorious vineyards. || Nestled in the gardens, the buildings are unobtrusive and meld into the landscape. ||| Unsurprisingly, both food and wine are of exceptional quality. |||| Asian décor is dotted around the spa. ||||| The elegant treatment rooms come equipped with showers. |||||| The luxurious and stylish lounge offers space for relaxation.

specific skin types. The day starts with a gentle steam and continues with a choice of body scrub. With the body prepared a wrap is prescribed to the skin's needs. Guests can enjoy this whilst the scalp is massaged. Midway, a light yet satisfying lunch is served using only the freshest ingredients cooked in simple, clean flavours. After lunch, a nourishing facial treatment and relaxing massage completes the experience, leaving guests to rebalance their senses in the spa's relaxation and serenity area.

At night, guests can retire to their luxurious accommodations that are set amidst the emerald vineyards. Dining options include the hotel's intimate Vineyard Restaurant or a picnic on the banks of the crystal clear stream can be arranged. The seasonal menu offers only the best in local and imported ingredients, with a strong focus on flavours that allow the freshness of the produce to shine through. All said and done, the Spa du Vin experience offers unsurpassed luxury in the vineyards—this is an unforgettable wellness retreat that will leave you coming back for more.

Spa Statistics

TYPE OF SPA
Resort spa

SPA AREA
500 sq m (5,380 sq ft)

FACILITIES
7 single indoor treatment rooms, 1 double indoor treatment room; consultation room; relaxation room; 2 Jacuzzis; 2 steam rooms; 2 nail salon stations; cardio studio, pilates studio; indoor swimming pool; 3 tennis courts; library

SIGNATURE TREATMENTS
Body Sculpting in NeoQi Cocoon, Thermal Regenerative Facial, Sodashi Signature Body Massage, Pregnancy Perfect

OTHER TREATMENTS AND THERAPIES
Anti-aging treatments, anti-cellulite treatments, aqua therapy, aromatherapy, baths, body bronzing, body wraps, eye treatments, facial treatments, firming and slimming, hand and foot treatments, hydrotherapy, lymphatic drainage, manicures/pedicures, massages, pre- and post-natal treatments, salon services, scalp treatments, waxing

PROVISIONS FOR COUPLES
1 couples-only therapy room

SPA CUISINE
Available at the Spa Café or in the Vineyard Restaurant

ACTIVITIES
Archery, biking, claypigeon shooting, croquet, golf, horse riding, hiking, kayaking, life enhancement classes, petanque, pilates, talks by visiting consultants, tennis, 12 hectares (30 acres of vineyards for walking)

SERVICES
Babysitting, childcare, body composition analysis, skincare analysis, corporate programmes, day use rooms, gift certificates, personal training

MEMBERSHIP/ADMISSION
Not required

CONTACT
Lyons Road R.D.1
Pokeno, New Zealand
T +64 9 233 6780
F +64 9 233 6781
E spa@duvin.co.nz
W www.spaduvin.co.nz

Hideaway Spa by Mandara at Island Hideaway Spa Resort and Marina

MALDIVES

Set on the Maldivian island of Dhonakulhi, which measures some 23½ hectares (58 acres), the exclusive Island Hideaway Spa Resort and Marina is magnificence redefined. The entire lagoon, with its glittering emerald waters, is the private domain of its guests; and its guest villa complexes are the largest of any resort in the Maldives. Still, despite its extensive facilities and services, The Island Hideaway takes up barely five per cent of the island and lagoon, leaving the remaining 95 per cent in its original state, untouched by the human hand.

Tucked away in the lush foliage of the island or scattered along the pristine beach, the Island Hideaway's majestic chalets each boast jaw-droppingly beautiful panoramic views of the Indian Ocean. At the heart of this exquisite boutique resort is the Hideaway Spa, operated by the internationally acclaimed spa and wellness company, Mandara Spa. Here, design emphasis has been placed on space,

privacy and luxury, accompanied by a level of service that pays extraordinary attention to delivering unobtrusive pampering.

Fittingly, its spa menu was created to match its exclusive nature. Combining traditional Asian favourites with Elemis Spa therapy, the treatments reflect the themes of the ocean, nature and indigenous Maldivian traditions. Massages, facial treatments, body wraps, detox treatments and body scrubs were all created using Elemis products combined with natural ingredients such as milk, coconut, seaweed, ginger, salt and clay. These signature treatments soothe, revitalize and invigorate the body leaving guests basking in an afterglow of serene contentment.

Also unique to The Island Hideaway are the Spa Water Villas that are the first of its kind in the Maldives, and quite possibly, the world. Perched on wooden stilts above the shallow, crystal clear waters

of the lagoon, these timber deck villas encompass their own private ocean-view treatment room, steam room, outdoor 'hanging' Jacuzzi whirlpool, sundeck, lagoon access and complete in-villa spa treatment facilities. In these villas, the spa comes to you, with the full menu at your service, administered by a dedicated team of spa specialists.

Two Lagoon Spa Pavilions and four expansive Spa Land Villas are also available for the unbeatable private spa experience—the Pavilions come with an outdoor terrazzo dip pool, while the Land Villas boast handcrafted bathtubs built romantically for two. From here guests can enjoy the wonderfully exotic tropical fruit from the spa's fruit bar.

After your wonderfully relaxing treatments, the sea below offers superb diving opportunities. There are at least 20 untouched dive sites for you to explore, always in the capable hands of the resort's trained and experienced dive masters. Open to everyone, from beginners to experienced divers, a trip under the ocean is an absolute must.

At the end of the day head to the Hideaway's Matheefaru restaurant to sample true Maldivian cuisine. With the sea right at its doorstep, it is no surprise that a great deal of the menu focuses on the freshest catches of the day. Then lounge at the private beach at sunset with a mocktail in hand and watch the darkness smudge dusk away into night. Indeed, life should always be this good.

| The Hideaway Palaces are the epitome of privacy and luxury. Raised on wooden decks, the views are breathtaking. || The resort's private beach is the perfect setting to enjoy the spa treatments. ||| One of the Jasmine Garden Villas, complete with swimming pool and private beach area, offers a place entirely your own. |||| From inside the luxury villas, the beach entices you outside. ||||| The Hideaway Spa by Mandara aims to provide an outstanding spa experience every time.

Spa Statistics

SPA AREA
235 square metres (2,500 sq ft)

FACILITIES
4 double indoor treatment villas each with private steam shower, 2 Lagoon Spa Pavilions, 2 Spa Water Villas, with Jacuzzi

SIGNATURE TREATMENT
Massage Rituals

OTHER TREATMENTS AND THERAPIES
Aromatherapy, Ayurveda, body scrubs, body wraps, Chinese therapies, facial treatments, hot stone therapies, manicures/pedicures, massages, movement therapies, reflexology, Thai therapies

PROVISIONS FOR COUPLES
6 double indoor treatment villas

ACTIVITIES
Silat

MEMBERSHIP/ADMISSION
Not required

CONTACT
Island Hideaway at Dhonakulhi, Maldives,
Spa Resort & Marina
2nd floor, (East Wing), Aage
12 Boduthakurufaanu Magu, Henveiru
Male 20094, Maldive Islands
T +960 650 15 15
F +960 650 16 16
E mandaraspa@island-hideaway.com
W www.mandaraspa.com/www.island-hideaway.com

The Island Spa at Four Seasons Resort at Kuda Huraa

MALDIVES

The journey to The Island Spa begins the moment guests step aboard The Four Seasons Resort's spa dhoni, a traditional Maldivian wooden boat. As it glides across the turquoise waters towards the private island of Huraa Fundhu, its gentle motion soothes your spirit, while the balmy breezes whisper against the skin.

Upon arrival at the spa jetty, guests stroll along a gorgeous wooden deck lined with thick rope rails. This leads to the breathtaking lounge pavilion, where jaws often drop at the impressive sight of an expansive white cloth tent rising seven metres from the ground. Billowing curtains lend an air of romance to the surroundings while the enticing scent of sandalwood wafts through the air.

The Island Spa menu is elegantly simple. Guests can choose from Ayurvedic, Maldivian, Thai and Indonesian body elixirs, scrubs, massages, facial treatments and salon treatments. A tribute to the surrounding ocean, the spa's innovative treatments celebrate the power of marine elements.

Signature treatments like the Tropical Glow sees seawater crystals blended with mandarin, neroli and palmarosa essential oils to stimulate and condition the skin. A revitalizing fresh lime rinse and nourishing ocean body milk skin application completes this treatment.

For a more native experience, the Maldivian Monsoon Ritual begins with a Kela Gana, or ground sandalwood body scrub. This is followed by a soothing simulation of a gentle monsoon rain (by way of a Vichy shower) falling on the skin. A refreshing rosewater rinse then creates a meditative experience, while a restorative warm herbal oil massage nourishes and detoxifies the nervous system. The indulgent ritual continues with a relaxing

Spa Statistics

SPA AREA
502 sq m (5,380 sq ft)

FACILITIES
5 double indoor treatment villas; medical consultation room; relaxation lounge; 5 steam rooms; 2 hair salon stations, 2 nail salon stations; spa boutique; library

SIGNATURE TREATMENT
Aloe & Lavender, Maldivian Monsoon Ritual, Oceanic Ritual, Tropical Glow

OTHER TREATMENTS AND THERAPIES
Aromatherapy, Ayurveda, body scrubs, body wraps, facial treatments, hair treatments, Indonesian therapies, make-up services, manicures/pedicures, massages, reflexology, salon services, Thai therapies, waxing

PROVISIONS FOR COUPLES
Available

SPA CUISINE
Not available
Provisions for dietary requirements available upon request

ACTIVITIES
Beach walks, cooking classes, fishing and fish talks, meditation classes, nature walks, parasailing, sailing, scuba diving, snorkelling, sports instruction, surfing, yoga, yoga talks

SERVICES
Babysitting, childcare, day use rooms, gift certificates, personal training, private spa parties (by request and subject to availability)

MEMBERSHIP/ADMISSION
For Resort guests only

CONTACT
Four Seasons Resort Maldives
North Male Atoll
Republic of Maldives
T +960 6644 888 ext 20
F +960 6644 800
E spa.maldives@fourseasons.com
W www.fourseasons.com/maldives

steam bath before a frankincense sandalwood body lotion brings the treatment to a close.

All treatments are taken in one of five pavilions perched at the edge of the private island's white-sanded beach. Designed with couples in mind, they include separate bathing and treatment pavilions, each topped by natural grass thatched roofs and lined with dark timber floorboards.

The overall ambience is perhaps best described as an eclectic mix of design influences from India and Morocco. The Island Spa's soothing colour palette of sand, turquoise and cream complement the wooden floor decking and heavy textured walls. Arabic design accents on doorways, walls, furniture and accessories lend an enigmatic flavour to the atmosphere, matched by fish motifs on lamps, heavy roping wrapped around table legs and aromatic burners which truly extend the sensory experience.

The Spa's staff were specially chosen for their multi-cultural expertise in the native healing arts of their respective homelands. Their hands-on knowledge and dedication are matched by The Island Spa's signature product line that draws from the best of the ocean and its rich, natural bounty of healing elements. These are then fused with natural herbs and spices of the surrounding lands to complement every exquisite treatment available here.

When your Island Spa experience is complete, stroll back onto the dhoni that brought you here and return to Four Seasons Resort Maldives at Kuda Huraa. There, the pampering experience continues, with unbeatable service, beautiful surrounds and activities that will fuel memories for a lifetime.

| Arrival at The Spa is by dhoni—a traditional Maldivian wooden boat—which ensures a magical and unique experience right from the start. || The monsoon treatment entails a healing rain shower just above the beautiful waters of the Maldives. ||| The spa pavilion where couples can enjoy the ultimate spa experience whilst overlooking the ocean outside. |||| Massages can best be enjoyed outside in the fresh air with the soft sounds of the waves lapping at the shore. ||||| Yoga is an important part of the well-being programme.

Six Senses Spa
at Soneva Fushi Resort

MALDIVES

On the privately owned tropical island of Kunfunadhoo in the Baa Atoll of the Maldives hides the Soneva Fushi Resort & Six Senses Spa. Blessed with crystal clear waters and lush vegetation, this stylish hideaway is the perfect spot to get away from it all while getting in touch with yourselves and with nature.

Its über luxurious cabins are scattered strategically along the beach. Each is tucked into its own slice of verdant greenery, thus ensuring unbridled privacy to do whatever you will.

Also within this exclusive property is the award-winning Six Senses Spa. Enter its doors and a water passage strewn with smooth stepping stones greets you. The spa has a 'no shoe' policy, so whatever your bare feet touch within these walls are surely exquisite sensory experiences unto themselves. Sip a glass of herbal tea or fresh fruit juice as you decide on your choice of treatment from the spa's extensive menu. If you can't decide, the spa offers consultations with its highly trained therapists to help you select what would best suit your needs.

A particular favourite is the Maldivian Treatment. Cool, wet sand is used to exfoliate the skin before an acupressure treatment focuses on the body's energy meridians. Pure coconut oil is then applied to soften the skin before guests return to their plush cabins to face the rest of the blissfully lazy day.

Equally exquisite and certainly more exotic is the Planet Earth Core Treatment. This holistic face and body treat is a nod to the healing wisdom of ancient Arabia and is unique to Six Senses Spas. It begins with an exfoliation and wrap, both of which draw upon the healing powers of nature-flower poultices, energized water and mineral rich clays-to replenish and renew. A special massage follows using a fabulous blend of oils that contain precious gems like ruby, emerald, sapphire and diamond. Recognizing that every individual has his or her own unique needs, the blend of massage oil is determined based on a consultation when guests first enter the spa.

In keeping with their holistic approach to well-being, Soneva Fushi boasts an excellent spa menu that is based on the produce grown in its own

Spa Statistics

SPA AREA
800 sq m (8,600 sq ft)

FACILITIES
2 single indoor treatments villas, 2 double indoor treatment villas, 1 outdoor treatment pavilion; 1 Ayurvedic consultation room; 1 relaxation room; 1 watsu pool/room, 1 Jacuzzi, 1 plunge pool; 1 sauna, 1 steam room; 1 gymnasium, 1 tennis court, 1 spa boutique, library

SIGNATURE TREATMENT
In Villa Bath Menu, Maldivian Treatment, The Sensory Spa Journey

OTHER TREATMENTS AND THERAPIES
Anti-ageing treatments, anti-cellulite treatments, Ayurveda, baths, body scrubs, body wraps, facial treatments, firming and slimming treatments, hand and foot treatments, holistic treatments, hot stone therapies, Indonesian therapies, jet-lag treatments, manicures/pedicures, reflexology, scalp treatments, Thai therapies, waxing

PROVISIONS FOR COUPLES
Massage Workshop, Romantic Getaway package, Jungle Champa Pavilion

SPA CUISINE
Available in-villa and at all resort restaurants

ACTIVITIES
Sailing, scuba diving, snorkelling, spinning, tai chi, tennis, yoga, cooking classes, massage workshops, meditation classes, nailcare classes, sports instruction, stretching classes, talks by visiting consultants

SERVICES
Body composition analysis, day use rooms, general healthcare consultations, nutrition consultations, personal butler service, skin care consultations

MEMBERSHIP/ADMISSION
Not required

CONTACT
Kunfunadhoo Island
Baa Atoll
Republic of Maldives
T +960 660 0304
F +960 660 0374
E spa@sonevafushi.com.mv
W www.sixsenses.com

organic garden. Sup on island grown leaves with mustard marinated potatoes and goats cheese, dressed with crème fraiche and herbs. Hearty main dishes include the likes of penne pasta in a creamy blue cheese sauce and sautéed morning glory, as well as ratatouille of tomato, courgette and basil served with a morel mushroom cous cous and tomato-oregano sauce.

Naturally, meals can be taken in the privacy of your villa, with all kinds of cuisines, such as Ayurvedic, wheat-free, detoxifying and vegetarian, easily available. When your appetites are satiated, lie back in A Sense Of Guilt. Meaning lie back in a hot chocolate bath soak that comes with a mug of iced chocolate to drink as a decadent dessert.

| Each private villa comes complete with its own pool. || The spa lobby welcomes its guests with soft and inviting candlelight tones. ||| The suites blend in perfectly with the surrounding environment. |||| Tai chi is just one of the holistic activities available. ||||| The Sensory Spa Journey, the Six Senses Spas' signature treatment that includes a four-hand massage.

Six Senses Spa at Soneva Gili Resort

MALDIVES

Set on the private tropical island of Lankanfushi, just a 10-minute boat ride away from Male, is the Soneva Gili Resort & Six Senses Spa. The first of its kind in the Maldives, the resort features villas that are elegantly perched over the glittering sapphire lagoon. Indeed, seeing it for the first time from the outside makes for a brilliant sight.

At the spa, personal and unique journeys are tailored for each guest through holistic healings and a philosophy of balancing the senses. Expect the unexpected here, as even a massage is an utterly new and sensual experience. Beneath its massage tables are glass floor panels. This means that while luxuriating under the knowing hands of the spa's experienced therapists, guests can gaze at the soothing visionary feast of tropical fish in the waters below. Otherwise, look out to the uninterrupted views of the waters breaking over the sparkling coral reefs. With sights like these and the attention to detail, it's no wonder the spa has been awarded the prize for Best Spa Ambience in *Spa Asia* magazine's 2004 Spa Asia Crystal Awards.

Delightfully unique and natural treatments abound. The Six Senses Spa signature treatment, The Sensory Spa Journey, is one such example, promising an experience that continues long after guests leave. The five senses are piqued and harmonized through various stages—the Journey begins with a luxurious footbath and renewing skin treats to whet the sensory appetite for more exquisite things to come. Two therapists then work in tandem using long, smooth strokes that are synchronized with a cleansing facial and stress reliving massage. The natural desire to concentrate on the treatment soon vanishes, as the immensely pleasurable sequence of multiple hands on pressure points encourages the mind to let go of stress and induces a deep state of calm. When this complete mind-and-body encounter comes to a close, guests are presented with a special memento lovingly

handcrafted by workers of the Mae Fah Luang Foundation (an organization dedicated to promoting handicrafts of the hill tribes) in Thailand.

Couples are treated at the Six Senses Spa with various packages that encompass a four-night stay at the amazing resort. Mornings are spent using the spa's facilities, relaxing in the sauna or herbal steam room before soaking in the benefits of an intimate hydro bath. This is followed by a full body massage in the private Couples Suite and finishes with a revitalizing body treatment that includes an exfoliation and mask.

Massage workshops are also available to teach basic Swedish massage strokes over two guided sessions. Those more interested in advanced techniques can participate in a four-session master class to pick up unique and useful massage skills.

With the skills learnt at these classes, guests can then retire to their over-water cabins to test their flare for endowing pleasure on their appreciative partners. What better place to do this in, than the haven of romance that is Soneva Gili.

| As the plane arrives, the beauty of Soneva Gili immediately reveals itself. || The luxury villas sit over the sparkling ocean. ||| The spa sits magestically on the waters. |||| Making good use of the environment, one of the spa's treatments involves an exfoliating sand scrub. ||||| Massages are skilfully administered by the spa's qualified therapists.

Spa Statistics

SPA AREA
636 sq m (6,850 sq ft)

FACILITIES
10 indoor treatment rooms, 1 outdoor treatment room; 1 consultation champa; 1 chiller room, 1 relaxation area; 1 sauna, 2 steam rooms; 1 over-water gymnasium, yoga champa; 1 swimming pool, 1 tennis court; library

SIGNATURE TREATMENT
Pathfinder, Planet Earth Core Treatment, Polarity Therapy, The Sensory Spa Journey

OTHER TREATMENTS AND THERAPIES
Anti-ageing treatments, aromatherapy, Ayurveda, baths, body scrubs, body wraps, facials, firming and slimming treatments, hand and foot treatments, holistic therapies, hot stone therapies, Indonesian therapies, jet-lag treatments manicures/pedicures, massages, purifying back treatments, reflexology, scalp treatments, Thai therapies, waxing

PROVISIONS FOR COUPLES
Ever Soneva So Relaxing Package, massage workshop, Romance Package, Detox Revival Package

SPA CUISINE
Available upon request

ACTIVITIES
Biking, board games, boules, canoeing, cooking classes, jogging, massage workshops, meditation classes, nailcare classes, life coaching counselling, lifestyle management classes, sailing, scuba diving, snorkelling, tai chi, talks by visiting consultants, tennis, windsurfing and hobiecat, yoga

SERVICES
Babysitting, childcare, personal butler service, private spa parties, skincare consultations

MEMBERSHIP/ADMISSION
Not required

CONTACT
Lankanfushi Island
North Male Atoll
Republic of Maldives
T +960 664 0304
F +960 664 0305
E spa@sonevagili.com.mv
W www.sixsenses.com

Spa Speak

A glossary of common spa, treatment and fitness terms. Variations may be offered, so it's best to check with the respective spas when you make your booking.

Abyhanga Ayurvedic gentle, rhythmic massage in which therapists work warm oil into the body to help enhance the body's immune system and encourage the removal of accumulated toxins.

Acupoints Points along the meridian channels where the life force—qi (Chinese), prana (Indian) and ki (Japanese)—accumulates. Also known as sên (Thai).

Acupressure Application of fingertip (and sometimes palm, elbow, knee and foot) pressure on the body's acupoints to improve the flow of qi throughout the body, release muscle tension and promote healing.

Acupuncture Ancient Chinese healing technique in which fine needles are inserted into acupoints along the body's meridians to maintain health and correct any imbalance that causes illness.

Aerobics Fitness routine that involves a series of rhythmic exercises usually performed to music. Promotes cardiovascular fitness, improves the body's use of oxygen, burns calories and increases endurance.

Aerobics studio Area used for floor exercises.

Affusion shower massage Massage given as you lie under a relaxing, rain-like, warm shower of water or seawater. Increases blood circulation.

After-sun treatment Treatment that soothes skin that has been over-exposed to the sun, and cools the over-heated body. Treatment may include a cooling bath and a gentle massage with a lotion of soothing ingredients such as cucumber and aloe vera.

Aikido Japanese martial art that uses techniques such as locks and throws, and focuses on using the opponent's own energy against himself.

Alexander Technique Therapy developed by Australian F M Alexander in the 1890s that retrains you to stand and move in an optimally balanced way. Helps reduce physical and psychological problems brought on by bad posture.

Algotherapy Use of algae in treatments such as baths, scrubs, wraps and skin care.

Anapanasati Mind Training Meditation practise that involves breathing exercises that promote greater consciousness of the body, mind and spirit to maximize efficiency, and calm and clear the mind to find peace and happiness.

Anti-cellulite treatment Treatment that contours the body and reduces cellulite at various parts of the body.

Anti-stress massage Typically a 30-minute introductory massage, or one for those with limited time and who suffer from high levels of stress. Focuses on tension areas such as the back, face, neck and shoulders.

Aquaerobics Aerobic exercises performed in a swimming pool where the water provides support and resistance to increase stamina, and stretch and strengthen muscles.

Aquamedic pool Pool with specially positioned therapeutic jets for benefits such as relaxation and improving muscle tone.

Aromatherapy Ancient healing art that dates back to 4,500 BC. Refers to the use of essential oils from plants and flowers in treatments such as facials, massages, body wraps, foot baths and hydrobaths.

Aromatherapy massage Massage in which essential oils—either pre-blended or specially mixed for your needs—are applied to the body, typically applied with Swedish massage techniques.

Asanas Yoga postures.

Ashtanga A fast-paced form of yoga.

Aura An electromagnetic field or subtle body of energy believed to surround each living thing. Traditionally thought of as oval in shape and comprising seven layered bands. Its colour, shape, size and action are believed to reflect your physical, emotional, psychological and spiritual well-being.

Ayurveda Holistic system of healing in India that encompasses diet, massage, exercise and yoga.

Ayurvedic massage Massage performed by one or more therapists directly on the skin to loosen the excess doshas. Promotes circulation, increases flexibility, and relieves pain and stiffness. Applied with herbal oil.

Baby massage Infant massage that focuses on the special needs of newborns. Relaxes, improves circulation and relieves common infant ailments. Nurtures and bonds when performed by the infant's parent.

Bach Flower Therapies 38 flower remedies, each associated with specific negative feelings and emotions, developed by Dr Edward Bach in the 1930s. The remedies are derived from solarized flowers that work on a vibrational level to effect emotional change. Flower therapies are also known as flower essences.

Back treatment Deep cleansing skin treatment for the back, neck and shoulders that removes impurities and excess oils, eases tension, and leaves the skin soft and smooth. Also known as clarifying back treatment or purifying back treatment.

Balinese boreh Traditional warming Balinese mask made from herbs and spices which improve circulation and skin suppleness. The paste is lightly applied to the body, which is then wrapped in a blanket. The spices produce a sensation of deep heat.

Balinese coffee scrub Exfoliating scrub in which finely ground Balinese coffee beans are applied to the skin.

Balinese massage Relaxing traditional massage of Bali that uses rolling, long strokes, and finger and palm pressure. Applied with oil.

Balneotherapy Water treatments that use hot springs, mineral water or seawater to improve circulation, restore and revitalize the body, and relieve pain and stress. Also an invigorating, re-mineralizing treatment for muscles that uses water jets and a localized massage in a tub with a special hose administered by a therapist.

Bath Soaking or cleansing the body in water that is typically infused with salt, flowers, minerals or essential oils. May serve as a prelude to, or conclude a treatment.

Bikram Hot yoga, where yoga is practised in a room heated to 29°C–38°C (84°F–100°F).

Blisswork Deep tissue exercise that lengthens the body and seeks to restore it to its original design.

Blitz shower Standing body massage in which a high-pressure shower jet is directed at the body or specific parts of the body by a therapist who is about 3 metres (10 feet) away. Has a deep massaging effect, which increases circulation. Also known as douche au jet, jet blitz or jet massage.

Beauty treatment Treatment provided by spas to enhance beauty and overall well-being. Includes facial treatments, makeovers, manicures, pedicures and waxing.

Body bronzing Tanning treatment without the sun. May begin with a scrub to smooth the skin, which allows for an even tan.

Body composition analysis Evaluation of lean body mass to determine the percentage of body fat for the purpose of tailoring a nutrition and exercise programme.

Body mask Regenerating treatment in which the body is slathered with clay. The minerals in the clay—which may be mixed with essential oils—detoxify and hydrate the skin, leaving it radiant.

Body scrub Exfoliating body treatment, using products such as salt or herbs, that removes dry, dead skin cells and improves blood circulation. Scrubs soften the skin and give it a healthier glow. They are often used for preparing the skin to receive the benefits of massages and wraps. Also known as body polish.

Body treatment General term that denotes treatments for the body.

Body wrap Treatment in which the body is wrapped in linen, soaked in a herbal solution for about 20 minutes, and sometimes kept under a heated blanket. May be preceded by an application of fruit, herbs, mud or seaweed, and accompanied by a face, head and scalp massage. Detoxifies the system, soothes tired muscles and hydrates the skin.

Bodywork Therapeutic touching or manipulation of the body that uses massage or exercise to relax, ease tension and pain, and treat illnesses. May involve lessons in proper posture or movement. Some modes may treat both the body and mind.

Brush and tone Use of a loofah, special brush or rough cloth to rapidly brush the body to remove dead skin cells and impurities.

Often used to prepare the body for treatments such as masks and bronzing. Also known as dry brushing.

Bust treatment Treatment to firm and tone the bust and décolleté.

Chair massage Massage performed on you while you remain clothed and seated on a specially designed massage chair. The chair is portable so the massage can be performed almost anywhere. The massage typically concentrates on the back, neck, scalp and shoulders.

Chakras The seven energy centres in the body that are associated with the flow of the body's subtle energy.

Champissage Head massage that was developed by blind Indian therapist Nehendra Mehta, who popularized his technique in London in the 1980s.

Chi nei tsang Internal organ massage that focuses on the navel and surrounding abdominal area where stress, tension and negative emotions accumulate. Relieves illnesses, and releases negative emotions and tensions, bringing relief to the abdomen and vital energy to the internal organs. Effective in eliminating toxins in the gastrointestinal tract, promoting lymphatic drainage and treating digestive problems such as irritable bowel syndrome, bloating and constipation.

Coconut mangir Exfoliating and hydrating Indonesian scrub made from a paste of flowers, spices, ground rice and grated coconut.

Cold plunge pool Small pool filled with chilled water to stimulate blood and cool the body quickly, especially after a sauna.

Colour therapy Use of colour to bring about balance and well-being.

Complementary therapy Health care system not traditionally utilized by conventional Western medical practitioners, and which may complement orthodox treatments. Also known as alternative therapy.

Cranial-Sacral Therapy A gentle touch therapy that evaluates and enhances the cranio-sacral system (comprising the membranes and fluid that surround and protect the brain and spinal cord) to restore balance, ease stress and enhance the body's self-healing process. Developed in the mid-1970s by osteopathic physician John E Upledger.

Crème bath Hair and scalp conditioning treatment in which a rich cream is applied to the hair section by section. The hair may be steamed before being rinsed. Treatment sometimes includes a neck, scalp and shoulder massage.

Cupping Chinese treatment where small glass cups are attached to the skin by a vacuum that is created by placing a lit match inside each cup to burn the oxygen. The suction increases the circulation of qi and blood.

Dance movement therapy Dance as a therapy, with or without music, to help those with emotional problems. The therapist may suggest movements and encourage the participants to innovate their own to express themselves.

Dancercise Aerobic exercise derived from modified modern dance steps and movements.

Dead Sea mud treatment Application of mineral-rich mud from the Dead Sea. Detoxifies the skin and body and relieves rheumatic and arthritic pain.

Deep tissue massage Firm and deep massage using specific techniques to release tensions, blockages and knots that have built up over time. Believed to release emotional tension. May be adapted to a specific area of tension.

Do-in System of exercise resembling yoga postures that encourages physical and spiritual development. Balances the flow of energy through the meridian system.

Doshas In ayurveda, the three humours that make up the physical body. Also describes the three constitutional types.

Echocardiography Technique for diagnosing cardiovascular illness by examining the heart and its vessels using non-invasive equipment.

Effleurage Long, even strokes in the direction of the heart that helps push along the flow of blood and lymph.

Endermologie Massage therapy using the Cellu M6 machine to reduce the appearance of cellulite and refine the figure.

Energy balancing General term to describe a variety of practices aimed at balancing the flow of energy in and around the body. Practitioners generally try to remove blockages, and balance and amplify this energy flow.

EQ4 meridian testing Combination of traditional Chinese medicine, homeopathy, kinesiology, medical research and modern computing. A probe is applied to the acupoints to determine the areas that require treatment. It is believed that allergens, food and environmental stresses that weaken the body are reflected in energy levels that are higher or lower than normal.

Equilibropathy Treatment that encourages the body to function properly by relaxing tense muscle groups in order to regulate the body's systems and ensure they work together harmoniously. It begins with an examination of the spinal column and associated muscle groups to determine the cause of health problems and reveal asymptomatic illnesses. A modified acupuncture technique is then used to help release tense and knotted muscle groups. Breathing exercises are taught to stimulate the muscles to release tension and correct the body's structures.

Essential oils Oils, extracted from plants and flowers, that have specific characteristics that determine their use. They may be sedative or stimulating, and have antibacterial and therapeutic qualities. Usually inhaled or used in treatments such as massages, where they are absorbed by the skin.

Exfoliation Removal of dry, dead skin cells and impurities that impede oxygenation, using products such as salt or herbs, or techniques such as dry brushing.

Eyebrow shaping Grooming of the eyebrows, typically by tweezing, to suit the facial features.

Eye treatment Treatment that focuses on the delicate eye area, generally to combat signs of premature ageing, relieve tired eyes, and reduce puffiness and dryness.

Facial Treatment that cleanses and improves the complexion of the face using products that best suit a specific skin type. May include gentle exfoliation, steaming to open pores for extractions, application of a facial mask and moisturizer, and a facial massage. Types of facials include aromatic, oxygenating, whitening and deep cleansing facial treatments.

Facial mask Cleansing facial treatment where products are applied on the face and left on for a period of time to cleanse pores and slough off dead skin.

Facial scrub Exfoliating face treatment that uses products with abrasive ingredients to remove dry, dead skin cells and improve blood circulation. Softens the skin and gives it a healthier glow.

Fitness facial for men Facial that addresses men's skin types and needs, including shaving rash. May include a face, neck and shoulder massage.

Flotation therapy Treatment where you float on salt and mineral water at body temperature in an enclosed flotation tank (also known as an isolation tank). The feeling of weightlessness, and the isolation from external sensations and stimuli provide a deep feeling of relaxation and sensory awareness. May be done in complete silence and darkness, or with music and videos. A two-hour treatment is said to be the equivalent of eight hours sleep.

Floral bath Bath filled with flowers and essential oils.

Four-handed massage Massage performed in complete tandem by two therapists. Often uses a blend of massage techniques.

G5 vibro massage Deep vibrating massage using a G5 machine that relaxes, stimulates circulation and breaks down fatty deposits.

Glycolic facial Facial that uses glycolic acid to break down the bond which holds dry skin on to the face. Exfoliates the top layer, smoothes the skin and softens lines.

Golden spoons facial Facial using alternating hot and cold 23-karat gold-plated spoons to open and close the pores. Stimulates circulation and helps the skin absorb creams and lotions.

Gommage Massage-like treatment using creams to cleanse and moisturize.

Gong fu Generic term for martial arts that originated in China.

Gymnasium Workout room with weights, and a range of high-tech cardio and variable resistance equipment.

Hair services Services for the hair, including cutting, styling, deep conditioning, hair colouring, and washing and blow drying.

Hammam Arabic steam bath.

Hatha Common form of yoga, focuses on control through asanas and breathing techniques.

Hay diet Diet, devised by American physician Dr William Howard, that recommends carbohydrates are eaten at separate mealtimes from proteins and acidic fruit. Carbohydrates and proteins are not to be eaten within four hours of each other. Pulses and peanuts are not included in this diet.

Herbal bolus treatment Treatment where a heated muslin or cotton parcel of herbs and spices are placed on various parts of the body to relieve sore muscles, boost circulation and refresh the skin. The herbal packs are also used in place of hands to massage the body. Also known as herbal heat revival.

Herbal medicine Use of medicinal herbs and plant-based medicine to prevent and cure illnesses. Some healing systems, traditional Chinese medicine for instance, use mineral- and animal-based ingredients in herbal medicine. Herbal medicine is used by many complementary health disciplines including ayurveda, homeopathy, naturopathy, and Chinese, Indonesian and Japanese medicines. It may be prepared for internal and external uses through various forms such as pills, teas, oils or compresses. Also known as herbalism.

Herbal steam infusion Steaming with herbs. The heat, moisture and fragrance of the herbs help to open the skin's pores and promote relaxation.

Herbal wrap Treatment where the body is wrapped in hot cloth sheets that have been soaked in a herbal solution. Eliminates impurities, softens the skin, and detoxifies and relaxes the body.

Herbology Therapeutic use of herbs in treatments and diets.

High-impact aerobics High-energy aerobics involving jumping, jogging and hopping movements where both feet loose contact with the ground.

Hilot Indigenous Filipino massage treatment that uses banana leaf strips and extra virgin coconut oil. It can be followed with Filipino coco-cocoa scrub and coconut milk bath.

Holistic approach Integrated approach to health and fitness that takes into account your lifestyle, and mental, physical and spiritual well-being.

Homeopathy Holistic health care practice, based on the concept of 'like cures like', that treats diseases by using minute doses of natural substances that in a healthy person would produce symptoms similar to what is already being experienced. Developed by German physician Dr Samuel Hahnemann (1755–1843).

Hot plunge pool Pool of hot water that helps open the capillaries.

Hot spring Natural, sometimes volcanic, spring of hot mineral water.

Hot tub Wooden tub of hot or cool water to soak the body.

Hydrobath Bathtub with water jets that pummel all parts of the body. Seawater may be used, or the water may be infused with essential oils or mineral salts. Relaxes, and stimulates muscle tone and circulation.

Hydromassage Underwater massage in a hydrobath equipped with high-pressure jets and hand-manipulated hoses to stimulate the blood and lymphatic circulations.

Hydropool Pool fitted with various high-pressure jets and fountains.

Hydrotherapy Therapeutic use of water which includes baths, steam baths, steam inhalation, in- and under-water massage, soaking in hot springs, and the use of hot, cold or alternating shower sprays.

Indonesian massage Traditional massage of Indonesia that uses deep pressure and specially blended massage oils to ease tension and improve circulation.

Iridology Analysis of the marks and changes on the iris, which is divided into areas linked to specific body parts and functions, to diagnose a problem, or spot early signs of trouble, in order to recommend appropriate action.

Iyengar Form of yoga that focuses on symmetry and alignment. Props, such as head rests, are commonly used.

Jamu Traditional Indonesian herbal medicine.

Javanese lulur Traditional fragrant scrub originating from the royal palaces of Java. A blend of powdered spices, including turmeric and sandalwood, is rubbed on to the body. After the vibrantly coloured paste dries, it is removed with a gentle massage. The skin is then moisturized with yogurt. The lulur is often used to clean and pamper the bride during the week leading up to her wedding.

Jet-lag treatment Treatment that eases travel-associated aches, pains and stiffness, and helps the body to adjust to the new time zone.

Jin Shin Do Bodymind Acupressure Body-mind healing approach that combines gentle but deep finger pressure on the acupoints to help release physical and emotional tension. The practitioner may suggest that you participate through breathing or focusing techniques.

Kanpo Japanese traditional herbal medicine. Less commonly used to refer to the Japanese traditional healing system.

Ki The life force that sustains the body. Known as qi in traditional Chinese medicine.

Kinesiology Use of fingertip pressure to locate weakness in specific muscles and diagnose a problem or asymptomatic illnesses. The fingertips are used to massage the appropriate points to disperse toxins and revitalize the flow of energy.

Kneipp baths Herbal or mineral baths of varying temperatures combined with diet and exercise. Kneipp therapy uses hot and cold hydrotherapy treatments to improve circulation.

Kodo Massage technique of Aboriginal Australians that uses a combination of pressure point therapy with rhythmical movements and native essential oils.

Kundalini A form of yoga that combines chanting and breathing exercises with different asanas. Designed to awaken kundalini energy.

Kur Course of daily treatments using natural resources, such as algae and thermal mineral water, to re-mineralize and balance the body.

Labyrinth Ancient meditation tool in which a single winding path leads to a central goal and back out again. Walking it is a metaphor for journeying to the centre of understanding and returning with a broadened outlook.

Lap pool Swimming pool with exercise lanes. Standard lap pools are 25 metres in length.

Life coach counselling Counselling sessions that help to solve daily problems, develop harmony with the self and contribute to understanding life's natural philosophy.

Light therapy Use of natural or artificial light to heal.

Lomi Lomi Massage originating in Hawaii that uses the forearms and elbows, rhythmical rocking movements, and long and broad strokes.

Low-impact aerobics Form of aerobics with side-to-side marching or gliding movements which spare the body from excessive stress and possible injuries.

Lymphatic drainage massage Massage that uses a gentle pumping technique to stimulate lymphatic circulation, and thus reduce water retention and remove toxins from the body. Lymph drainage can be achieved through manual massage or hydromassage. May be performed on the face and neck, or on the body.

Lymphobiology Treatment that combines a massage with an application of biological products to improve the skin's condition. Provides a radiant glow, reduces cellulite, restores hydration, controls acne, balances oily or dry skin, minimizes lines and wrinkles, and corrects post-surgical bruising and swelling.

Macrobiotics Diet that aims to balance foods by their yin-yang qualities and according to your needs.

Malay massage Traditional massage that uses pressure and long, kneading strokes that focus on the body. May be applied with herbal oil.

Manicure Treatment that beautifies the hands and nails. Hands are soaked and exfoliated with a scrub to remove dead skin cells, cuticles are groomed, and nails are trimmed and shaped. Nails may be buffed to a shine or coated with a polish. May include a hand massage.

Manuluve Hand and arm treatment comprising a scrub and heated seaweed massage.

Marine aerosol treatment Inhalation of ionic seawater mist to cleanse the respiratory system. Alleviates breathing problems caused by asthma or smoking.

Marma point massage Ayurvedic massage in which the marma points are massaged with the thumb or index fingers in clockwise circles. Focuses on the face, neck, scalp and shoulders.

Marma points In ayurveda, these are the body's vital energy points. It is believed that the dysfunction of any of these points leads to illness.

Massage Therapy that uses manipulative and soft tissue techniques that are generally based on concepts of the anatomy, physiology and human function. Relaxes, creates a sense of well-being, eases strain and tension, mobilizes stiff joints, improves blood circulation, improves the digestive system, and encourages the removal of toxins from the body. Generally delivered by hand, though machines and high-powered water-jets are also used.

Masseur Male massage therapist.

Masseuse Female massage therapist.

Meditation Method of deep breathing, mental concentration and contemplation. During meditation, breathing, brain activity, and heart and pulse rates slow, encouraging the body to relax and achieve a greater sense of inner balance and peace. Relieves stress, removes pain and reduces blood pressure.

Meridians Pathways or channels through which the vital energy circulates throughout the body. All illnesses are believed to result from an imbalance or blockage of this flow.

Meridian stretching Stretching exercises designed to encourage physical and mental flexibility, for the body and mind to perform at their peak. Combines exercise, yoga and traditional Chinese medicine.

Microdermabrasion Clinical skin-resurfacing procedure where a jet of fine crystals is vacuumed across the surface of the face to remove the topmost layer of skin.

Mineralize Supply of minerals to the body.

Moxibustion Burning of the dried herb moxa around the acupoints to relieve pain. Applied using cones of moxa directly on the skin, or indirectly with an insulating layer of other herbs.

Muay Thai Thai boxing that involves the use of the upper and lower bodies. A cardiovascular and fat-burning exercise that helps relief stress.

Mud pool Pool with a central pedestal of volcanic mud. The mud is self applied to the body and left to dry in the sun before being rinsed off.

Mud treatment Mineral-rich mud used to detoxify, loosen muscles and stimulate circulation.

Mukh Lepa An ayurvedic facial treatment.

Myofacial release Use of the fingers, palms, forearms and elbows in long, deliberate, gliding strokes to stretch and mobilize the fascia (connective tissue that surrounds and supports the muscles, organs and bones) to provide long-term relief of pain and promote well-being.

Nail art Beautification of the nails with patterns, paintings or other decorative motifs.

Nasya Use of nasal medicated drops to clear the nasal passages to help allergies. One of the five purification techniques in panchakarma.

Naturopathy Holistic approach that believes in the body's ability to heal itself. Uses treatments not to alleviate symptoms, but to encourage the body's self-healing mechanism. Symptoms are viewed not as a part of the illness, but as the body's way of ridding itself of the problem. Also known as natural medicine.

Njavarakizhi Ayurvedic massage using small linen bags—filled with rice cooked in milk mixed with a herbal blend—to induce sweat. Applied with medicated oil. Strengthens and rejuvenates.

Nutritional consultation Consultation with a qualified nutritional practitioner to review eating habits and dietary needs. Taking into account your lifestyle, food intolerance, appetite control and weight goals, the nutritionist may compile a nutritionally balanced programme to help you attain optimal health and weight.

Onsen Japanese natural hot springs.

Organic food Food grown without the use of pesticides or other chemicals.

Ovo lacto vegetarian Vegan who consumes milk and egg products.

Ovo vegetarian Vegan who consumes egg products.

Panchakarma Ayurvedic therapy (vamana, virechana, vasti, nasya and raktamokshana) that helps rid the body of its toxins.

Paraffin treatment Application of warm paraffin wax on the hands and feet to the skin to absorb toxins. Treatment leaves the skin silky soft.

Pedicure Treatment that beautifies the feet and nails. Feet are soaked and exfoliated with a scrub to remove dead skin cells, cuticles are groomed, and nails are trimmed and shaped. Nails may be buffed to a shine or coated with a polish. May include a foot and calf massage.

Pediluve Treatment in which feet and legs are dipped in alternate tubs of bubbling jets of warm and cold seawater to improve blood circulation.

Personal fitness assessment Programme that assesses your current fitness levels to recommend a suitable exercise programme. May include tests for aerobic capacity, body composition, blood pressure, heart rate, and muscular endurance and strength.

Personal training One-on-one personalized workout with a qualified instructor.

Pescetarian Vegetarian who consumes fish.

Physiotherapy Rehabilitative therapy that helps recovery from injury, surgery or disease. Treatments—which include massage, traction, hydrotherapy, corrective exercise and electrical stimulation—help relieve pain, increase strength and improve the range of motion.

Pilates Exercise comprising slow, precise movements with special exercise equipment that engage the body and mind, and increase flexibility and strength without building bulk.

Pizhichil Ayurvedic massage in which lukewarm herbal oils are gently and rhythmically applied to the body by two to four therapists.

Pregnancy massage Pre-natal massage that deals with the special needs of a mother-to-be, and anti-natal massages that deal with her needs after she has delivered. Some spas have massage tables with a hole in the centre to accommodate a pregnant woman.

Pressotherapy Computerized pressure massage that uses a specially designed airbag that compresses and deflates to improve the circulation throughout the feet and legs.

Purvakarma Two Ayurvedic treatments (snehana and svedana) that soften and cleanse the skin in preparation for panchakarma.

Qi gong Chinese physical exercise of working with or mastering qi. Uses breathing and slow body movement to help develop a powerful qi.

Qi 'Vital energy' or 'life force' of the universe and the body. Also known as ki (Japanese) and prana (Indian).

Raktamokshana Blood purification treatment for illnesses such as skin problems using surgical instruments or leeches. One of the five purification techniques in panchakarma.

Rasul Tiled steam room in which different muds are applied to the body before being washed off.

Reflexology Application of finger-point pressure to reflex zones on the feet—and to a lesser extent, hands—to improve circulation, ease pain, relax the body and re-establish the flow of energy through the body. Its underlying theory is that specific areas on the feet and hands correspond with specific body parts, organs and glands, and that the manipulation of specific areas can bring about change associated with the corresponding parts.

Reiki Healing technique based on ancient Tibetan teachings. The practitioner places his palms over or on various areas of the body for a few minutes each to energize and balance the body, mind and spirit. Helps treat physical problems, heal emotional stresses and encourage personal transformation.

Salt glow Exfoliating treatment where the body is rubbed with a mixture of coarse salt and essential oils to remove dry, dead skin cells and stimulate circulation.

Samana Ayurvedic herbal medicine that works to balance the doshas.

Sauna Dry heat, wood-lined treatment room. The heat brings on sweating to help cleanse the body of impurities and relax the muscles. Usually followed by a cold plunge or shower.

Shiatsu Massage that uses finger pressure—and also the hands, forearms, elbows, knees and feet—on acupoints. Calms and relaxes.

Shirodhara Ayurvedic massage in which warmed medicated oil steadily drips on the forehead. Relieves mental tension and calms the mind.

Signature treatment Treatment specially created by a spa or spa group, often using indigenous ingredients.

Sivananda A form of yoga based on the 12 sun salutation postures.

Shirovasthi Ayurvedic treatment in which warm herbal medicated oil is massaged on to the head after which a closely fitted cap is worn for a while to retain the therapeutic benefits.

Snehana Ayurvedic oil therapy in which a mixture of herbs, oils and natural ingredients are massaged on to the body. The oils may also be taken orally or introduced as enemas. One of the two preparatory treatments in purvakarma.

Spa Term, originating from the name of a town in Belgium where people flocked to in the 17th century for its healing waters, that refers to anything from a mineral spring to an establishment which provides facilities and services that helps you achieve a sense of well-being. Many spas also provide fitness activities, classes on well-being and spa cuisine. Types of spas include day spas (spas for day use); hotel or resort spas (spas located within hotels or resorts); destination spas (spas with an all-round emphasis on a healthy lifestyle, and include on-site accommodation, treatments, programmes and spa cuisine); and mineral springs spas (spas with a natural source of mineral or thermal waters, or seawater).

Spa cuisine Light, healthy meals served at spas. Typically low in calories, fat and salt.

Spa menu Selection of treatments and therapies offered by a spa.

Spa package Two or more treatments offered together. Often longer in length and good value.

Sports massage Deep tissue massage directed at muscles used in athletic activities to help the body achieve its maximum physical efficiency. Before physical exertion, it buffers against pain and injury; after, it helps remove lactic acid and restore muscle tone and range of movement.

Steaming Use of hot steam—often infused with essential oils or herbs—to relax the body, soften the skin, and open up the pores to prepare the face or body for treatment. Hair may also be steamed by wrapping it in a hot towel or exposing it to steam.

Steam room Tiled room with benches in which steam is generated at high pressure and temperature. The steam opens the pores, eliminates toxins, cleanses the skin and relaxes the body.

Step aerobics Aerobic sessions done with a small platform for stepping up and down.

Stone therapy Massage where hot, warm or cold smooth stones are rubbed in long, flowing strokes on to the oiled body, then placed on energy points to ease away tension. Also known as hot stone massage or la stone® therapy.

Stress management Techniques to deal with stress and anxiety.

Stretching Flexibility workout where various parts of the body are stretched by assuming different positions. Helps increase flexibility, and relieve stress and tension.

Svedana Body purification method to cleanse and relax through sweat therapy. One of the two preparatory treatments in purvakarma.

Swedish massage Massage in which oils are applied to the body with techniques such as gliding, kneading, rubbing, tapping and shaking. Relieves stress, tension and muscle pain; improves circulation; increases flexibility; and induces relaxation.

Tai chi Graceful movement that combines mental concentration with deep, controlled breathing. Regular practice brings about relaxation and good health. Stimulates the body's energy systems and enhances mental functions.

Tantra A form of yoga that includes visualization, chanting, asana and strong breathing practices.

Tapik Kawayan Filipino therapy that uses a short bamboo stick to tap specific areas of the body to unblock flow of energy.

Thai herbal massage Massage using a warmed pouch of steamed Thai herbs pressed against the body's meridians.

Thai massage Traditional massage of Thailand, influenced by Chinese and Indian healing arts, that involves a combination of stretching and gentle rocking, and uses a range of motions and acupressure techniques. The massage is oil-free, and performed on a traditional Thai mattress on the floor. Loose pajamas are worn.

Thalassotherapy Treatments that harness mineral- and vitamin-rich seawater and seaweed for curative and preventive purposes. True thalassotherapy centres are located no more than 800 metres (2,625 feet) from the shore, and constantly pump fresh seawater filtered through large canals for use in the treatments.

Thermal bath Therapeutic use of thermal water rich in salts and minerals.

Traditional Chinese medicine (TCM) Holistic system of care that sees the body and mind as a whole. Treatments include herbal medicine, physical and mental exercises, and therapies such as acupuncture and moxibustion.

Treatments for couples Typically treatments that a couple can enjoy together with a therapist pampering each person. Treatments specially designed for couples usually use an aphrodisiac blend of essential oils.

Tui na Chinese system of manual therapy used to treat specific illnesses of an internal nature and musculoskeletal ailments. Principal hand strokes include pushing (tui), grasping (na), pressing (an), rubbing (mo), rolling (gun), pulling (qian), beating (da) and shaking (dou). The hands, arms, elbows and feet may be used.

Turkish bath Series of hot and humid steam rooms, each of which increases in heat. You spend several minutes in each room and finish with a cool shower.

Vamana The consumption of potions to induce vomiting to treat bronchitis, and throat, chest and heart problems. One of the five purification techniques in panchakarma.

Vasti Use of enemas to calm nerves and treat fatigue, dry skin and digestive imbalances. One of the five purification techniques in panchakarma.

Vegan Person who exclusively consumes a vegetable and fruit diet, and does not eat animal products such as butter, cheese, eggs and milk.

Vegetarian Person who consumes mainly vegetables, fruit, nuts, pulses and grains, and who does not eat meat or fish, but eats animal products such as butter, cheese, eggs and milk.

Vichy shower Spray of water from five micro-jets fixed to a horizontal rail which rain down on you while you lie on a table below. May also include a massage. Also known as affusion shower or rain shower.

Vietnamese massage Invigorating massage that uses a combination of deep stroking and percussive movements. Benefits include stimulating the blood and lymphatic circulation, improving the skin texture and tone, as well as warming and relaxing the muscle tissue.

Virechana Drinking a herb tea to help flush out elements that may clog the digestive tract. One of the five purification techniques in panchakarma.

Visualization Technique that involves focusing the mind by consciously creating a mental image of a desired condition to bring about change. May be self-directed or therapist guided. Also known as imaging.

Watsu Therapy where you float in a swimming pool, supported by a therapist who manipulates your body with stretches, rhythmic movements and pressure point massage to bring deep relaxation.

Waxing Temporary hair removal method. Warm or cool wax, usually honeycomb blended with oils, is applied on to areas of unwanted hair. A cloth is smoothed on to the area and quickly whisked off, pulling the hair off with the wax.

Wet area Area in a spa where Jacuzzis, saunas, cold tubs, hot tubs, steam baths and pressure showers are located.

Whirlpool Tub of hot water with high-pressure jets on the sides and bottom that circulate the water. Massages muscles and relaxes the body.

Whitening treatment Treatment that brightens the skin, restores lost radiance and tones pigmentation marks.

Yin and yang Yin is the universal energy force whose characteristics are feminine, cold, dark, quiet, static and wet. Yang is masculine, warm, bright, dynamic and dry. In traditional Chinese medicine, true balance and health are achieved when these two opposing forces are in balance. Also known as in and yo (Japanese).

Yoga Ancient Hindu practice comprising focused deep breathing, and stretching and toning the body using various postures. The ultimate goal is to reach full physical, mental and spiritual potential. Relaxes and improves circulation, flexibility and strength.

Spa Directory

A comprehensive listing of the spas in the book and their sister spas in Asia. Page references indicate where the entries appear in the book.

AUSTRALIA

Sydney

Angsana Spa Double Bay (pp 232–233)
15 Bay Street
Double Bay
Sydney
NSW 2028
Australia
Tel: (61 2) 9328 5501
Fax: (61 2) 9328 5517
Email: spa-doublebaysydney@angsana.com
Website: www.angsanaspa.com

Daintree

Daintree Spa (pp 236–237)
Daintree Eco Lodge & Spa
20 Daintree Road, Daintree
Queensland 4873
Australia
Tel: (61 7) 4098 6100
Fax: (61 7) 4098 6200
Email: info@daintree-ecolodge.com.au
Website: www.daintree-ecolodge.com.au

Melbourne

Chuan Spa (pp 234–235)
Langham Hotel, Melbourne
One Southgate Avenue
Southbank, Victoria 3006
Australia
Tel: (61 3) 8696 8111
Fax: (61 3) 9690 6581
Email: mel.info@chuanspa.com
Website: www.chuanspa.com

CAMBODIA

Phnom Penh

RafflesAmrita Spa
Raffles Hotel Le Royal
92 Rukhak Vithei Daun Penh
Sangkat Wat Phnom
Phnom Penh, Cambodia
Tel: (855 23) 981 888
Fax: (855 23) 981 168
Email: amrita-spa.leroyal@raffles.com
Website: www.amritaspas.com

Siem Reap

RafflesAmrita Spa
Raffles Grand Hotel d'Angkor
1 Vithei Charles De Gaulle
Khum Svay Dang Kum
Siem Reap, Cambodia
Tel: (855 63) 963 888
Fax: (855 63) 963 168
Email: amrita-spa.grandhotel@raffles.com
Website: www.amritaspas.com

Angkor Spa (pp 156–157)
Sofitel Royal Angkor Golf & Spa Resort
Vithei Charles de Gaulle
Khum Svay Dang Kum
Siem Reap, Cambodia
Tel: (855 63) 96 46 00
Fax: (855 63) 96 46 10
Email: angkor.spa@sofitel-royal-angkor.com
Wesbite: www.accorhotels.com/asia

CHINA

Beijing

Palms Spring Spa at Palms Spring Beijing
Palm Springs International Club
No. 8, South Road of Chao Yao Park
Chao Yang District
Beijing, People's Republic of China
Tel: (86 10) 8595 7777
Fax: (86 10) 6539 8338
Email: infochina@minornet.com
Website: www.mspa-international.com

Hainan

Mandara Spa at Sheraton Sanya Resort
Sheraton Sanya Resort
Yalong Bay National Resort District, Sanya
Hainan Island 572000
People's Republic of China
Tel: (86 898) 8855 8855 ext. 8497, 8498
Fax: (86 898) 8855 8499
Email: infochina@minornet.com
Website: www.mspa-international.com

Hong Kong

Angsana Spa Park Island
Hong Kong
Blue Blue Club, Park Island
8 Pak Lai Road
Ma Wan, New Territories, Hong Kong
Tel: (852) 2296 4228
Fax: (852) 2296 4198
Email: spa-parkislandhk@angsana.com
Website: www.angsana.com

Chuan Spa (pp 136–137)
Langham Place Hotel
Level 41, 555 Shanghai Street
Mongkok, Kowloon
Hong Kong
Tel: (852) 3552 3510
Fax: (852) 3552 3529
Email: hkg.lph.info@chuanspa.com
Website: www.chuanspa.com

I-Spa at InterContinental (pp 138–139)
18 Salisbury Road
3rd floor, InterContinental Hong Kong
Kowloon, Hong Kong
Tel: (852) 2721 1211
Fax: (852) 2739 4546
Email: hongkong@interconti.com
Website: www.hongkong-ic.intercontinental.com

The Oriental Spa (pp 140–141)
The Landmark Mandarin Oriental
15 Queen's Road Central
The Landmark
Central, Hong Kong
Tel: (852) 2132 0011
Fax: (852) 3127 8011
Email: lmhkg-spa@mohg.com
Website: www.mandarinoriental.com/landmark

Plateau at The Grand Hyatt (pp 142–143)
11th floor Grand Hyatt Hong Kong
1 Harbour Road, Hong Kong
Tel: (852) 2584 7688
Fax: (852) 2584 7738
Email: plateau@grandhyatt.com.hk
Website: www.plateau.com.hk

Macau

The Spa at Mandarin Oriental (pp 144–145)
Mandarin Oriental, Macau
956-1110 Avenida da Amizade
Macau
Tel: (853) 793 4824
Fax: (853) 713 168
Email: momfm-spa@mohg.com
Website: www.mandarinoriental.com/macau

Shanghai

Banyan Tree Spa Shanghai
Level 3, The Westin Shanghai
Bund Centre
88 Henan Central Road
Shanghai, 200002
People's Republic of China
Tel: (86 21) 6335 1888
Fax: (86 21) 6335 1113
Email: spa-shanghai@banyantree.com
Website: www.banyantree.com

Club Oasis
Grand Hyatt Shanghai
Jin Mao Tower
88 Century Boulevard, Pudong
Shanghai, 200121
People's Republic of China
Tel: (86 21) 5049 1234
Fax: (86 21) 5049 1111
Email: info@hyattshanghai.com
Website: www.shanghai.hyatt.com

Mandara Spa at JW Marriott (pp 134–135)
JW Marriott Hotel Shanghai
6th Floor, 399 Nanjing West Road
Shanghai, 200003
People's Republic of China
Tel: (86 21) 5359 4969 ext 6798, 6799
Fax: (86 21) 5852 1155
Email: infochina@minornet.com
Website: www.mspa-international.com

Suzhou

Angsana Spa Suzhou, China
Suzhou, China
Suzhou Baodao Garden Hotel
Changsha Island
Taihu National Tourism Resort District
Suzhou, Jiangsu Province 215164
People's Republic of China
Tel: (86 512) 6651 5999
Fax: (86 512) 6651 5000
Email: spa-suzhou@angsana.com
Website: www.angsana.com

Yunan Province

Angsana Spa Gyalthang, China
Shangri-La, Yunnan China
Gyalthang Dzong Hotel
Shangri-La Diqing Tibetan Autonomous
Prefecture, Yunnan 674400
People's Republic of China
Tel: (86 887) 822 3646
Fax: (86 887) 822 3620
Email: spa-gyalthang@angsana.com
Website: www.angsana.com

Banyan Tree Spa Ringha
Hong Po Village, Jian Yang Town
Shangri-La County
Diqing Tibetan Autonomous Prefecture
Yunnan Province
People's Republic of China 674400
Tel: (86 887) 828 8822

Fax: +86 887 828 8911
Email: spa-ringha@banyantree.com
Website: www.banyantree.com

INDIA

Bangalore

Angsana Oasis Spa & Resort Bangalore
Northwest Country
Main Doddaballapur Road
Addevishwanathapura Village
Rajankunte
Bangalore 560064, India
Tel: (91 80) 846 8893
Fax: (91 80) 846 8897
Email: spa-bangalore@angsana.com
Website: www.angsana.com

Kerala

Somatheeram Ayurvedic Beach Resort
Chowara, South of Kovalam, Via Balarampuram
Trivandrum 695501
Kerala, South India
Tel: (91 471) 2268 101
Fax: (91 471) 2267 600
Email: somatheeram@vsnl.com
Website: www.somatheeram.com

Uttaranchal

Ananda – In the Himalayas (pp 130–133)
The Palace Estate
Narendra Nagar
Tehri-Garhwal
Uttaranchal 249175, India
Tel: (91 1378) 227 500
Fax: (91 1378) 227 550
Email: sales@anandaspa.com
Website: www.anandaspa.com

INDONESIA

Bali

Jamu Traditional Spa
AlamKulKul Resort
Jalan Pantai Kuta
Legian
Bali 80361, Indonesia
Tel: (62 361) 752 520
Fax: (62 361) 66 377
Email: jamubali@jamutraditionalspa.com
Website: www.jamutraditionalspa.com

Mandara Spa
Alila Manggis
Buitan Manggis, Karangasem
Bali 80871, Indonesia
Tel: (62 363) 41 011
Fax: (62 363) 41 015
Email: infoasia@mandaraspa.com
Website: www.mandaraspa.com

Mandara Spa (pp 210–211)
Alila Ubud
Desa Melinggih Kelod Payagan

Gianyar
Bali 80572, Indonesia
Tel: (62 361) 975 963
Fax: (62 361) 975 968
Email: infoasia@mandaraspa.com
Website: www.mandaraspa.com
www.alilahotels.com

Mandara Spa
Bali Golf & Country Club
Kawasan Wisata Nusa Dua
Bali 80363, Indonesia
Tel: (62 361) 771 791
Fax: (62 361) 771 797
Email: infoasia@mandaraspa.com
Website: www.mandaraspa.com

Mandara Spa
Hotel Padma Bali
1 Jalan Padma
Legian
Bali 80361, Indonesia
Tel: (62 361) 752 111
Fax: (62 361) 752 140
Email: infoasia@mandaraspa.com
Website: www.mandaraspa.com

Mandara Spa
Ibah Ubud
Jalan Raya Campuhan
Ubud
Bali 80571, Indonesia
Tel: (62 361) 974 466
Fax: (62 361) 974 467
Email: infoasia@mandaraspa.com
Website: www.mandaraspa.com

Mandara Spa
Waterbom Park & Spa
Jalan Kartika Plaza
Tuban
Bali 80361, Indonesia
Tel: (62 361) 758 241
Fax: (62 361) 733 517
Email: infoasia@mandaraspa.com
Website: www.mandaraspa.com

Parwathi Spa (pp 214–215)
Matahari Beach Resort & Spa
Pemuteran Village
Singaraja
Bali 81155, Indonesia
Tel: (62 362) 92 312
Fax: (62 362) 92 313
Email: mhr-bali@indo.net.id
Website: www.matahari-beach-resort.com

**Pita Maha & Tjampuhan Resort & Spa
(pp 216–217)**
Jalan Sanggingan, Ubud
Bali 80571, Indonesia
Tel: (62 361) 974 330
Fax: (62 361) 974 329
Email: pitamaha@indosat.net.id
Website: www.pitamaha-bali.com

Prana Spa at the Villas (pp 218–219)
Jalan Kunti 118X
Seminyak
Bali, Indonesia
Tel: (62 361) 730 840
Fax: (62 361) 734 758
Email: spa@thevillas.net
Website: www.thevillas.net

The Spa (pp 222–223)
Four Seasons Resort Bali at Jimbaran Bay
Jimbaran
Bali 80361, Indonesia
Tel: (62 361) 701 010
Fax: (62 361) 701 020
Email: fsrb.jimbaran@fourseasons.com
Website: www.fourseasons.com/jimbaranbay

The Spa (pp 334–225)
Four Seasons Resort Bali at Sayan
Sayan, Ubud, Gianyar
Bali 80571, Indonesia
Tel: (62 361) 977 577
Fax: (62 361) 977 588
Email: fsrb.sayan@fourseasons.com
Website: www.fourseasons.com/sayan

Spa at Maya (pp 212–213)
Maya Ubud Resort & Spa
Jalan Gunung Sari
Banjar Ambengan, Ubud
Bali 80571, Indonesia
Tel: (62 361) 977 888
Fax: (62 361) 977 555
Email: spa@mayaubud.com
Website: www.mayaubud.com

The Spa
The Legian
Jalan Laksmana
Seminyak Beach
Bali 80361, Indonesia
Tel: (62 361) 730 622
Fax: (62 361) 730 623
Email: legian@ghmhotels.com
Website: www.ghmhotels.com

**The Ritz-Carlton, Bali Thalasso
Resort & Spa (pp 220–221)**
Jalan Karang Mas Sehahtera
Jimbaran
Bali 80364, Indonesia
Tel: (62 361) 702 222
Fax: (62 361) 701 555
Email: spa.reservation@ritzcarlton-bali.com
Website: www.ritzcarlton.com

Tjampuhan Spa
Hotel Tjampuhan & Spa
Jalan Raya Campuhan, Ubud
Bali 80571, Indonesia
Tel: (62 361) 975 368
Fax: (62 361) 975 137
Email: tjampuan@indo.com
Website: www.indo.com/hotels/tjampuhan

Bintan Island, Riau
Angsana Spa Bintan
Angsana Resort & Spa Bintan
Site A4, Lagoi
Bintan Island, Indonesia
Tel: (62 770) 693 111
Fax: (62 770) 693 222
Email: spa-bintan@angsana.com
Website: www.angsana.com

Asmara at Nirwana
Nirwana Resort Hotel
Nirwana Gardens, Bintan Utara
Riau 29152, Indonesia
Tel: (62 770) 692 566
Fax: (62 770) 692 602
Email: bookingsms@asmaraspas.com
Website: www.asmaraspas.com

Asmara Ria
Ria Bintan Golf Club
Jalan Perigi Raja, Parcel A11
Lagoi, Bintan Utara
Riau 29152, Indonesia
Tel: (62 770) 692 851
Fax: (62 770) 692 602
Email: bookingsms@asmaraspas.com
Website: www.asmaraspas.com

Banyan Tree Spa Bintan
Banyan Tree Bintan
Site A4, Lagoi
Tanjong Said
Bintan Island, Indonesia
Tel: (62 770) 693 100
Fax: (62 770) 693 151
Email: spa-bintan@banyantree.com
Website: www.banyantree.com

Lombok, Nusa Tenggara Barat
Mandara Spa
Novotel Coralia Lombok
Mandalika Resort
Pantai Putri Nyale
Pujut, Lombok Tengah 83111
Nusa Tenggara Barat, Indonesia
Tel: (62 370) 653 333
Fax: (62 370) 653 555
Email: infoasia@mandaraspa.com
Website: wwwl.mandaraspa.com

Mandara Spa
Senggigi Beach Hotel
Jalan Raya Senggigi Km 8
Lombok 83010, Indonesia
Tel: (62 370) 693 210
Fax: (62 370) 693 200
Email: infoasia@mandaraspa.com
Website: www.aerowisata.co.id/seng.html

East Java
Apsara Residence & Spa
Hotel Tugu Malang
Jalan Tugu Number 3
Malang 65119

East Java, Indonesia
Tel: (62 34) 1363 891
Fax: (62 34) 1362 747
Email: malang@tuguhotels.com
Website: www.tuguhotels.com

Martha Tilaar Spa
Mandarin Oriental Hotel, Majapahit
65 Jalan Tanjungan
Surabaya 60275
East Java, Indonesia
Tel: (62 31) 545 9002
Fax: (62 31) 545 9003
Email: mosub-reservations@mohg.com
Website: www.mandarinoriental.com

Jakarta
Taman Sari Royal Heritage Spa
Jalan K H Wahid Hasyim Number 133
Jakarta Pusat 10240, Indonesia
Tel: (62 21) 314 3585
Fax: (62 21) 330 100
Email: spa@mustika-ratu.co.id
Website: www.mustika-ratu.co.id

West Java
Javana Spa (pp 208–209)
Cangkuang-Cidahu, Sukabumi
West Java, Indonesia
Tel: (62 21) 719 8327/8
Fax: (62 21) 719 5555
Email: javana@indo.net.id
Website: www.javanaspa.com

The Malya
56–8 Jalan Ranca Bentang
Ciumbuleuit
Bandung 40142, West Java, Indonesia
Tel: (62 22) 203 0333
Fax: (62 22) 203 0633
Email: reservation@malyabandung.com
Website: www.malyabandung.com

JAPAN

Gora
Banyan Tree Spa (pp 146–147)
Level 2 Granforet Villa Gora Club
1320-123 Aza-Mukoyama, Gora,
Hakone-machi
Ashigarashimo-gun, Kanagawam
250-0408 Japan
Tel: (81 460) 2 7790
Fax: (81 460) 2 7791
Email: spa-gorahakone@banyantree.com
Website: www.banyantreespa.com

Miyazaki
Banyan Tree Spa Phoenix Seagaia Resort
Sheraton Grande Ocean Resort
Hamayama Yamazaki-cho
Miyazaki-shi Miyazaki, 880-8545 Japan
Tel: (81 985) 211 351
Fax: (81 985) 211 394
Email: spa-phoenixseagaia@banyantree.com
Website: www.banyantree.com

Tokyo

Mizuki Spa at Conrad Tokyo (pp 148–149)
Tokyo Shiodome Building 29F
1-9-1 Higashi Shinbashi,
Minato-ku, Tokyo 105-7337, Japan
Tel: (81 3) 6388 8620
Fax: (81 3) 388 8001
Email: mizuki.conradtokyo@hilton.com
Website: www.conradhotels.jp

The Spa at Mandarin Oriental (pp 150–151)
2-1-1 Nihonbashi Muromachi
Chuo-ku, Tokyo 103-8328, Japan
Tel: (81 3) 3270 8800
Fax: (81 3) 3270 8308
Website: www.mandarinoriental.com

LAOS

Angsana Spa Luang Prabang, Laos
Maison Souvannaphoum Hotel
Rue Chao Fa Ngum
Banthatluang, PO Box 741
Luang Prabang, Laos PDR
Tel: (856) 7125 4609
Fax: (856) 7121 2577
Email: spa-luangprabang@angsana.com
Website: www.angsana.com

MALAYSIA

Borneo

Mandara Spa
Magellan Sutera Hotel & Spa
1 Sutera Harbour Boulevard
Sutera Harbour 88100
Kota Kinabalu, Sabah
Borneo, East Malaysia
Tel: (60 8) 831 8888
Fax: (60 8) 831 7777
Email: mssutera@myjaring.net
Website: www.mandaraspa.com

Johor

Mandara Spa
Sofitel Palm Resort
Jalan Pesiaran Golf
(off Jalan Jumbo)
Senai 81250
Johor Darul Ta'zim, Malaysia
Tel: (60 7) 599 6000
Fax: (60 7) 599 7028
Email: mspasof@pd.jaring.my
Website: www.mandaraspa.com

Kuala Lumpur

Angsana Spa (pp 192–193)
Level 5 Crowne Plaza Mutiara, Kuala Lumpur
Jalan Sultan Ismail
50250 Kuala Lumpur
Malaysia
Tel: (60 3) 2141 4321
Fax: (60 3) 2141 1321
Email: spa-kualalumpur@angsana.com
Website: www.angsanaspa.com

Mandara Spa (pp 196–197)
Prince Hotel & Residence
Level 10, Jalan Conlay
50450 Kuala Lumpur
Malaysia
Tel: (60 3) 2170 8777
Fax: (60 3) 2170 8776
Email: infoasia@mandaraspa.com
Website: www.mandaraspa.com

The Spa at Mandarin Oriental, Kuala Lumpur
Mandarin Oriental, Kuala Lumpur
Kuala Lumpur City Centre
50088 Kuala Lumpur
Malaysia
Tel: (60 3) 2179 8700
Fax : (60 3) 2179 8777
Email:asharo@mohg.com
Website: www.mandarinoriental.com

Spa Village at The Residences (pp 200–201)
4th floor, The Residences
The Ritz-Carlton, Kuala Lumpur
168 Jalan Imbi
55100 Kuala Lumpur
Malaysia
Tel: (60 3) 2782 9090
Fax: (60 3) 2782 9099
Email: spavillagekl@ytlhotels.com.my
Website: www.ytlhotels.com

Langkawi Island, Kedah

Chavana Spa
Sheraton Langkawi Beach Resort
Teluk Nibong
07000 Langkawi Island
Kedah Darul Aman
Malaysia
Tel: (60 4) 955 1901
Fax: (60 4) 955 1968
Email: mspasher@tm.net.my
Website: www.mandaraspa.com

The Spa (pp 194–195)
Four Seasons Resort Langkawi
Jalan Tanjung Rhu
07000 Langkawi
Kedah Darul Aman
Malaysia
Tel: (60 4) 950 8888
Fax: (60 4) 950 8899
Email: spa.langkawi@fourseasons.com
Website: www.fourseasons.com/langkawi

Mandara Spa
The Datai
Jalan Teluk Datai
07000 Langkawi Island
Kedah Darul Aman
Malaysia
Tel: (60 4) 959 2500
Fax: (60 4) 959 2600
Email: infoasia@mandaraspa.com
Website: www.mandaraspa.com

The Spa
The Andaman Datai Bay
Jalan Teluk Datai
07000 Langkawi Island
Kedah Darul Aman, Malaysia
Tel: (60 4) 959 1088
Fax: (60 4) 959 1168
Email: reservations@theandaman.com
Website: www.theandaman.com

The Spa
Berjaya Langkawi Beach & Spa Resort
Karong Berkunci 200
Burau Bay
07000 Langkawi Island
Kedah Darul Aman
Malaysia
Tel: (60 4) 959 1888 ext 701
Fax: (60 4) 959 1886
Email: resvn@b-langkawi.com.my
Website: www.berjayaresorts.com

Pahang

Club Med Spa
Club Med Malaysia
Holiday Villages of Malaysia
Kuantan 25710
Pahang Darul Makmur
Malaysia
Tel: (60 9) 581 9133
Fax: (60 9) 581 9172
Email: checfitn01@clubmed.com
Website: www.mandaraspa.com

Pangkor Laut Island, Perak

Spa Village (pp 198–199)
Pangkor Laut Resort
Pangkor Laut Island
32200 Lumut
Perak, Malaysia
Tel: (60 5) 699 1100
Fax: (60 5) 699 1025
Email: spavillageplr@ytlhotels.com.my
Website: www.pangkorlautresort.com

THE MALDIVES

Baa Atoll

The Nautilus Spa
Coco Palm Resort & Spa
Dunikolu Island
Baa Atoll, The Maldives
Tel: (960) 230 011
Fax: (960) 230 022
Email: cocopalm@sunland.com.mv
Website: www.mandaraspa-asia.com

Six Senses Spa (pp 246–247)
Soneva Fushi Resort & Spa
Kunfunadhoo Island
Baa Atoll, The Maldives
Tel: (960) 660 0304
Fax: (960) 660 0374
Email: spa@sonevafushi.com.mv
Website: www.sixsenses.com

Male

Mandara Spa
Club Med Faru
Farukolufushi Island, Male, The Maldives
Tel: (960) 337 848
Fax: (960) 312 120
Email: stephanieb@mandaraspa.com
Website: www.mandaraspa.com

Hideaway Spa by Mandara (pp 242–243)
Island Hideaway Spa Resort and Marina
2nd floor, (East Wing), Aage
12 Boduthakurufaanu Magu, Henveiru
Male 20094, Maldive Islands
Tel: (960) 650 15 15
Fax: (960) 650 16 16
Email: mandaraspa@island-hideaway.com
Website: www.mandaraspa.com

Meemu Atoll

Mandara Spa
Medhufushi Island Resort
Meemu Atoll, The Maldives
Tel: (960) 460 026
Fax: (960) 460 027
Email: medhu@mandaraspa.com.mv
Website: www.mandaraspa.com

North Male Atoll

Angsana Spa Maldives Ihuru
Angsana Resort & Spa Maldives Ihuru
Ihuru Island
North Male Atoll, The Maldives
Tel: (960) 664 3502
Fax: (960) 664 5933
Email: spa-maldives@angsana.com
Website: www.angsana.com

Banyan Tree Spa Maldives
Banyan Tree Maldives Vabbinfaru
Vabbinfaru Island
North Male Atoll, The Maldives
Tel: (960) 664 3147
Fax: (960) 664 3843
Email: spa-maldives@banyantree.com
Website: www.banyantree.com

The Island Spa (pp 244–245)
Four Seasons Resort at Kuda Huraa
Four Seasons Resort Maldives
North Male Atoll
The Maldives
Tel: (960) 664 4888 ext 20
Fax: (960) 664 4800
Email: spa.maldives@fourseasons.com
Website: www.fourseasons.com/maldives

Mandara Spa
Club Med Kani
Kanifinolhu Island
North Male Atoll, The Maldives
Tel: (960) 443 152
Fax: (960) 443 859
Email: cmkani@mandaraspa.com
Website: www.mandaraspa.com

Mandara Spa
Taj Coral Reef Resort
PO Box 20117
North Male Atoll
The Maldives
Tel: (960) 442 200
Fax: (960) 442 211
Email: tajc@mandaraspa.mv
Website: www.mandaraspa.com

Six Senses Spa (pp 248–249)
Soneva Gili Resort & Spa
Lankanfushi Island
North Male Atoll
The Maldives
Tel: (960) 664 0304
Fax: (960) 664 0305
Email: spa@sonevagili.com.mv
Website: www.sixsenses.com

South Male Atoll

Mandara Spa
Taj Spa by Mandara
Taj Exotica Resort & Spa
PO Box 20117
South Male Atoll
The Maldives
Tel: (960) 442 200
Fax: (960) 442 211
Email: spa@tajexotica.com.mv
Website: www.mandaraspa.com

Reflections Spa at Bodu Huraa Resort & Spa
Bodu Huraa Resort & Spa
P.O.Box 2014,
South Male Atoll
The Maldives
E-mail: ms_bodu@minornet.com
Website: www.mspa-international.com

New Zealand

Pokeno

Spa Du Vin (pp 240–241)
Lyons Road R.D.1
Pokeno, New Zealand
Tel: (64 9) 233 6780
Fax: (64 9) 233 6781
Email: spa@duvin.co.nz
Website: www.spaduvin.co.nz

Queenstown

Hush Spa (pp 238–239)
Level Two - The Junction
Corner Gorge & Robins Road
Queenstown 9197
New Zealand
Tel: (64 3) 409 0901
Fax: (64 3) 409 0902
Email: relax@hushspa.co.nz
Website: www.hushspa.co.nz

THE PHILIPPINES

Boracay

Mandala Spa (pp 230–231)
Boracay Island
Malay Aklan 5608
Philippines
Tel: (63 36) 288 5858
Fax: (63 36) 288 3531
Email: info@mandalaspa.com
Website: www.mandalaspa.com

Batangas

The Farm at San Benito (pp 228–229)
119 Barangay Tipakan, Lipa City
Batangas
PO Box 39676
Philippines
Tel: (63 2) 751 3498/696 3795
Fax: (63 2) 751 3497/696 3175
Email: info@thefarm.com.ph
Website: www.thefarm.com.ph

Cebu

CHI Spa Village (pp 226–227)
Shangri-La's Mactan Island Resort and Spa
Punta Engano Road
PO Box 86,
Lapu Lapu City 6015
Cebu, Philippines
Tel: (63 32) 231 0288
Fax: (63 32) 495 1259
Email: mac@shangri-la.com
Website: www.shangri-la.com/spa

Manila

The Oriental Spa, Manila
Mandarin Oriental, Manila
Makati Avenue,
Makati City 1226
Metro Manila, Philippines
Tel: (63 2) 867 4461 - 63
Fax: (63 2) 810 6582
E-mail: momnl-reservations@mohg.com
Website: www.mandarinoriental.com

SINGAPORE

The Oriental Spa (pp 202–203)
Level 5, The Mandarin Oriental
5 Raffles Avenue
Marina Square
Singapore 039797
Tel: (65) 6885 3533
Fax: (65) 6885 3542
Email: orsin-spa@mohg.com
Website: www.mandarinoriental.com

RafflesAmrita Spa (pp 204–205)
Raffles The Plaza
Level 6, 80 Bras Basah Road
Singapore 189560
Tel: (65) 6336 4477
Fax: (65) 6336 1161
Email: enquiries@amritaspas.com
Website: www.amritaspas.com

Spa Botanica (pp 206–207)
The Sentosa Resort and Spa
2 Bukit Manis Road, Sentosa
Singapore 099891
Tel: (65) 6275 0331
Fax: (65) 6275 0228
Email: thesentosa@beaufort.com.sg
Website: www.spabotanica.com

SRI LANKA

Galle
Angsana Spa City Club & Spa Crescat City
75B, Galle Road
Colombo 3
Sri Lanka
Tel: (94 11) 242 4245
Fax: (94 11) 242 4255
Email: spa-crescatcity@angsana.com
Website: www.angsana.com

Polonnaruwa
Angsana Spa Giritale, Sri Lanka
Giritale, Sri Lanka
Deer Park Hotel
Giritale, Polonnaruwa, Sri Lanka
Tel: (94 27) 224 6272/7685/7686
Fax: (94 27) 224 6470
Email: spa-giritale@angsana.com
Website: www.angsana.com

THAILAND

Bangkok
Banyan Tree Spa Bangkok
Banyan Tree Bangkok
21/100 South Sathon Road
Bangkok 10120
Thailand
Tel: (66 2) 679 1052
Fax: (66 2) 679 1053
Email: spa-bangkok@banyantree.com
Website: www.banyantree.com

CHI Spa (pp 162–163)
Shangri-La
89 Soi Wat Suan Plu
New Road, Bangrak
Bangkok 10500
Thailand
Tel: (66 2) 236 7777
Fax: (66 2) 236 8579
Email: chi.bangkok@shangri-la.com
Website: www.shangri-la.com/chiopa

Devarana Spa (pp 174–175)
The Dusit Thani Hotel
946 Rama IV Road
Silom, Bangrak
Bangkok 10500
Thailand
Tel: (66 2) 636 3596
Fax: (66 2) 636 3597
Email: bangkok@devaranaspa.com
Website: www.devaranaspa.com

The Spa at Four Seasons Hotel (pp 190–191)
Four Seasons Bangkok
155 Rajadamri Road
Bangkok 10330
Thailand
Tel: (66 2) 652 9311
Fax: (66 2) 651 9314
Email: ms_fsbk@minornet.com
Website: www.mspa-international.com

Imperial Mandara Spa
Imperial Queen's Park Hotel
199 Sukhumvit Soi 22
Bangkok 10110, Thailand
Tel: (66 2) 261 9000
Fax: (66 2) 258 2327
Email: ms_impq@minornet.com
Website: www.mspa-international.com

Mandara Spa
Bangkok Marriott Resort & Spa
257/1-3 Charoen Nakorn Road
At the Krungthep Brigde, Thonburi
Bangkok 10600, Thailand
Tel: (66 2) 476 0021
Fax: (66 2) 476 1120
Email: ms_bmrs@minornet.com
Website: www.mspa-international.com

Oriental Spa at The Oriental (pp 182–183)
597 Charoennakorn Road
Khlongsan
Bangkok 10600, Thailand
Tel: (66 2) 439 7613/4
Fax: (66 2) 439 7885
Email: orbkk-spa@mohg.com
Website: www.mandarinoriental.com

The Royal Orchid Mandara Spa
The Royal Orchid Sheraton Hotel
2 Captain Bush Lane, New Road, Siphaya,
Bangkok 10500, Thailand
Tel: (66 2) 266 0123
Fax: (66 2) 639 5478
Email: ms_rosh@minornet.com
Website: www.mspa-international.com

Spa Athénée at Plaza Athénée Bangkok, a Royal Meridien Hotel
Plaza Athénée, a Royal Meridien Hotel
Wireless Road, Bangkok 10330, Thailand
Tel: (66 2) 650 8800 Ext 5010
Email: ms_mepa@minornet.com
Website: www.mspa-international.com

Chiang Mai
Dheva Spa (pp 168–169)
Mandarin Oriental Dhara Dhevi
51/4 Chiang Mai - Sankampaeng Road
T Tasala A Muang
Chiang Mai 50000, Thailand
Tel: (66 53) 888 888
Fax: (64 53) 888 978
Email: mocnx-dhevaspa@mohg.com
Website: www.mandarinoriental.com

The Spa at Four Seasons (pp 178–179)
Mae Rim-Samoeng Old Road
Mae Rim
Chiang Mai 50180, Thailand
Tel: (66 53) 298 181
Fax: (66 53) 298 189
Email: spa.chiangmai@fourseasons.com
Website: www.fourseasons.com/chiangmai

Chiang Rai
Anantara Spa (pp 158–159)
Anantara Resort and Spa Golden Triangle
299 Moo 1, T Wiang Chiangsen
Chiang Rai 57150, Thailand
Tel: (66 53) 784 084
Fax: (66 53) 784 090
Email: ms_argt@minornet.com
Website: www.mspa-international.com

Hua Hin
Anantara Spa
Anantara Resort & Spa
43/1 Phetkasem Beach Road
Hua Hin 77110, Thailand
Tel: (66 32) 520 250
Fax: (66 32) 520 259
Email: anantara@mandaraspa.com
Website: www.mspa-international.com

Chiva-Som International Health Resort (pp 164–167)
73/4 Petchkasem Road
Hua Hin 77110, Thailand
Tel: (66 3) 253 6536
Fax: (66 3) 251 1154
Email: reserv@chivasom.com
Website: www.chivasom.com

Devarana Spa (pp 170–171)
Dusit Resort Hua Hin
1349 Petchkasem Road
Cha-Am, Petchburi 76120, Thailand
Tel: (66 3) 244 2494
Fax: (66 3) 244 2495
Email: huahin@devaranaspa.com
Website: www.devaranaspa.com

The Earth Spa by Six Senses (pp 176–177)
Evason Hideaway at Hua Hin
9/22 Moo 5 Paknampran, Pranburi
Prachuap Khiri Khan 77220
Thailand
Tel: (66 32) 618 200
Fax: (66 32) 618 201
Email: spahuahin@evasonhuahin.com
Website: www.sixsenses.com

Mandara Spa
Hua Hin Marriott Resort & Spa
107/1 Phetchkasem Beach Road
Hua Hin 77110, Thailand
Tel: (66 32) 511 882
Fax: (66 32) 512 422
Email: ms_hmrs@minornet.com
Website: www.mspa-international.com

Six Senses Spa (pp 186–187)
at Evason Hua Hin Resort
9 Moo 3 Paknampran, Pranburi
Prachuap Khiri Khan 77220
Thailand
Tel: (66 32) 632111
Fax: (66 32) 632112
Email: spahuahin@evasonhauhin.com
Website: www.sixsenses.com

Krabi
Mandara Spa
Sheraton Krabi Beach Resort
Klong Muang Beach
Krabi 8100
Thailand
Tel: (66) 7562 8000
Fax: (66) 7562 8028
Email: ms_shkr@minornet.com
Website: www.mspa-international.com

Pimalai Resort & Spa (pp 184–185)
99 Moo 5, Kan Tiang Beach
Koh Lanta
Krabi 81150
Thailand
Tel: (66) 7560 7999 ext 1999
Fax: (66) 7560 7998
Email: spa@pimalai.com
Website: www.pimalai.com

Pattaya
Devarana Spa (pp 172–173)
Dusit Resort Pattaya
Dusit Resort 240/2
Pattaya Beach, Cholburi 20150
Thailand
Tel: (66 3) 837 1044
Fax: (66 3) 837 1045
Email: pattaya@devaranaspa.com
Website: www.devaranaspa.com

Royal Garden Spa at Pattaya Marriott Resort & Spa
Pattaya Marriott Resort & Spa
218/2-4 M.10 Beach Road
Pattaya 20260
Thailand
Tel: (66) 3841 2120
Fax: (66) 3841 1753
Email: ms_pmrs@minornet.com
Website: www.mspa-international.com

Phuket
Angsana Spa Allamanda Laguna Phuket
Phuket, Thailand
29/98 Moo 4, Srisoonthorn Road
Cherngtalay, Amphur Talang,
Phuket 83110
Thailand
Tel: (66 76) 324 359
Fax: (66 76) 325 764
Email: spa-allamandaphuket@angsana.com
Website: www.angsana.com

Angsana Spa Dusit Laguna Resort
Phuket, Thailand
390 Srisoonthorn Road
Cherngtalay, Amphur Talang
Phuket 83110
Thailand
Tel: (66 76) 324 320
Fax: (66 76) 271 002
Email: spa-dusitphuket@angsana.com
Website: www.angsana.com

Angsana Spa Laguna Beach Resort
Phuket, Thailand
323/2 Moo 2, Srisoonthorn Road
Cherngtalay, Amphur Talang
Phuket 83110
Thailand
Tel: (66 76) 325 405
Fax: (66 76) 325 407
Email: spa-lagunabeachphuket@angsana.com
Website: www.angsana.com

Angsana Spa Sheraton Grande Laguna Phuket
Phuket, Thailand
10 Moo 4, Srisoonthorn Road
Cherngtalay, Amphur Talang
Phuket 83110
Thailand
Tel: (66 76) 324 101
Fax: (66 76) 324 368
Email: spa-sheratonphuket@angsana.com
Website: www.angsana.com

Banyan Tree Spa (pp 160–161)
Banyan Tree Phuket
33 Moo 4, Srisoonthorn Road
Cherngtalay, Amphur Talang
Phuket 83110
Thailand
Tel: (66 76) 324 374
Fax: (66 76) 271 463
Email: spa-phuket@banyantree.com
Website: www.banyantree.com

Pearl Spa by Mandara
Pearl Village Hotel Phuket
Nai Yang Beach and National Park
Phuket 83140
Thailand
Tel: (66 76) 327 006
Fax: (66 76) 327 338/9
Email: ms_pear@minornet.com
Website: www.mspa-international.com

Mandara Spa
JW Marriott Phuket Resort & Spa
Moo 3, Mai Khao, Talang
Phuket 83140
Thailand
Tel: (66 0) 7633 8000
Fax: (66 0) 7634 8349
Email: ms_jwmp@minornet.com
Website: www.mspa-international.com

Six Senses Spa (pp 188–189)
The Evason Phuket Resort
100 Vised Road
Tambon Rawai, Muang District
Phuket 83100
Thailand
Tel: (66 76) 381 010
Fax: (66 76) 381 018
Email: spa@evasonphuket.com
Website: www.sixsenses.com

Samui
Anantara Spa
Anantara Resort & Spa Koh Samui
101/3 Bophut Bay, Samui Island
Suratthani 84320
Thailand
Tel: (66) 7742 8300-9
Fax: (66) 7742 8310
Email: anantarasm@mandaraspa.com
Website: www.mspa-international.com

The Hideaway Spa (pp 180–181)
Sila Evason Hideaway at Samui
9/10 Moo 5, Baan Plai Laem
Bophut, Koh Samui
Suratthani 84320
Thailand
Tel: (66) 7724 5678
Fax: (66) 7724 5671
Email: silaspa@evasonhideaways.com
Website: www.sixsenses.com

Mandara Spa
SALA Samui Resort & Spa
10/9 Moo 5 T. Bophut, Koh Samui
Suratthani 84320
Thailand
Tel: (66) 7724 5888
Fax: (66) 7724 5889
Email: ms_ssam@minornet.com
Website: www.mspa-international.com

VIETNAM

Nha Trang
Six Senses Spa (pp 152–153)
Ana Mandara Evason Resort
Beachside, Tran Phu Boulevard
Nha Trang
Vietnam
Tel: (84 58) 829 829
Fax: (84 58) 829 629
Email: resvana@dng.vnn.vn
Website: www.six-senses.com

Six Senses Spa at Evason Hideaway at Ana Mandara (pp 154–155)
Beachside, Tran Phu Boulevard
Nha Trang
Vietnam
Tel: (84 58) 728 222 ext 677
Fax: (84 58) 728 223
Email: sixsensesspa@evasonhideaways.com
Website: www.sixsensesspa.com

Bibliography

Alphen, Jan Van and Aris, Anthony (General Editors), *Oriental Medicine: An Illustrated Guide to the Asian Arts of Healing*, Shambhala Publications, 1995

Archipelago Guides *Bali: A Traveller's Companion*, Archipelago Press, an imprint of Editions Didier Millet Pte Ltd, 1995

Archipelago Guides *Thailand: A Traveller's Companion*, Archipelago Press, an imprint of Editions Didier Millet Pte Ltd, 2001

Beers, Susan-Jane, *Jamu: The Ancient Indonesian Art of Herbal Healing*, Periplus Editions (HK) Ltd, 2001

Benge, Sophie, *The Tropical Spa*, Periplus Editions (HK) Ltd, 1999

Cash, Mel, *Sport & Remedial Massage Therapy*, Ebury Press, an imprint of Random House, 1996

Chapman, Jessie, *Yoga: Postures for Body, Mind and Soul*, HarperCollinsPublishers (Australia), 2000

Claire, Thomas, *Bodywork: What Type of Massage to Get and How to Make the Most of it*, Quill, an imprint of William Morrow and Company, Inc., 1995

Cummings, Joe and Martin, Steven, *Thailand*, Lonely Planet Publications, 2001

Dr Duo Gao (Consultant Editor), *The Encyclopedia of Chinese Medicine*, Sevenoaks Ltd, 1997

Jonas, Steven M.D. and Gordon, Sandra, *30 Secrets of the World's Healthiest Cuisines*, John Wiley & Sons, Inc., 2000

Mitchell, Stewart, *The Complete Illustrated Guide to Massage*, Element Books Limited, 1997

Nash, Barbara, *From Acupressure to Zen: An Essay of Natural Therapies*, Hunter House, 1996

National Museum of the Republic of Indonesia, *Pusaka: Art of Indonesia*, Archipelago Press, an imprint of Editions Didier Millet Pte Ltd, 1992

O' Brien, Kate with Sing OMD Troy, *Qi! Chinese Serets of Health, Beauty & Vitality*, C-Licence 2005

Ody, Penelope, with Lyon, Alice Lyon and Vilinac, Dragana, *The Chinese Herbal Cookbook: Healing Foods from East and West*, Kyle Cathie Ltd, 2000

Pierce Salguero, C, *A Thai Herbal - traditional recipes for health and harmony*, Findhorn Press 2003

Plants, *Indonesian Heritage Series Vol 4*, Archipelago Press, an imprint of Editions Didier Millet Pte Ltd, 1996

Purchon, Nerys, *Health and Beauty the Natural Way*, MetroBooks, an imprint of Friedman/Fairfax Publishers, 1997

Rister, Robert, *Japanese Herbal Medicine: The Healing Art of Kampo*, Avery Publishing Group, Inc., 1999

Ryrie, Charlie, *Healing Energies of Water*, Journey Editions, an imprint of Periplus Editions (HK) Ltd, 1999

Shealy, C Norman, *The Complete Family Guide to Alternative Medicine*, Element Books Ltd, 1996

The Complete Illustrated Encyclopedia of Alternative Healing Therapies: A Complete Guide to Natural Healing, Element Books Ltd, 1999

The Encyclopedia of Alternative Medicine, Journey Editions, an imprint of Charles E Tuttle Co., Inc., 1996

Vyas, Bharti and Warren, Jane, *Simply Ayurveda*, HarperCollinsPublishers (UK), 2000

Warrier, Gopi and Gunawant, Deepika, *The Complete Illustrated Guide to Ayurveda: The Ancient Indian Healing System*, Element Books Ltd, 1997

Woodham, Anne and Dr Peters, David, *Encyclopedia of Natural Healing: The Definitive Home Reference Guide to Treatments for Mind and Body*, Dorling Kindersley Ltd, 2000

Young, Jacqueline, *The Healing Path: The Practical Guide to the Holistic Traditions of China, India, Tibet and Japan*, Thorsons, an imprint of HarperCollinsPublishers (UK), 2001

Picture Credits

Index

Page numbers in bold type refer to an illustration.
Readers should refer to individual spa entries for
guidance on treatments and therapies offered by
the spas.